AF476971

# ALAN PHELAN

## Fragile Absolutes

Irish Museum of Modern Art

CHARTA

/

# Contents

/

/

# Foreword

/

We are delighted to present at IMMA a new commission and solo exhibition project by Irish artist Alan Phelan (Dublin, 1968). Continuing a strand of programming which showcases emerging Irish and International artists, Phelan belongs to a generation of artists who have exhibited recently at IMMA including Shahzia Sikander, Ulla von Brandenburg, Orla Barry and Paul Morrison.

Alan Phelan's practice creates relationships between quite disparate elements of political history, cultural theory, popular culture, science fiction, and modified cars. These and other elements explore the potential for different and sometimes conflicting sources of knowledge to create new meanings. Many times the works approach specific contexts with ideas, narratives and motifs that overlap, encouraging a dialogue between the disparate components. The relationships generated are multi-faceted, with individual works and installations forming a visual coherence yet projecting a complexity that captures a sense of the subject addressed. Straddled between discourses of representation and production Phelan explores how meanings are generated by locating references in real historical fact and invented or fictive scenarios.

This publication accompanies a solo exhibition project and a new commission for the Formal Gardens at IMMA which takes the form of the framework for a Yugo car, suspended over the fountain of the Formal Garden. *Goran's Stealth Yugo*, 2009, was made in collaboration with Goran Krstić, a car designer from the Zastava/Yugo car factory in Kragujevac, Serbia. This work continues Phelan's ongoing investigations into car culture where he has in the past worked with modified car enthusiasts on several projects. Over the past two years Phelan and IMMA have been working in unique collaboration with Goran Krstić and Zastava, manufacturers of the infamous Yugo car, once a proud yet conflicted symbol of the former Yugoslavia. As Dušan I. Bjelić writes in his essay which is included in this publication: *Goran's Stealth Yugo*,

2009 represents the "complex totality of geopolitics, history, industrial production, and aesthetics using the car as a central metaphor". He concludes Phelan's art "allows industrial materials, machines, blueprints, trees, tools, to tell their version of history and so seriously challenge post-Yugoslav aesthetics grounded in the hegemony of the symbolic of the national subject".

Alan Phelan studied at Dublin City University, Dublin and Rochester Institute of Technology, New York. He has exhibited widely internationally including Whitney Museum of American Art, New York; Škuc Gallery, Ljubljana; Feinkost, Berlin; SKC, Belgrade. In Ireland he has exhibited at mother's tankstation, Solstice Arts Centre, Navan; MCAC, Portadown; and LCGA Limerick. He was editor/curator for Printed Project, issue 5, launched at the 51st Venice Biennale, and has curated exhibitions at the RHA, Dublin, Project, Dublin and Rochester, New York. Phelan was short-listed for this exhibition for the AIB Art Prize in 2007.

I would like to thank each of the authors in the catalogue: curator of the exhibition, Seán Kissane; Medb Ruane, writer, psychoanalytic practitioner and columnist; Tony White, novelist and literary editor of The Idler; and Dušan I. Bjelić, associate professor of criminology at the University of Southern Maine. Each of these writers has given their unique perspective on Phelan's work, greatly enhancing our enjoyment and understanding of his practice. The design of the book is the work of Ajdin Bašić, who was born in Sarajevo but is based in Ljubljana – further extending the Balkan theme of this project. I would also like to thank Giuseppe Liverani and his team at Charta.

At IMMA the exhibition was curated by Seán Kissane, Curator of Exhibitions, alongside Marianne Kelly, Exhibitions Assistant. I would like to thank them for their commitment to the project as well as Gale Scanlon, Head of Operations and Tony Checkley of the OPW for facilitating the commission.

We are delighted that the exhibition will have a longer life through our collaboration with Chapter Arts Centre in Cardiff, and Limerick City Gallery of Art who will exhibit sections of the exhibition later in the year. I would like to thank Hannah Firth, Curator at Chapter and Mike Fitzpatrick, Director of LCGA for making this possible.

Particular thanks are due to Goran Krstić, the designer of Goran's Stealth Yugo for the enormous amount of time and effort which he dedicated to this project. We would also like to thank Marija Aleksandrović for her valuable support.

Finally I would like to thank the artist Alan Phelan. Over the past two years there has been a constant and open collaboration between him and the IMMA curators while this project and commission have evolved. He has remained a constant source of vision, enthusiasm and inspiration.

Enrique Juncosa
Director

p.9

/

# Fragile Absolutes

/

fully endorsing what one is accused of should there is no Christ outside of Saint Paul persist down there Mitteleuropa flair finesse Europe's ghost displaced racism Underground The Balkans constitute a place of exception with regard to which the tolerant multiculturalist is allowed to act out his/her repressed racism respect The Phantom Menace Star Wars nothing but global reflexivization/mediatization generates its own brutal immediacy Id-Evil Id-Evil class multiculturalist hatred tolerance even more hatred political

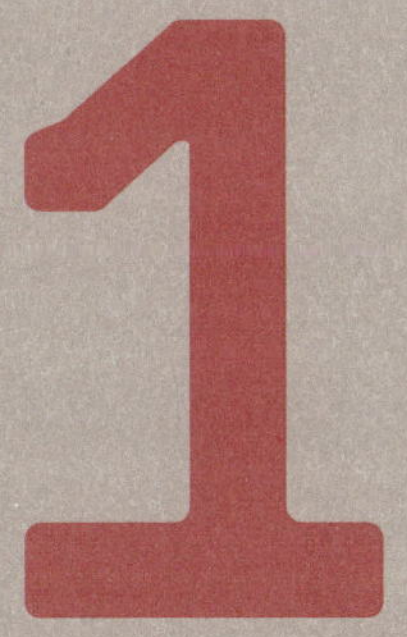

Live/Evil, 2002
deteriorated paper, balsa wood, linen
tape, glue
20 x 20 x 4 cms

Phantom Blanket (there is no Christ
outside of Saint Paul), 2008
orange blanket, push-pins
180 x 120x 40 cms

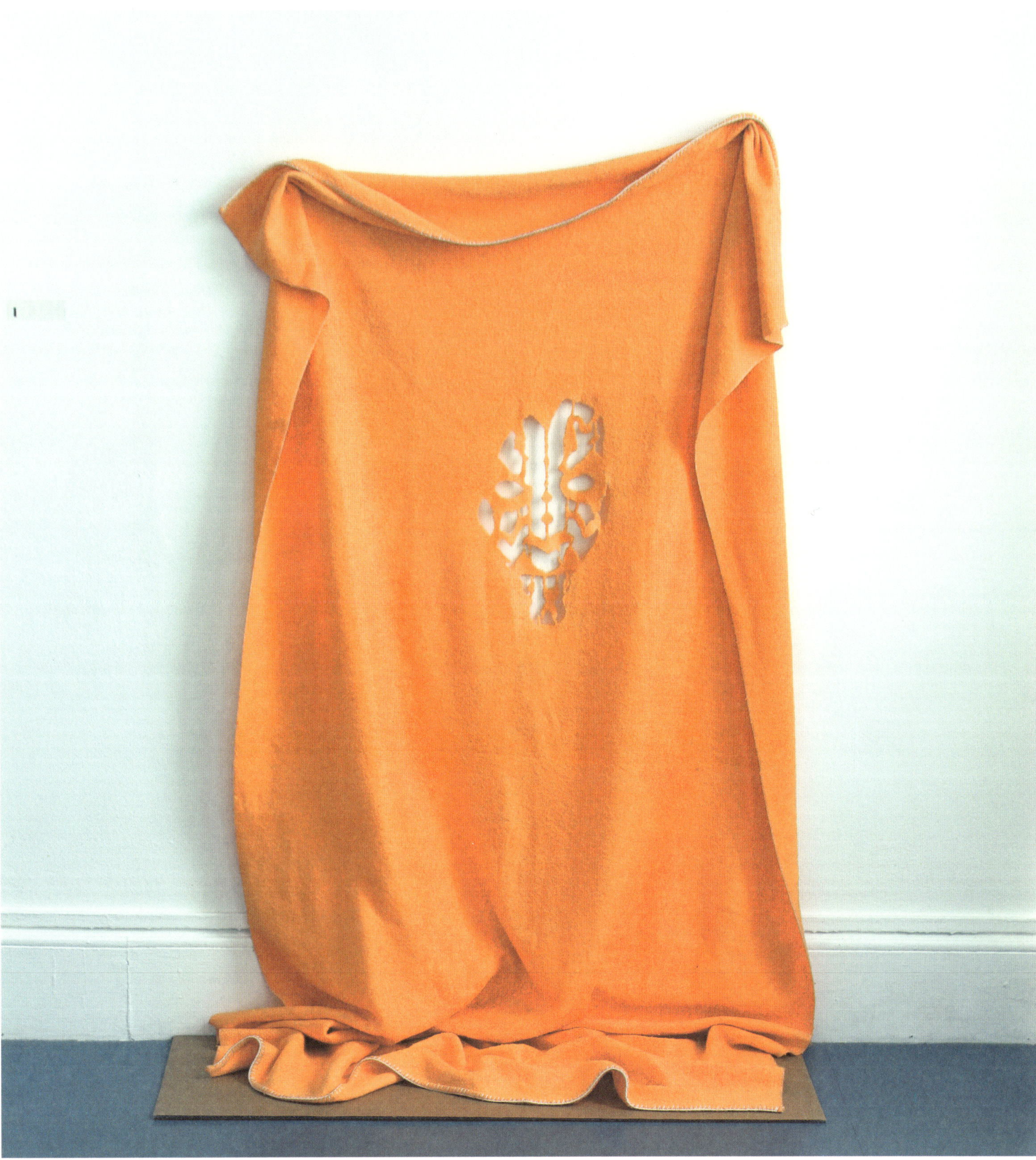

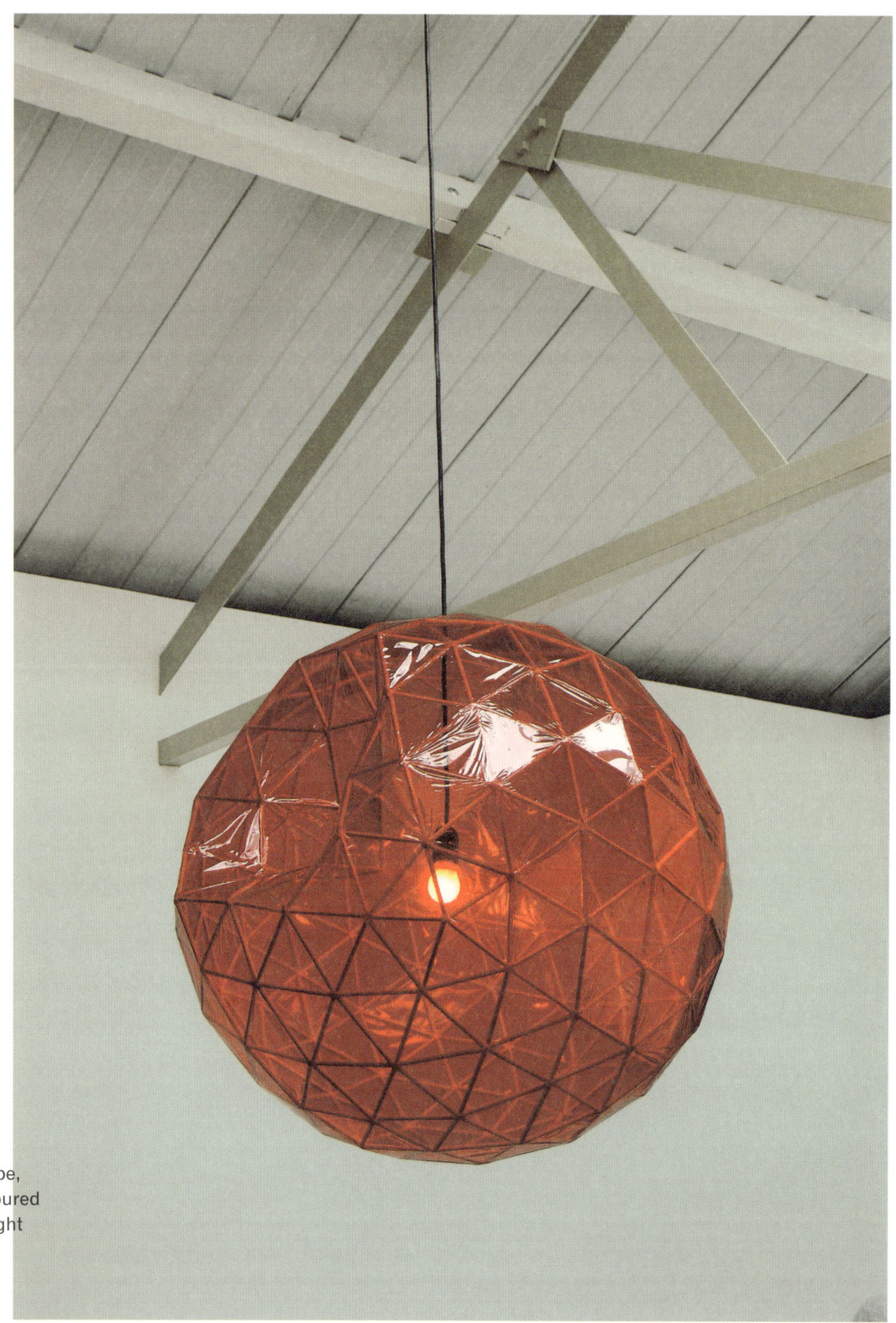

Red Star Death Star, 2007
balsa wood, card, paper tape, cocktail sticks, glue, coloured polyester thermal film, light fixture, cable
75 x 75 x 75 cms

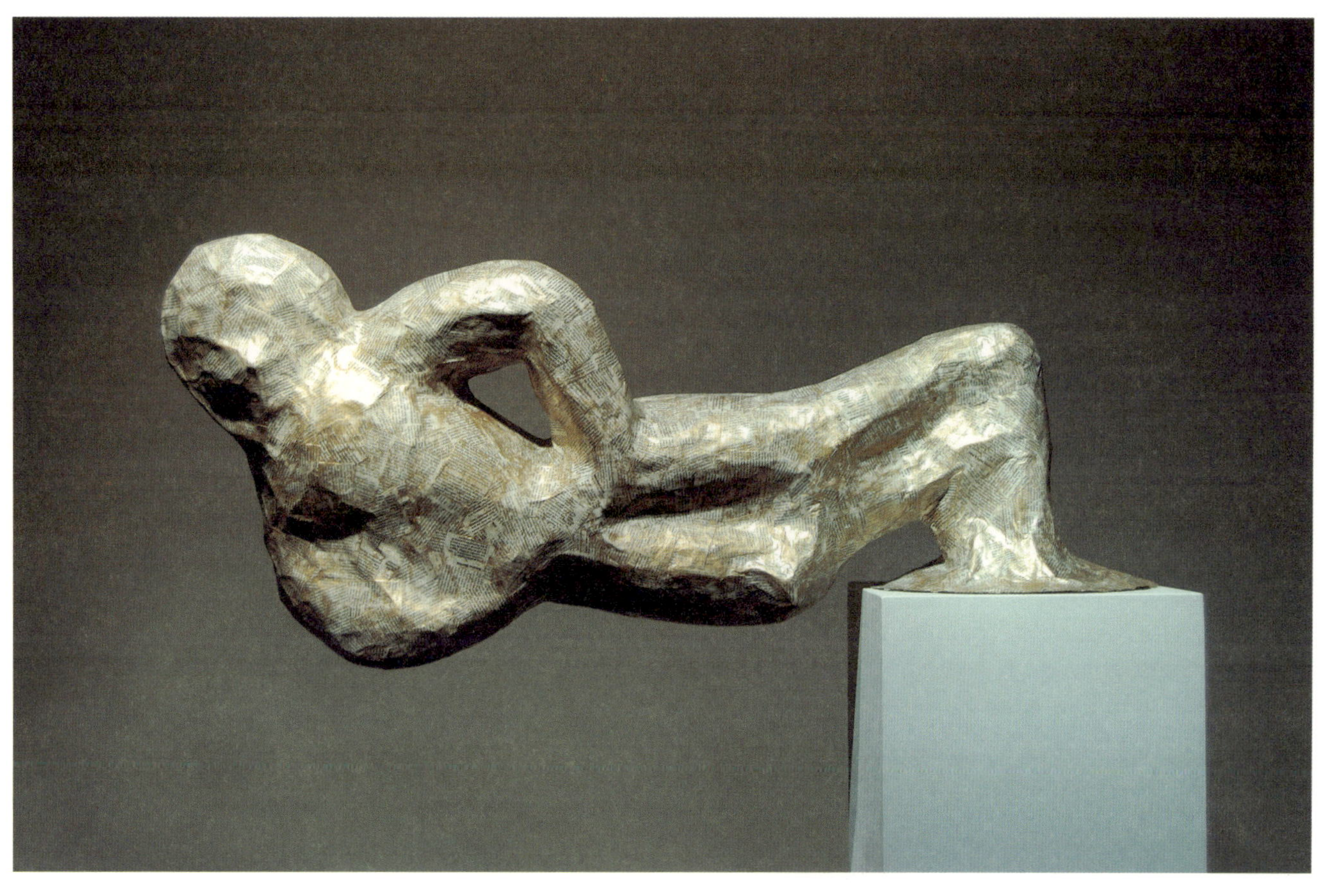

Barbara's Boy (The Alternate), 2007
archival paper, toner, EVA glue,
plastic blow-up hen party doll,
gold paint, metal support, pedestal
49 x 104 x 32 cms
pedestal 124 x 33 x 33 cms

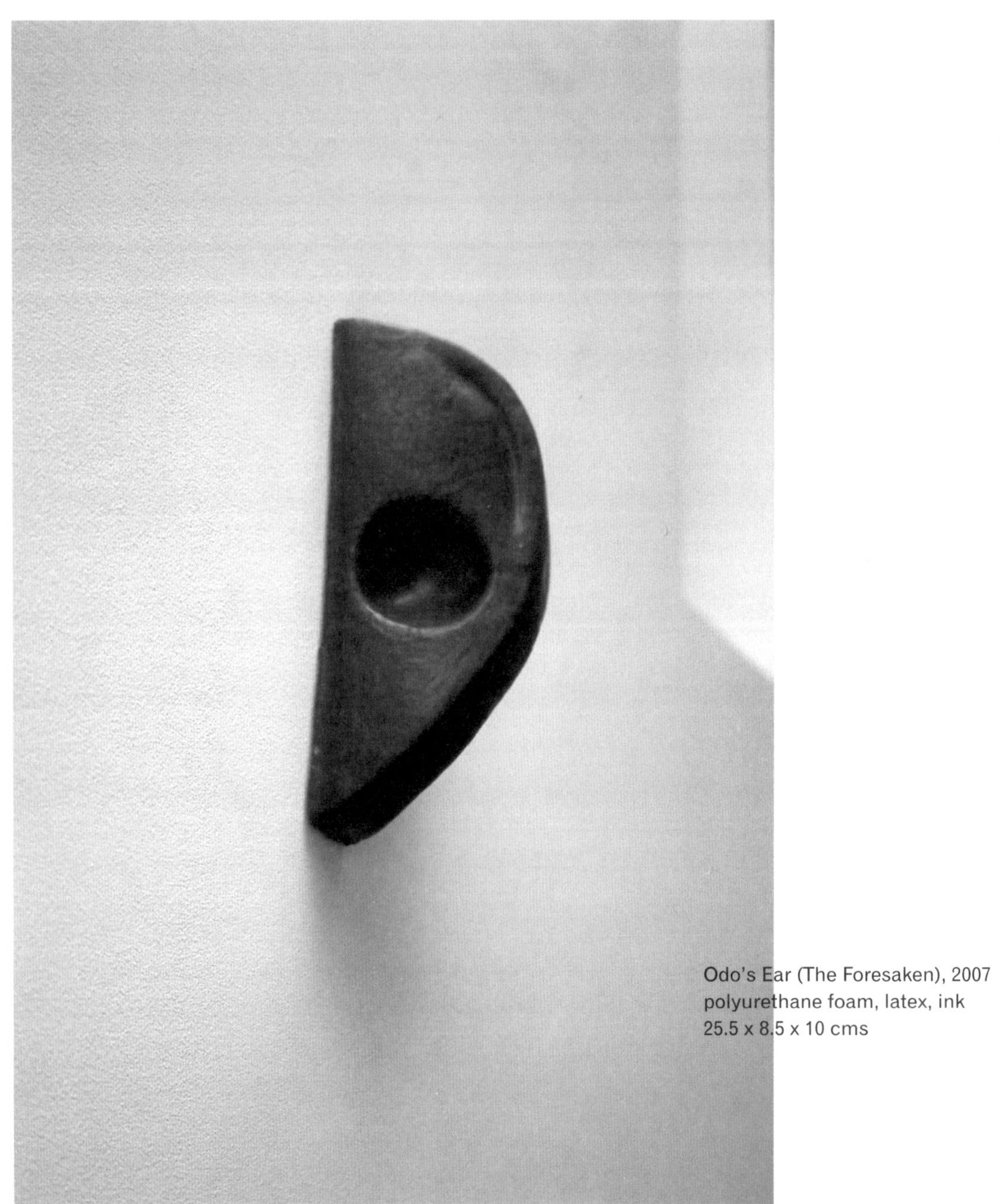

Odo's Ear (The Foresaken), 2007
polyurethane foam, latex, ink
25.5 x 8.5 x 10 cms

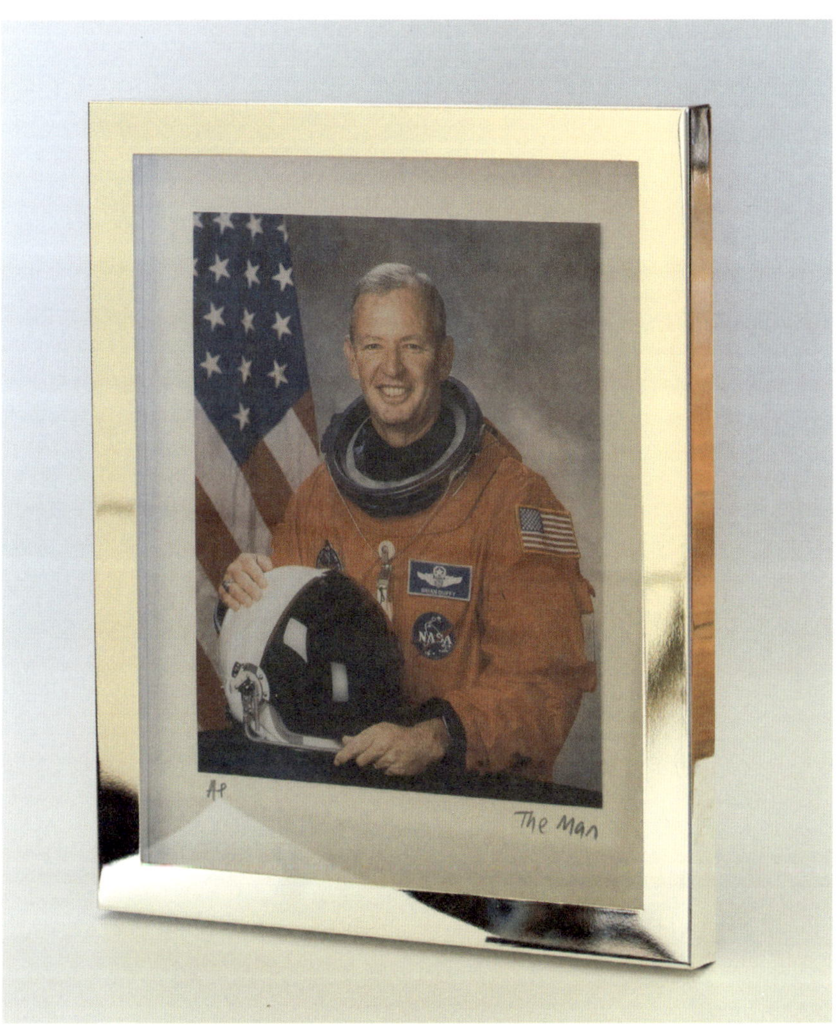


The man who ruins my break, 2007
c-type print, metal frame
photo: 19 x 15  cms
frame 27.5 x 22.5 x 1.5 cms

its own ghosts The Communist Manifesto
The Manifesto wrong The Manifesto
The Manifesto today
The Manifesto sexual The Manifesto
'spiritualization' of the very material process of production
The Manifesto this reduction of
all heavenly chimeras to brutal economic reality generates a spectrality of
its own this today both
sides are wrong outside capitalist
ideological the only possible
framework of the actual material existence of a society of permanent self-
enhancing productivity utopian radical
enough repeat repeat
without premodern
object cause obstacle
Vertigo objet petit a cause
make the cause of desire directly into our object of desire
Vertigo the object of desire deprived of
its cause distance desire
coincide for itself
from which objcct

2

p.24

Ralph Gifford
Servicemen on Whiddy Island,
Ireland, 1910-1919
scan from nitrate negative

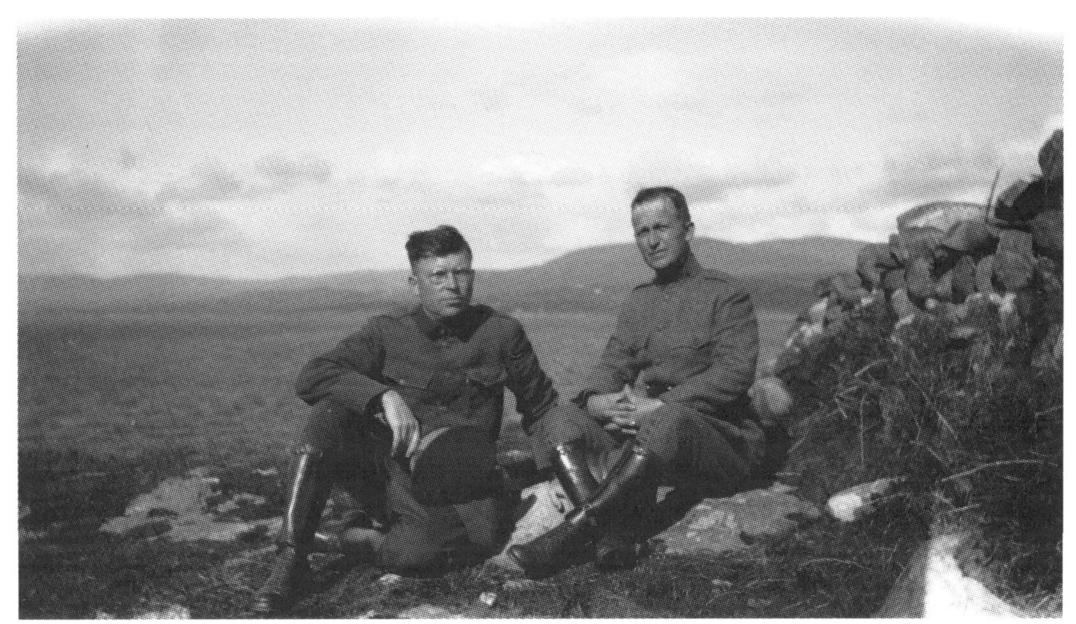

include me out of the

# partisans manifesto

# Include Me Out

Tony White

I was in the kitchen separating the CDs and DVDs into their constituent parts. 'All of this can be recycled,' I said, loudly enough that Sally could hear me from the next room, 'once I've separated out the paper, polystyrene, paint, lacquer and the aluminium or gold or whatever.'

I couldn't hear what she was saying in reply.

It wasn't a political act. Not a protest against 'the star system' or anything like that. It wasn't ideological or anti-capitalist. Nor anti-narrativist. I didn't have a manifesto. It was more kind of, 'include me out.'

There was a brutal immediacy to it though.

The jewel cases are my favourite. Nice and simple. You can mash them up with any mortar and pestle-type of arrangement. I like to start things off with a fairly heavy-duty stone affair that we were given as a wedding present. There's no skill involved, no special, I don't know, hand-swing technique. No sighing the maker's sigh. I'll put the jewel case in there, cover the whole thing with a tea towel, then bash it. Gently at first, finding the correct amount of force. Letting the contents settle slightly so that the rigid pieces of plastic find any number of random contacts against the curvature of the mortar's interior and the other pieces of plastic that are in there. The movement and pressure of the pestle creating what I suppose would be a species of shear stress; a more complex and distributed version of what happens when you break a stick over your knee.

When I've gone as far as I can with mortar number one, I tip the pieces out into a smaller one, repeat the process and so on.

Sally was speaking in the next room, but I still couldn't hear what she was saying.

If money were no object and I'd had a more hi-tech set-up, or if there were compliance and quality-certification or licensing issues, I'd probably have wanted to chuck the bits through a laser filter at the end, to remove any contaminants. That would have left me with a really high quality crystal polystyrene pellet – and don't tell me that couldn't be used to make a whole range of products: jars, insulating foam, windshield units for toy cars, whatever. Even without such a filter I was getting a pretty good result, but a certain amount of foreign particulate matter did creep in. Dust maybe, or perhaps the substance of the mortars themselves, loosened by some inevitable abrasion between the plastic and the stone, wood or ceramic. Scale that up and I could see that this wouldn't be a pure enough product for commercial applications.

Ditto the polycarbonate bodies of the discs themselves.

But here they were on my, *our* kitchen table: *Star Wars IV*, *Vertigo*, *The Last Tycoon*, *Blade Runner*, *My Best Friend's Wedding*, *The Cabinet of Dr Caligari*. I wasn't doing them in any particular order. These were just as they came. Nearest first. The order they were in on the shelf. Did they have anything in common other than the fact that we had chosen them? That we'd stood there in the shop on a series of Saturday afternoons when we were feeling flush, or when one or other of us wanted to buy a present for the other one? That we'd paid for them and brought them home? Was there any other unifying strand running through this seemingly arbitrary selection?

Maybe not.

The fact that we'd sat and watched them all?

Well, that. Yes.

I pictured the two of us sitting side by side on the sofa on a weekend evening with a bottle of wine. Did I say *Vertigo*? Not that titles mattered much now. These discs were on their way to being stripped of their transcendent freight, disconnected from their own ghosts and reduced to, what? Something more than soulless husks? Raw materials, perhaps? To make what? Ingredients to be mixed and shaped how, exactly?

The handful of paper sleeves and covers that awaited shredding were as meaningless to me now as takeaway flyers on someone else's doormat. Once I had done enough I would soak them for a day or so, then boil them to a paste. Spread this out to dry on a clean cloth over the bath to make a thick wad of soft card, pending further decisions.

A ceramic mixing bowl full of gritty and irregularly shaped crystal polystyrene chunks, the best of which were the density of fine gravel.

A bucket full of black, clear and translucent variations on the DVD case that had been rough-cut into rigid polypropylene *tagliatelle* ready to be wilted in boiling water and pressed while still warm into tangled rubbery cakes, like oversized dried egg noodles.

The discs themselves were more complicated, comprising a 1.2mm thick wafer of polycarbonate, a reflective layer, a lacquer layer to prevent oxidation and then a layer of paint: the label or artwork.

First I tried scraping off one layer at a time. Not good. A few clumsy attempts with a variety of improvised tools later, it occurred to me that I could simply use a domestic rotary sander to grind off 'the label side' of the disc with a fine abrasive. I'd have to tap the sander wheel carefully onto a sheet of paper to get the dust out, then lift the paper and gently start to roll it to create a kind of spout. Tip it into a glass jug or something. I'd probably need to wear a mask. The dust could then be dissolved in ethanol and exposed to a series of reagents in order to separate the metals from the dyes and paints blah blah. The polycarbonate core could itself probably be given a final clean with ethanol to remove any lingering particles of paint, metal, whatever, allowed to dry and then broken up in the same way as the jewel cases.

I could hear the squeak of a chair as she stood up in the next room; footsteps in the hall. 'Couldn't we just watch them one more time?' Her voice getting closer. 'Watch them one by one? Couldn't we do that at least.'

Then, there she was, standing there with a *Star Wars: The Phantom Menace* in one hand. She looked like she'd seen a ghost. 'Put them away until we want to watch them again? Aren't there any that you actually want to watch again?'

There she was interrupting my circular logic and what was I doing at this point? I was looking at her, holding a pestle and saying, 'Sweetie.'

'It'd be different if you could *do* anything with this stuff.' Sally picked up a big chunk of chopped-up DVD case and waved it about half-heartedly: 'I mean...' Looking at the piece of polypropylene in her hand she turned it around: 'It does look a bit like a horse.'

She was right. Something about the way the secateur cut had negotiated the moulded corner.

'Sweetie,' I said again.

'Don't "sweetie" me. Look at you! Turning our kitchen into a place where you just act out out this fantasy of work to avoid reality, it seems like. And you expect me to shut my eyes, or look the other way while all the fun drains out of our relationship.'

She looked really feminine; *une vraie femme*.

I couldn't say that I fully endorsed what Sally was accusing me of. 'Granted,' I said, 'that it's not exactly full unconstrained enjoyment or permanent self-enhancing productivity...'

The process was radical enough to generate ghosts of its own, but I didn't tell her about that. I'd have needed the help of interpreters.

A memory of a lorry laden with fragrant pine branches. A piece of smooth stone. A symbolic suicide.

Confessions written in chalk or soapstone pencil. The taste of tamarind at Shabazar near Tarkeswar. Types of pasta named after national holidays and dates in the revolutionary calendar.

Broadcasting in the rain. Large bundles of twigs. Two people looking through a photo album that's spread across both their knees.

Ephemeral associations and inaccessible fragments.

A man in a gorilla suit copulating with a woman in a robot outfit.

High-bandwidth nonsenses of this kind.

Monstrosities too. Bombed factories. More real than reality itself.

Fleeting images too rich and vast to be taken in in their entirety. Ideas the simplest of which I knew would be impossible to approximate with even fifty, a hundred-times more crystal polystyrene granules or paper shreddings.

What was I thinking?

The enormity of the task.

Shooting myself in the foot.

Again.

'I think I need your help,' I said. 'Maybe let's watch a film first, then carry on with...?' I tried to remember what else was on the shelf.

'I never liked this anyway,' Sally said, opening the DVD case in her hand and flexing the cover back so she could slide out the sleeve artwork. She put on a funny voice: 'How did Darth Vader become Darth Vader?'

'*Stalker*? I could watch that again,' I said. 'Nothing but Tarkovsky, way I'm feeling.'

Sally put *The Phantom Menace* down on the table and thought for a second, then disappeared off to the other room. I could hear the sound of DVDs being moved, the soft rattle of discs rocking gently on their clip-mountings. Footsteps coming back down the hall. A little more brightly this time, I thought.

'Here,' she said. '*Stalker* I've left where it is.' She started flicking through them and read out the first few titles as if they were questions: '*The Woman in the Window*? *The Strange Affair of Uncle Harry*? *Life is Beautiful*?' Then: '*Satyricon. The Usual Suspects. Ransom. The Shawshank Redemption. Blue...*'

'Jarman?'

'Mm-hmm.'

I shrugged. 'Please continue!'

'*Ben Hur. The Others. Sophie's Choice. Beloved.*'

She put the pile down and straightened it. We looked at each other for a second, searching each others faces.

I shrugged again, raising my eyebrows as if to say, 'What?'

As if to say, 'I rest my case!'

Sally smiled quickly then glanced out of the kitchen window, frowning. I took the bait and turned to look in the same direction, but as I did so she pushed past me in a kind of play slow-motion, her left hand pressing me back, keeping me in the kitchen while her body angled towards the door. I ducked, holding my body low, then followed her, reaching out like a footballer in an action replay, as if I was trying to get an arm in front of her to hold her back.

We 'ran' back towards the sitting room like that. Like characters in a sit-com who are pretending to have a race, pretending they're in an action movie. Our movements were slow and heavy and our arms were outstretched, like Picasso's *Women Running on the Beach*.

— Notes —

'Include Me Out' was written by cutting-up, remixing and renarrativising fragments of the following sources to create a completely new story:

Anonymous, 'CD's [*sic.*] Can be Recycled into Other Materials for Re-use', London Recycling Limited.
http://www.london-recycling.co.uk/special/cds.php
Accessed 19 January 2009

Frances Kinsley Hutchinson, *Motoring in the Balkans: Along the Highways of Dalmatia, Montenegro, The Herzegovina and Bosnia*. Chicago: A.C.McClurg & Co., 1909, p.66-67.

ICTY, 'Slobodan Milošević (IT-02-54) Kosovo, Croatia and Bosnia', 14 February 2002, pages 225, 249-250, 311-313. http://www.icty.org/x/cases/slobodan_milosevic/trans/en/020214IT.htm
Accessed 19 January 2009

D.N.Mookerji, M.A., Full text of '*A Monograph on Paper and Papier-Mache in Bengal*, Calcutta: The Bengal Secretariat Book Depot, 1908.' San Francisco: The Internet Archive, 2007.
http://www.archive.org/stream/monographonpaper00mookrich/monographonpaper00mookrich_djvu.txt
Accessed 19 January 2009

Alan Phelan, *15 Fragile Absolutes* (all the words in italics from Slavoj Žižek's book, *The Fragile Absolute: Or, Why is the Christian Legacy Worth Fighting For?*), Dublin: Irish Museum of Modern Art, 2008.
www.alanphelan.com/15/15%20fragile%20absolutes.pdf
Accessed 19 January 2009

Sing Yin Secondary School, 'New Strategies for Compact Disc Recycling', Riyadh: King Saud University, 2006.
http://faculty.ksu.edu.sa/othman/CHE498/Forms/AllItems.aspx
Accessed 19 January 2009

Young Marble Giants, 'Include Me Out', *Colossal Youth*, London: Rough Trade 1980.

Slavoj Žižek, *The Fragile Absolute: Or, Why is the Christian Legacy Worth Fighting For?* London: Verso Books, 2001

p.37

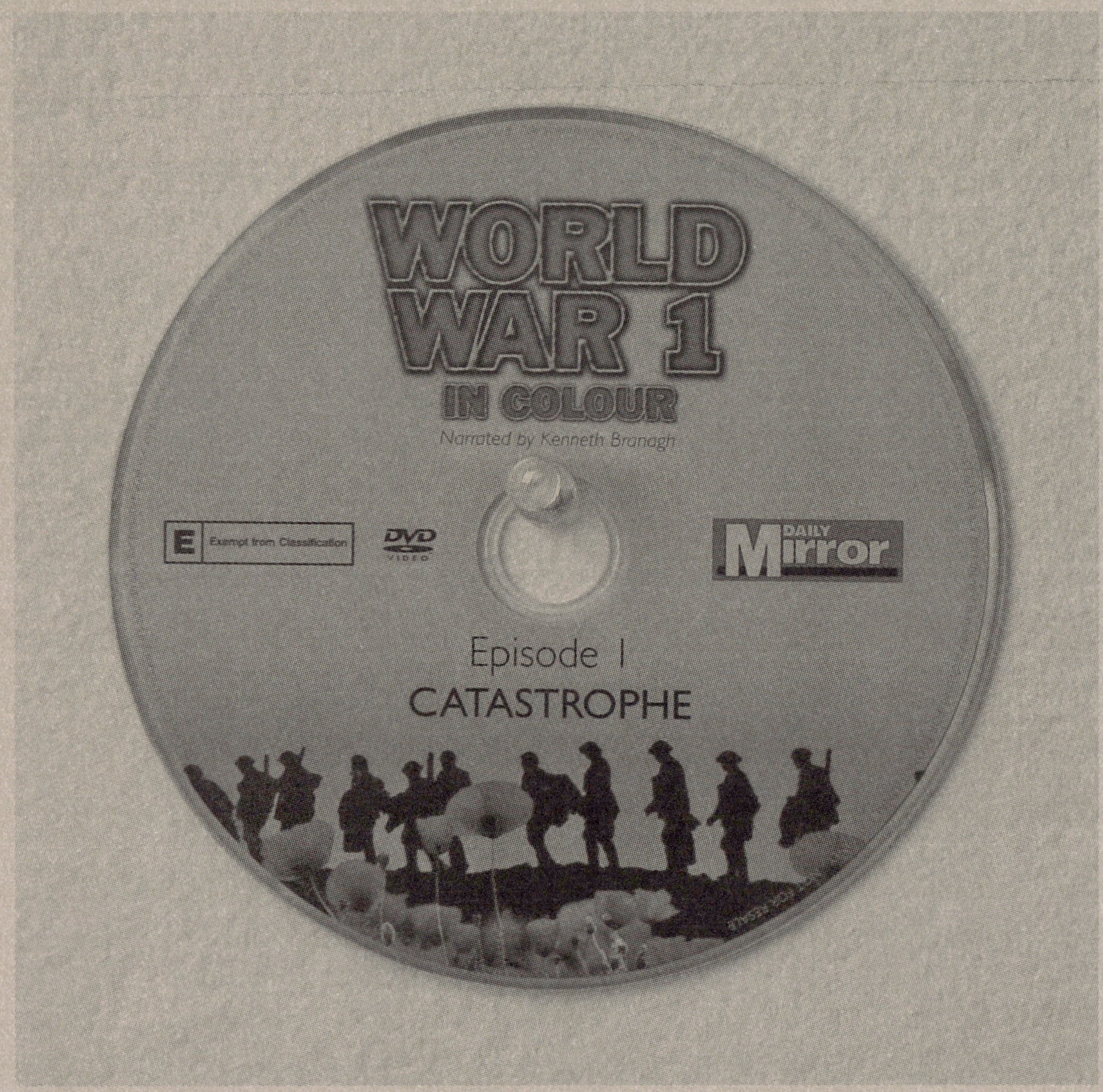


World War 1 in colour,
narrated by Kenneth Branagh, Episode 1 Catastrophe,
free with the Daily Mirror, 2008
(public screening prohibited)
DVD
12 x 12 cms

3

it it it more!
did drink the Nothingness itself objet petit
opposite 'culturalization' of the market
economy itself place objet petit a
horror vacui creating empty,
unoccupied place occupant without a place
correlative only an element which is
thoroughly 'out of place' can sustain the void of
an empty place rien n'aura eu lieu que le lieu
suicide imaginary
imagined Real passage à l'acte
resists cannot
resists internal
passage à l'acte direct
directly same passage à l'acte
passage à l'acte symbolic almost-nothing
opposite this
L'objet du siècle future anterior
rien n'aura eu lieu que le lieu takes place
save its own à la
'objectively' ugly 'represents' the function of ugliness
irrelevant Verweisung
The Last Tycoon But behind
desublimation directly depicting
had to be accomplished
the Void itself trash itself
within directly

p.40

World War 1 in Colour (the void itself), 2009
inkjet billboard sheets
each 92 x 133 cms

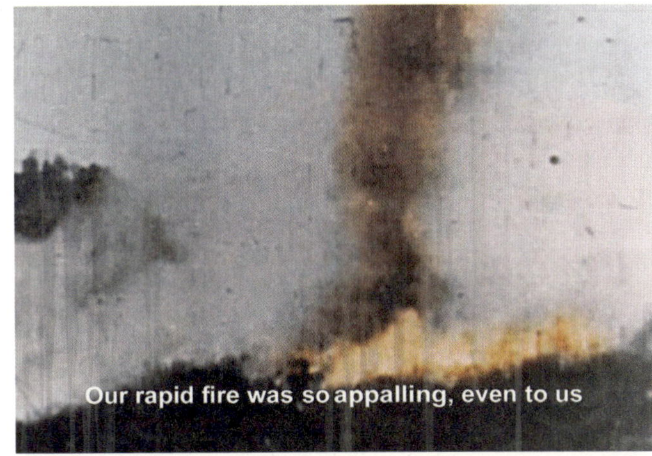
Our rapid fire was so appalling, even to us

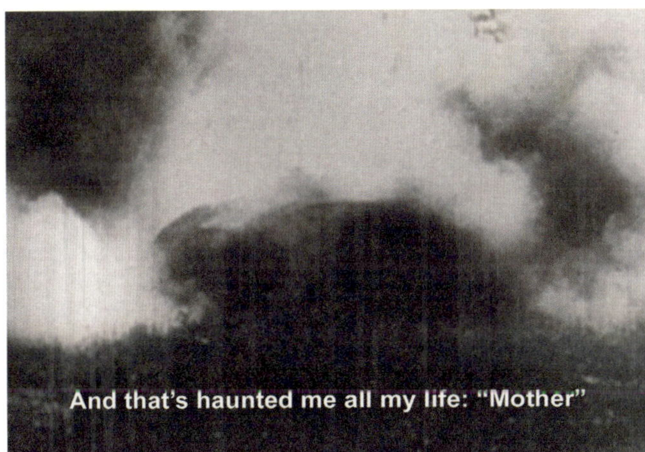
And that's haunted me all my life: "Mother"

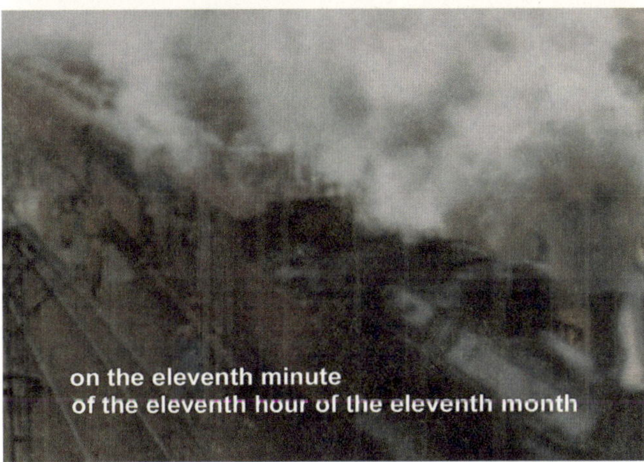
on the eleventh minute
of the eleventh hour of the eleventh month

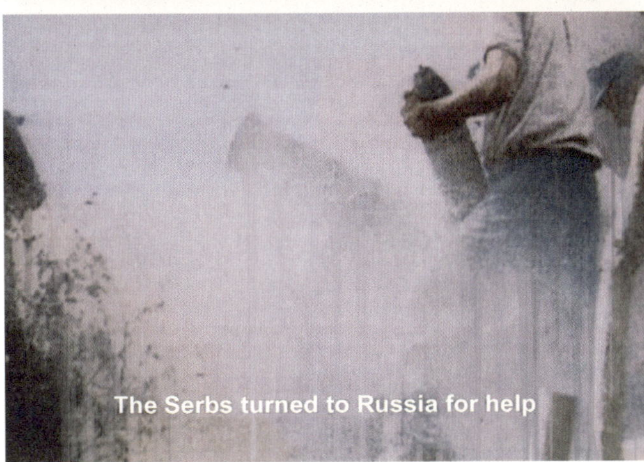
The Serbs turned to Russia for help

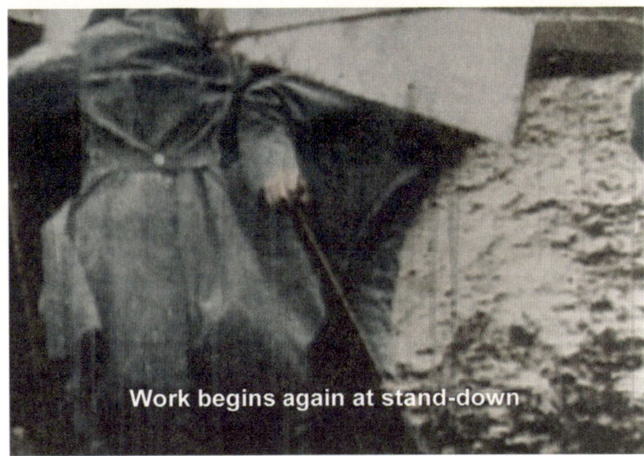
Work begins again at stand-down

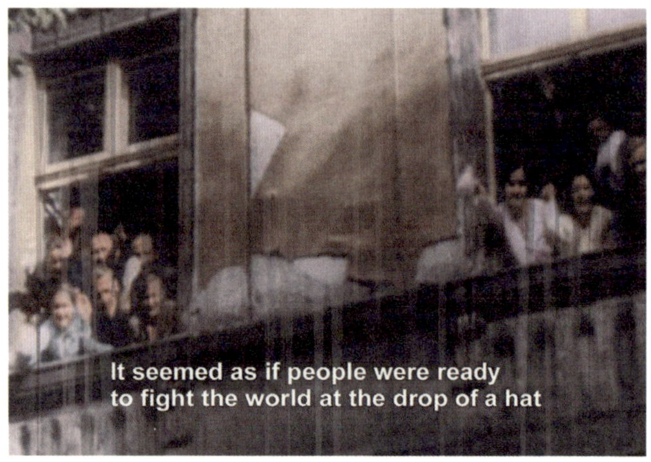
It seemed as if people were ready
to fight the world at the drop of a hat

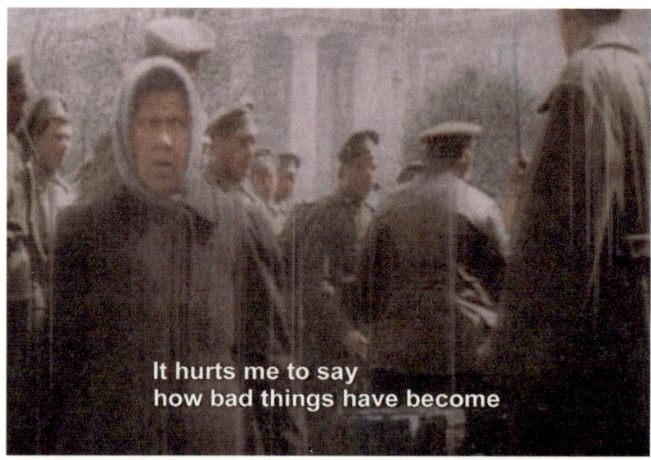
It hurts me to say
how bad things have become

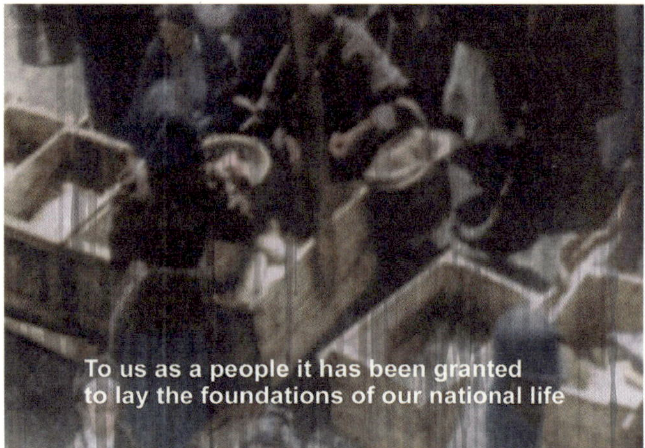
To us as a people it has been granted
to lay the foundations of our national life

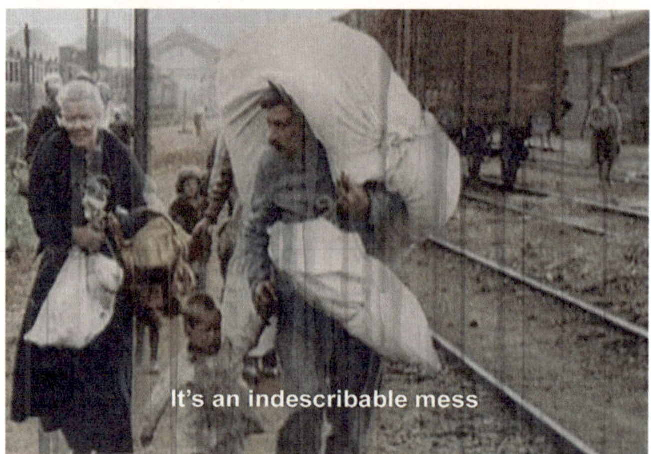
It's an indescribable mess

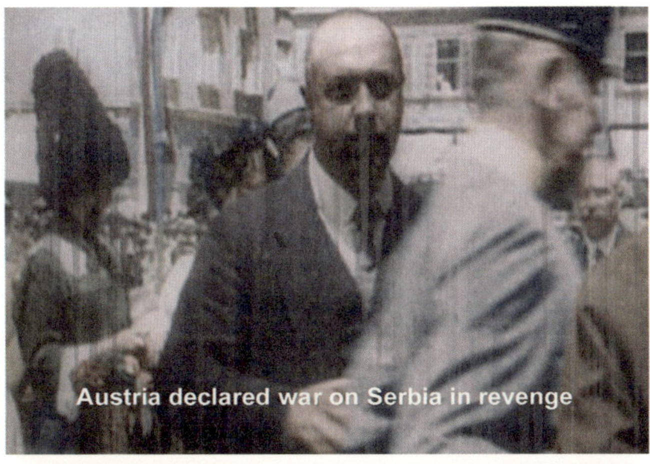
Austria declared war on Serbia in revenge

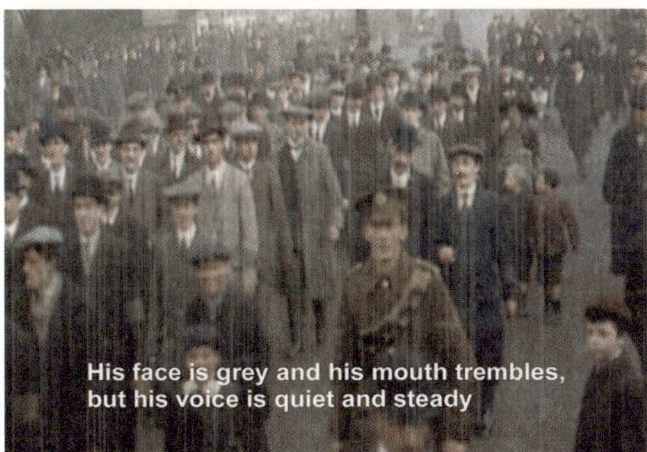
His face is grey and his mouth trembles,
but his voice is quiet and steady

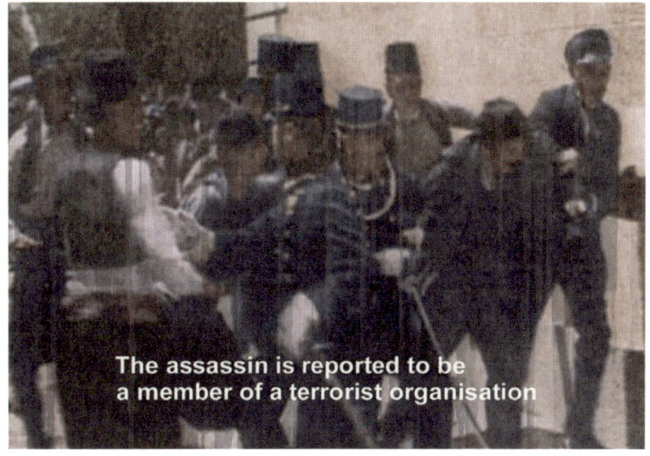
The assassin is reported to be
a member of a terrorist organisation

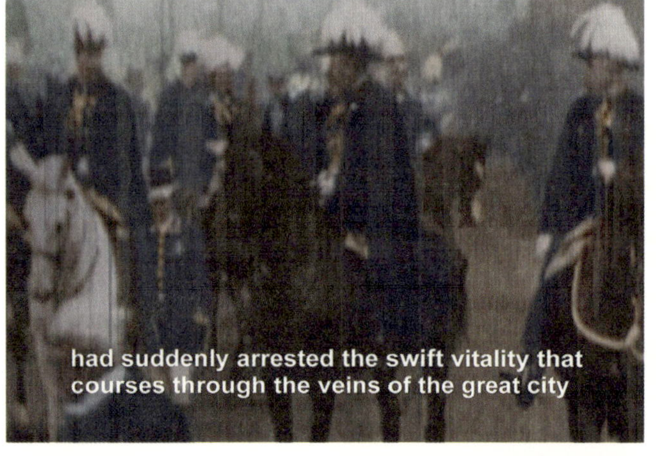
had suddenly arrested the swift vitality that
courses through the veins of the great city

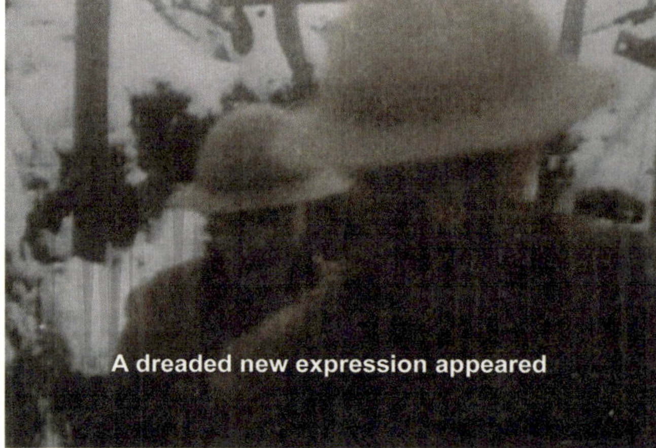
A dreaded new expression appeared

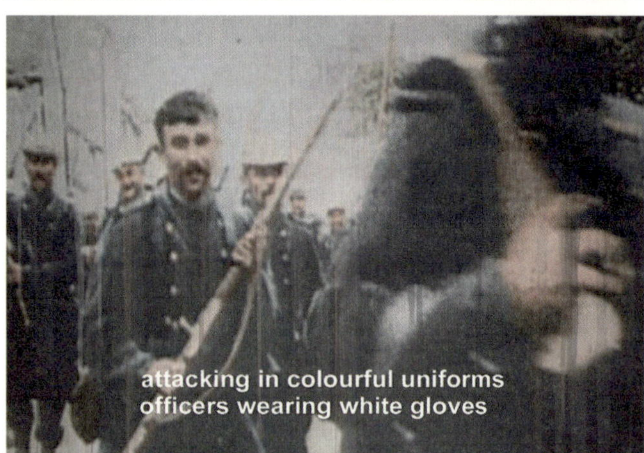
attacking in colourful uniforms
officers wearing white gloves

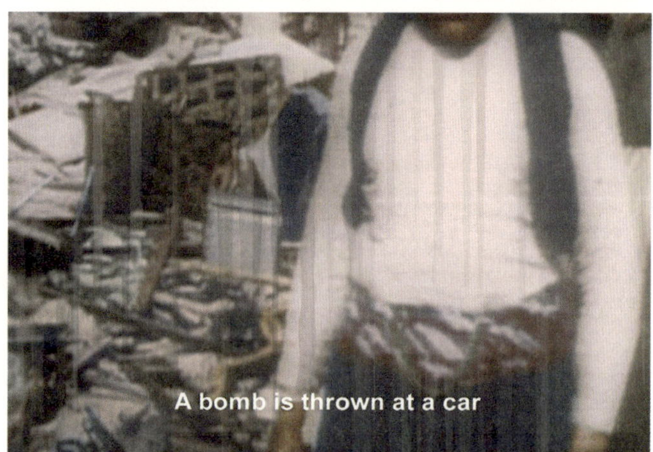
A bomb is thrown at a car

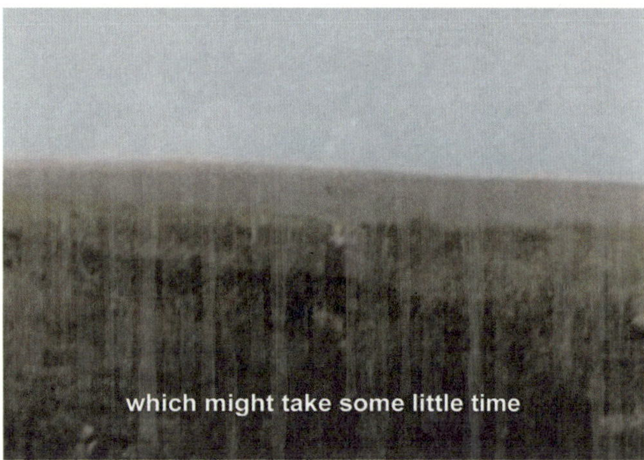
which might take some little time

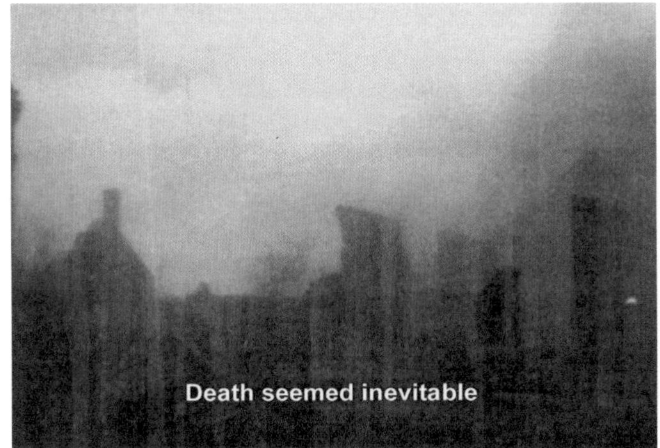
Death seemed inevitable

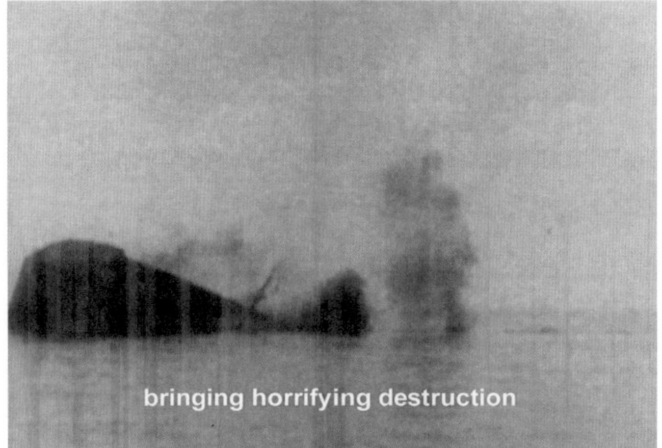
bringing horrifying destruction

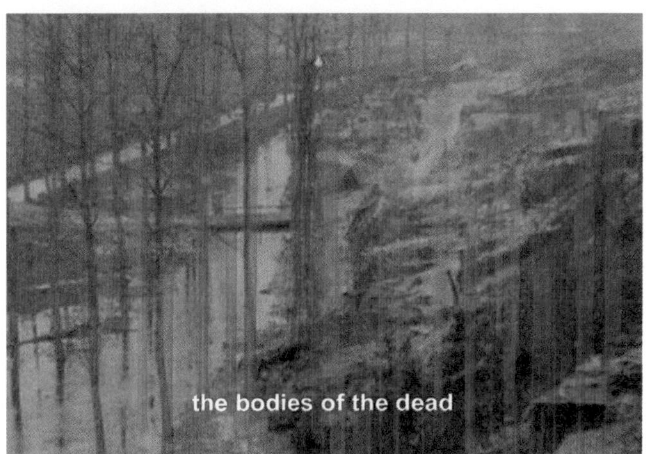
the bodies of the dead

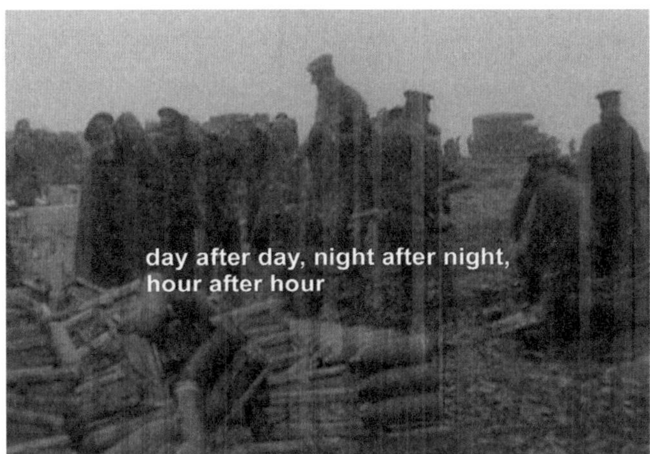
day after day, night after night,
hour after hour

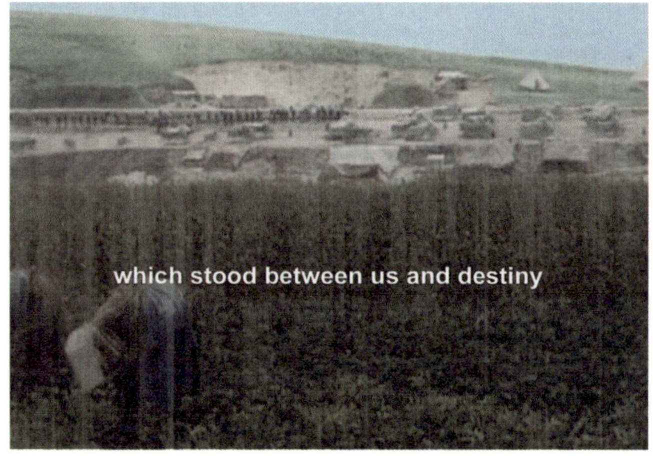
which stood between us and destiny

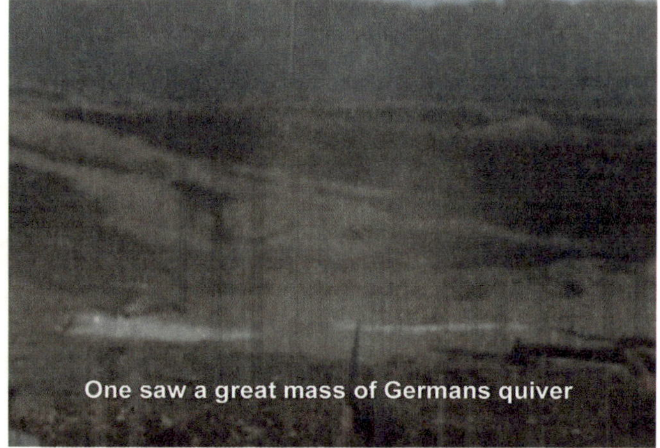
One saw a great mass of Germans quiver

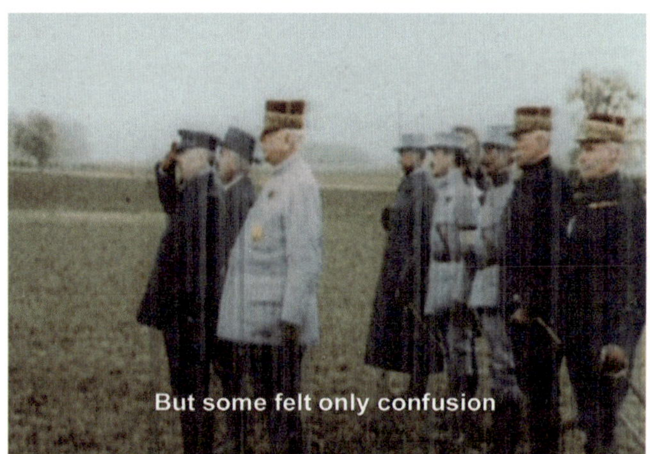
But some felt only confusion

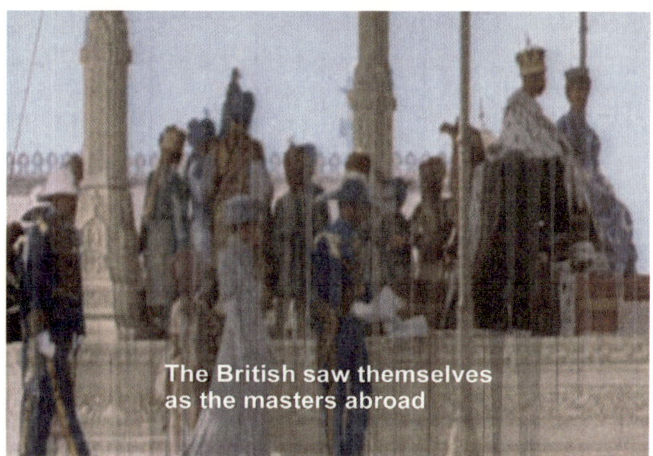
The British saw themselves
as the masters abroad

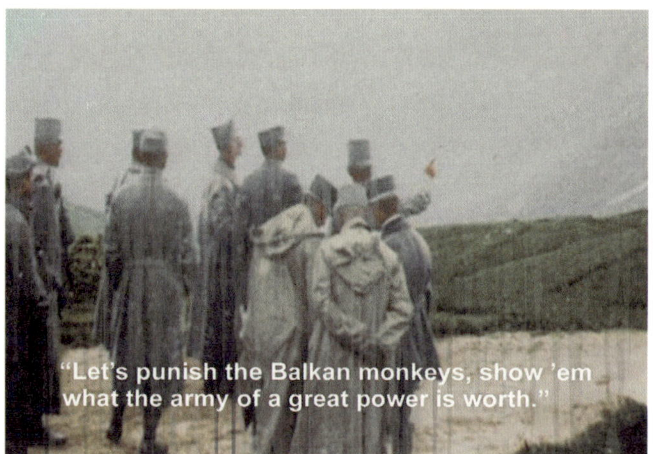
"Let's punish the Balkan monkeys, show 'em
what the army of a great power is worth."

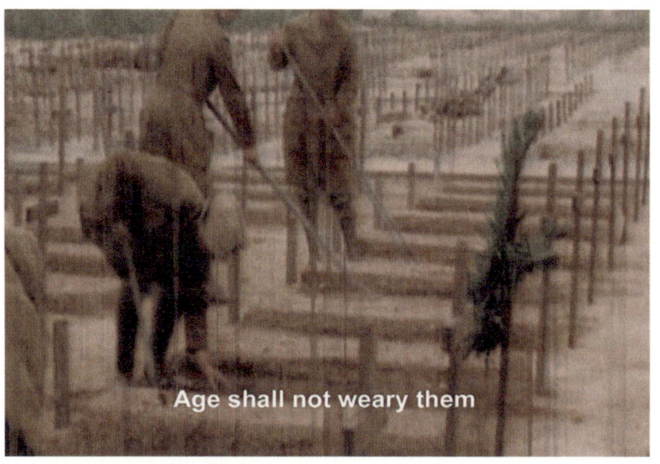
Age shall not weary them

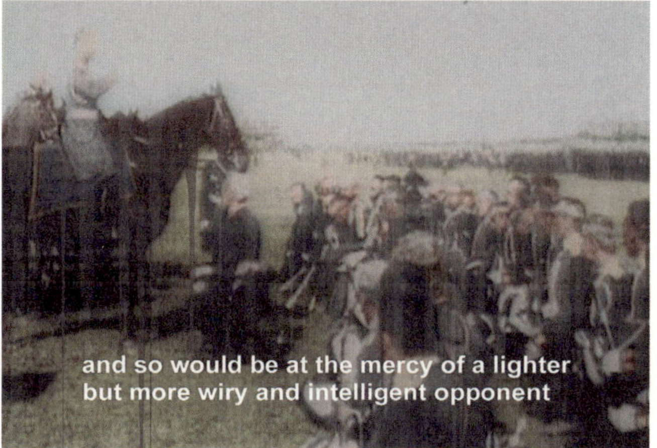
and so would be at the mercy of a lighter
but more wiry and intelligent opponent

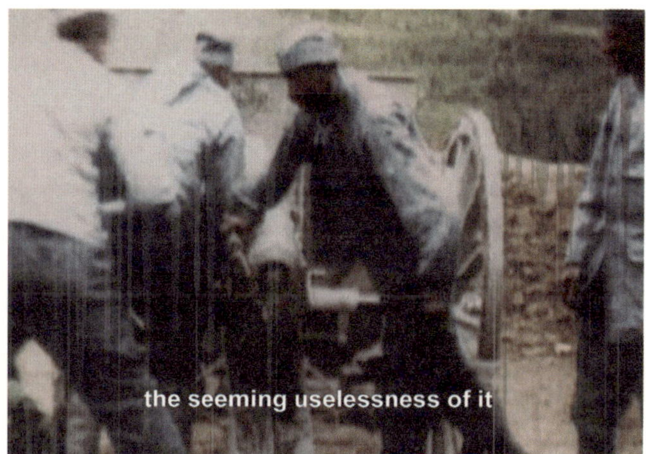
the seeming uselessness of it

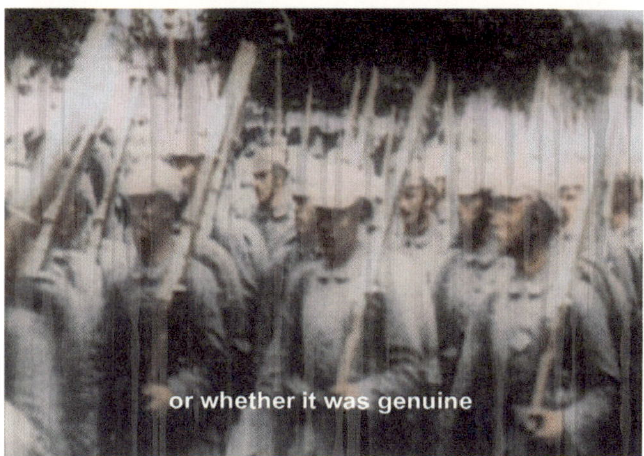
or whether it was genuine

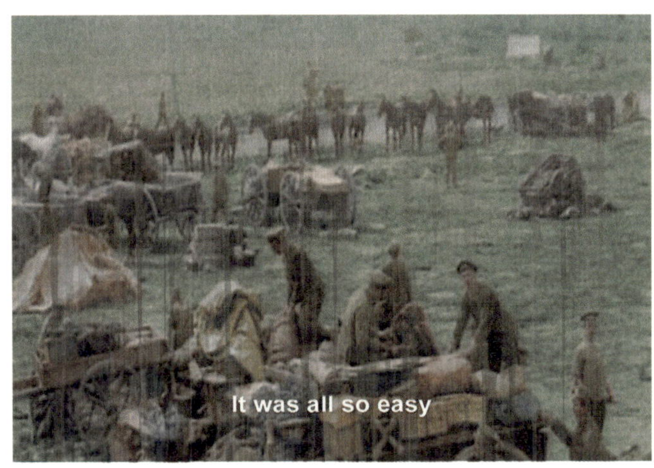
It was all so easy

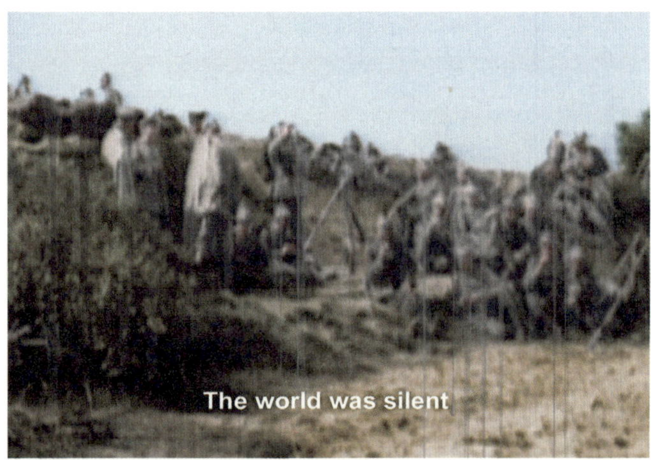
The world was silent

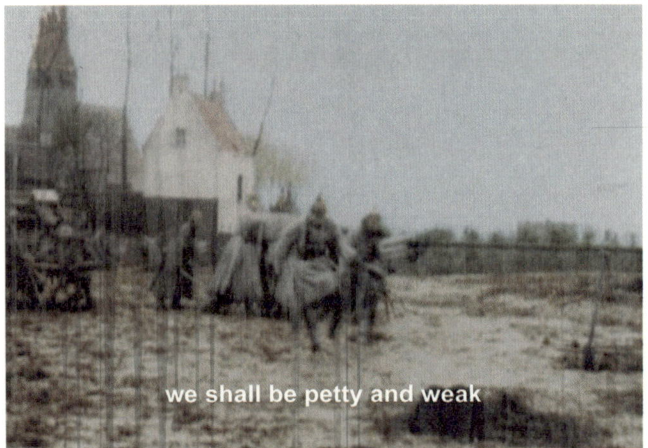
we shall be petty and weak

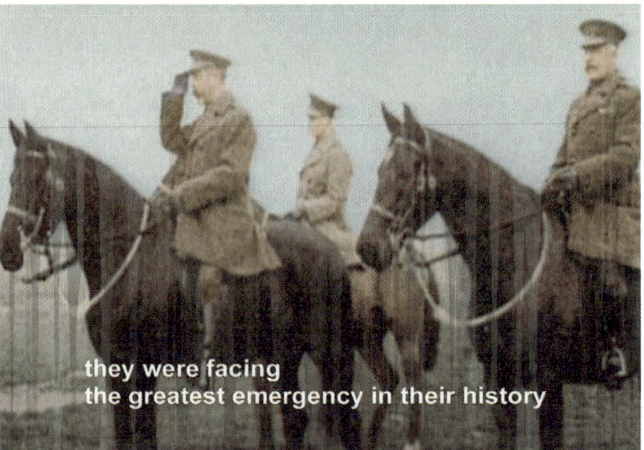
they were facing
the greatest emergency in their history

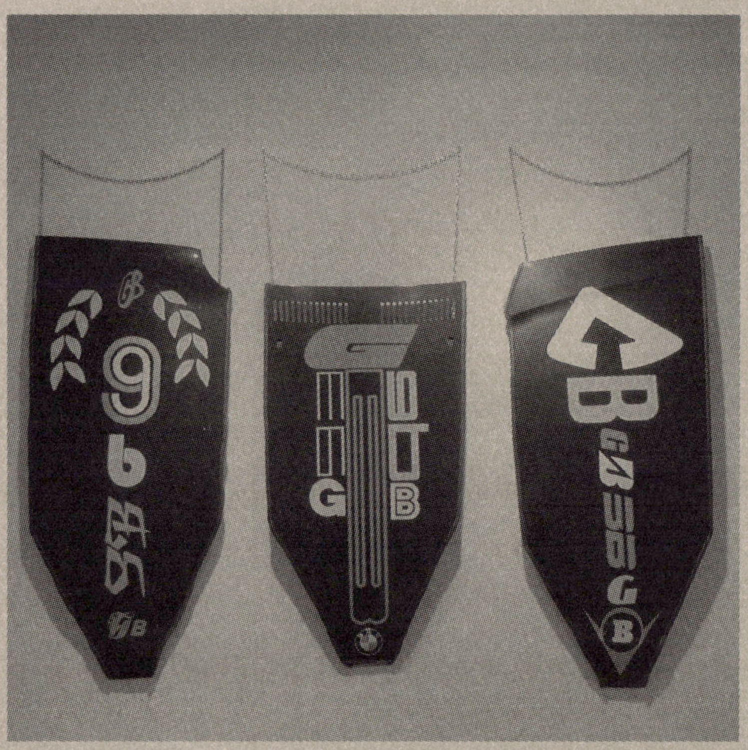

GB Shields, 2004
metal, rubber, vinyl adhesive stickers
various sizes, approx. 250 x 50 x 4 cms

objet petit a The Manifesto Stalker
not objet petit a
Oedipus at Colonus Oedipus the King
tragique moque-comique? Phenomenology
tragique moque-comique?
Nephew of Rameau Eighteenth Brumaire
repeats grandeur passage
from which the
avoid emphasizing assuming
not Rameau not radical enough
remains the same nothing
money das Selbst
sustains do objet petit a
objet petit a objet petit a expected
as such two objet petit a
tragique moque-comique
objet petit a objet petit a symbolic
identification with the way the Other(s) misperceive(s) me
misperception objet petit a
all the time horse look like
resemble the guarantor of non-identity
signifier ad infinitum nothing
as such absence object
all excluding himself in

4

Insert:
Poster for the Second Gordon Bennett Show & Shine, 2006

Second Gordon Bennett Memorial Show and Shine
Modified car event - Sunday, 29 October 2006

Scent of Orange Rim Cleaner (object petit object), 2009
scent, delivery system
developed by Demeter Fragrance Library

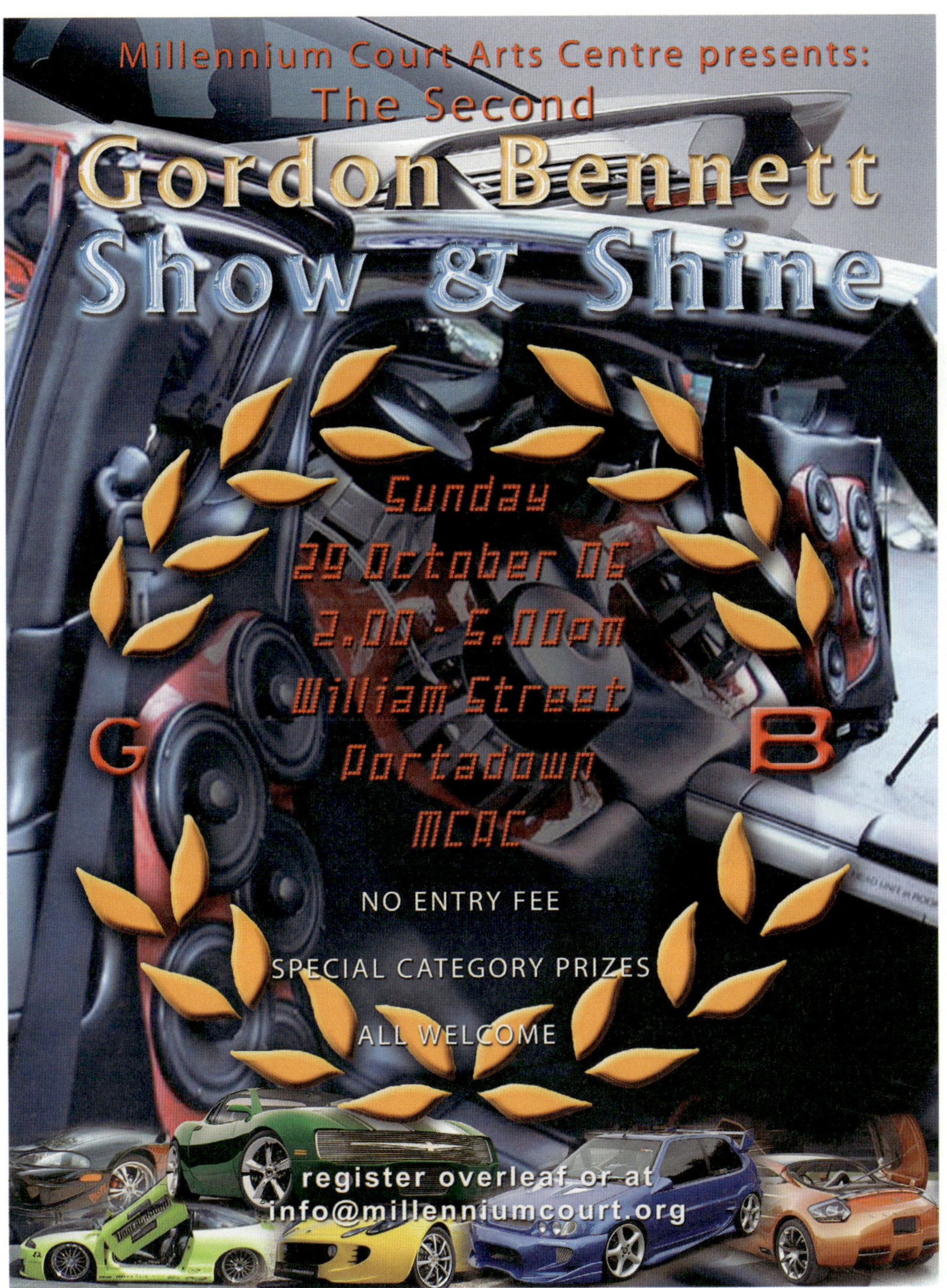
Millennium Court Arts Centre presents:
The Second
Gordon Bennett
Show & Shine
Sunday
29 October 06
2.00 - 5.00pm
William Street
Portadown
MCAC
G
B
NO ENTRY FEE
SPECIAL CATEGORY PRIZES
ALL WELCOME
register overleaf or at
info@millenniumcourt.org

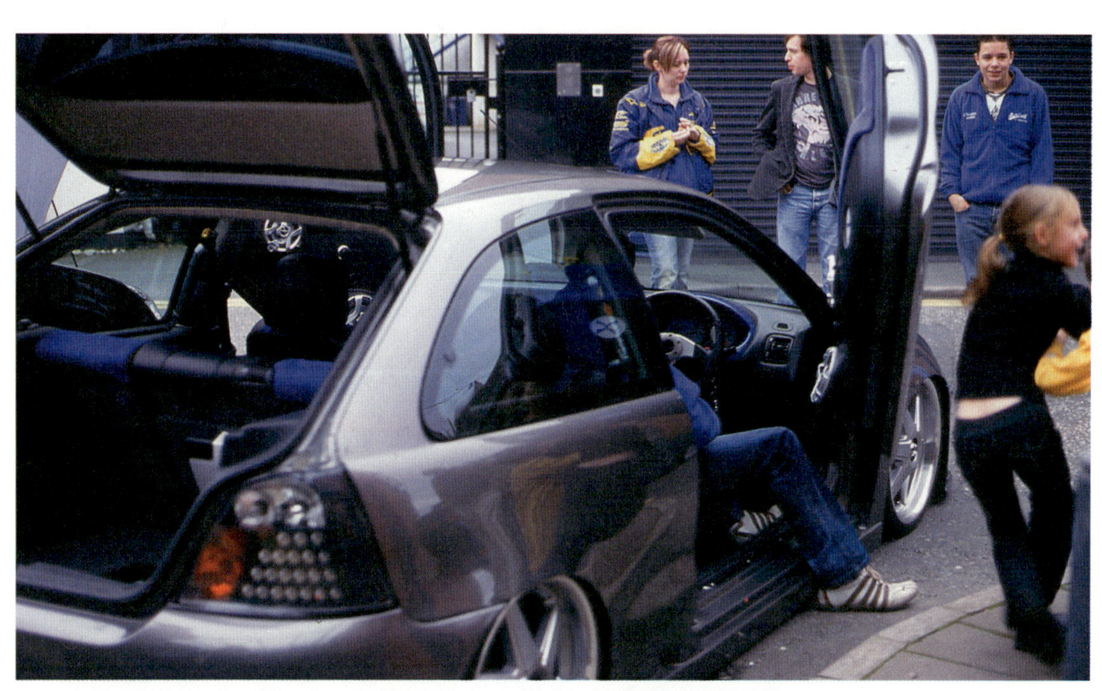

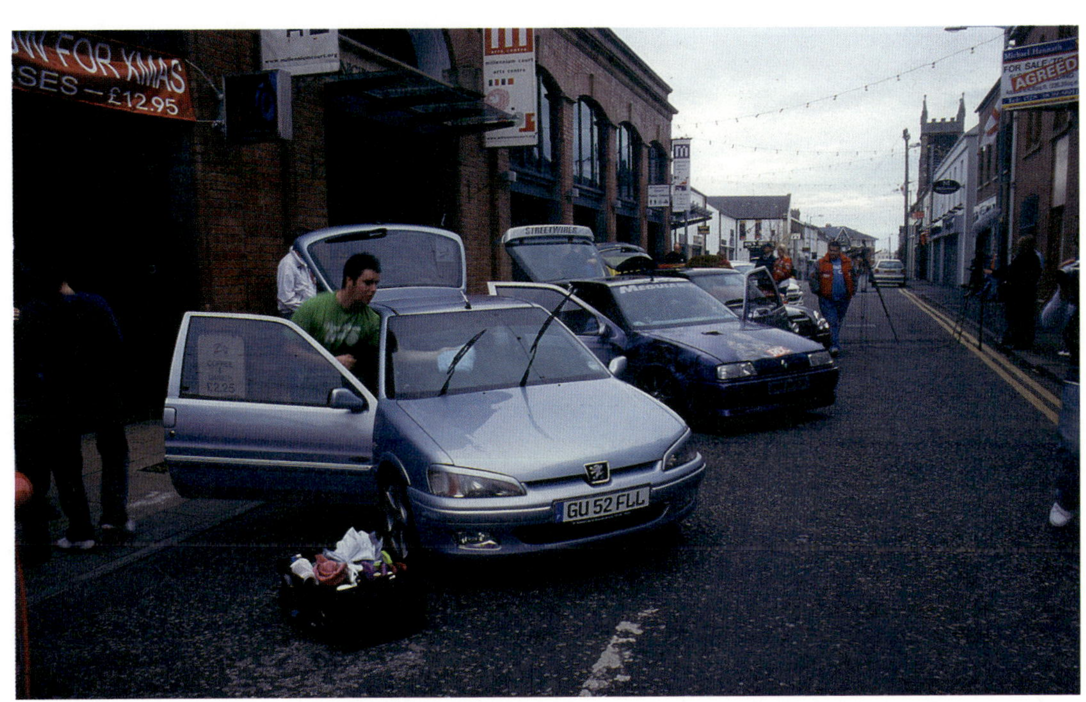
W FOR XMAS
SES – £12.95
FOR SALE
AGREED
GU 52 FLL

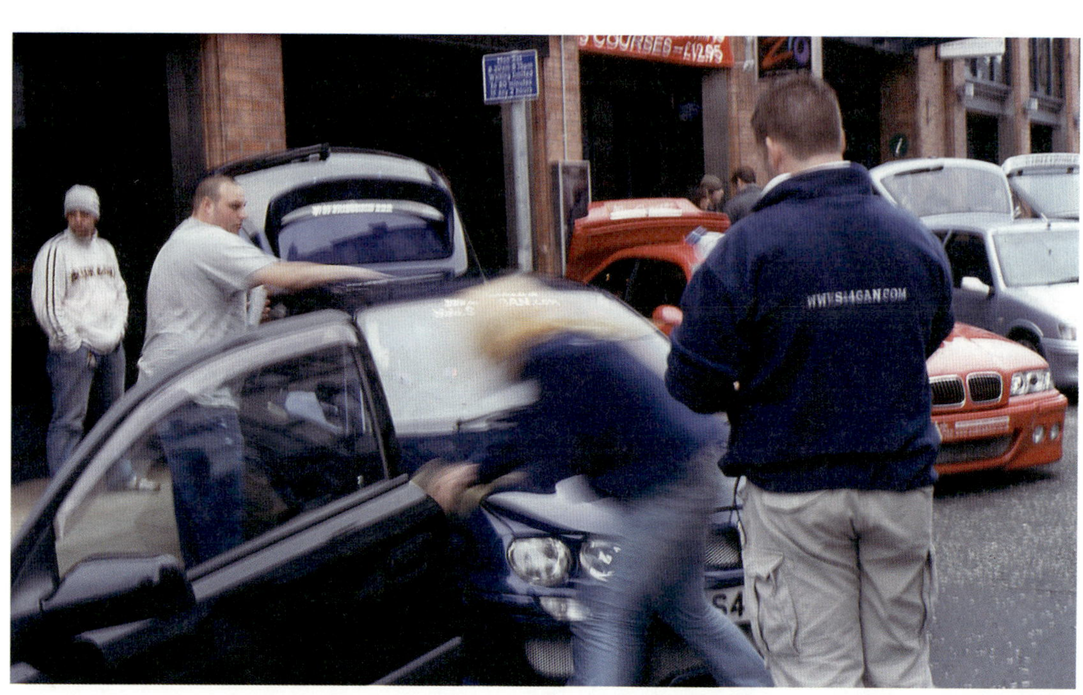

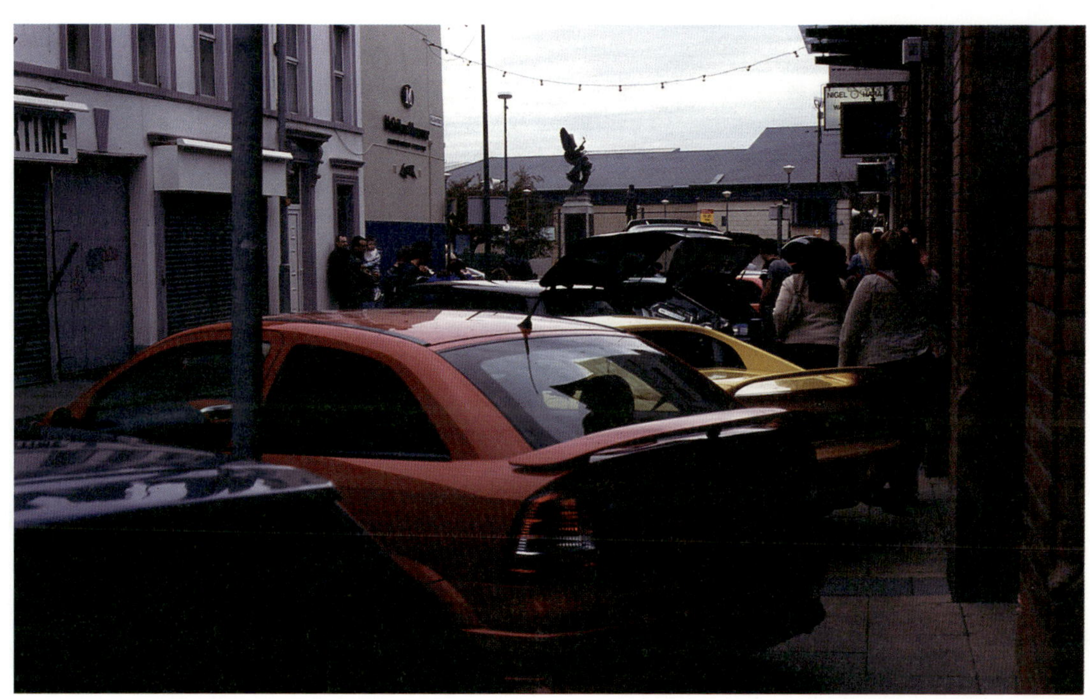
RTIME
NIGEL

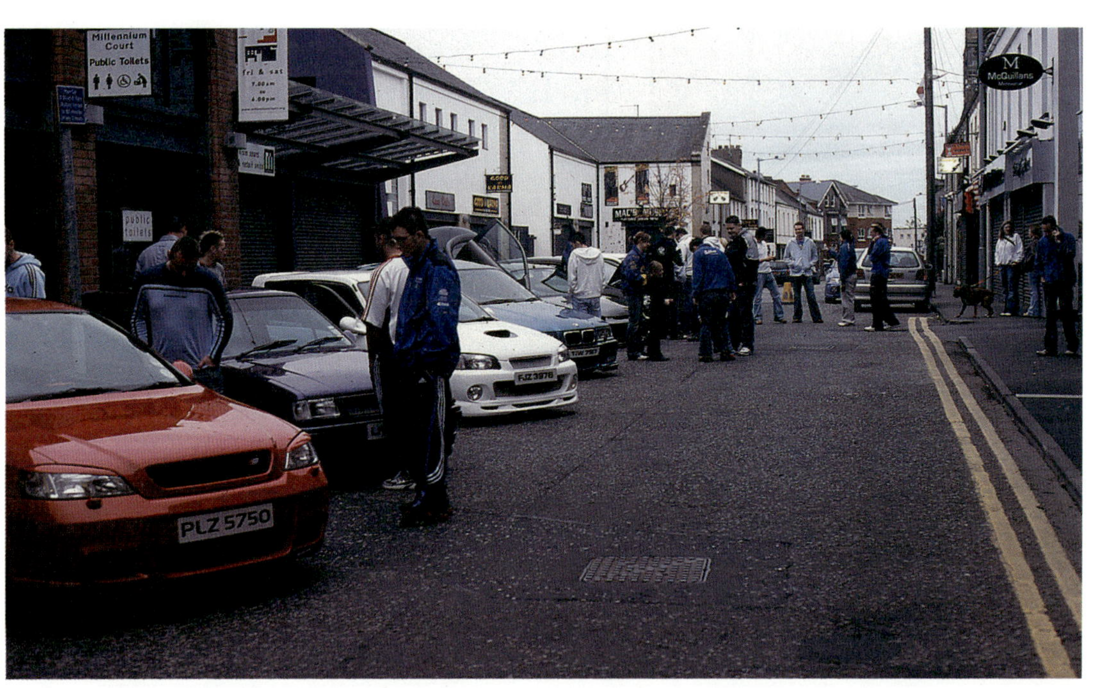
Millennium Court
Public Toilets
fri & sat
public toilets
McQuillans
PLZ 5750

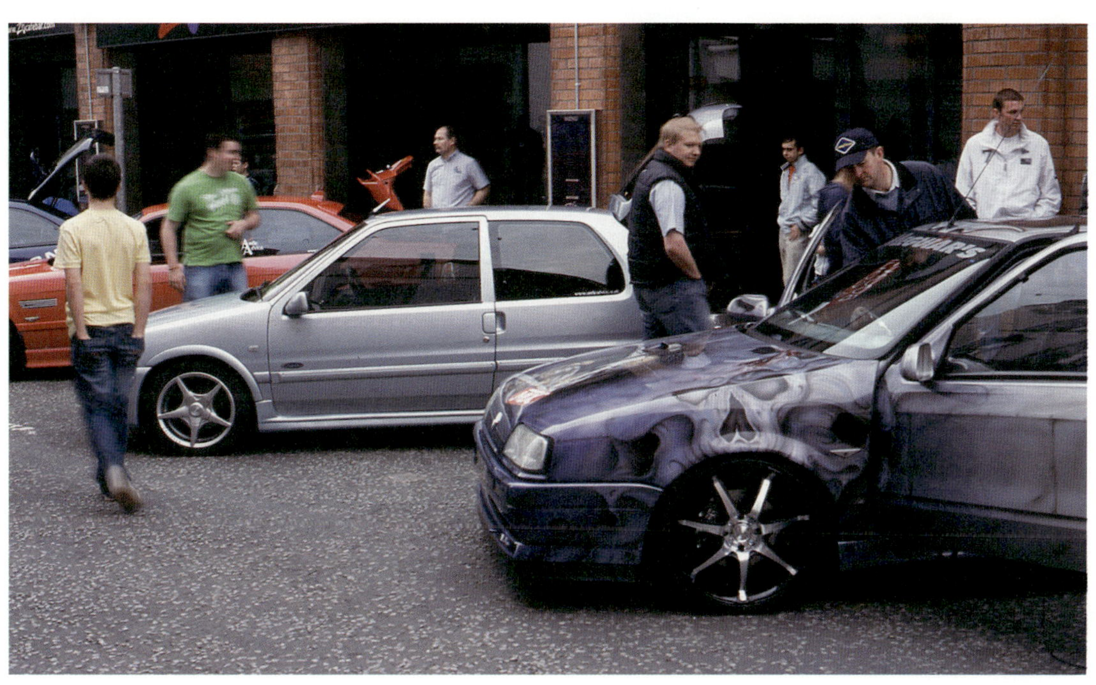

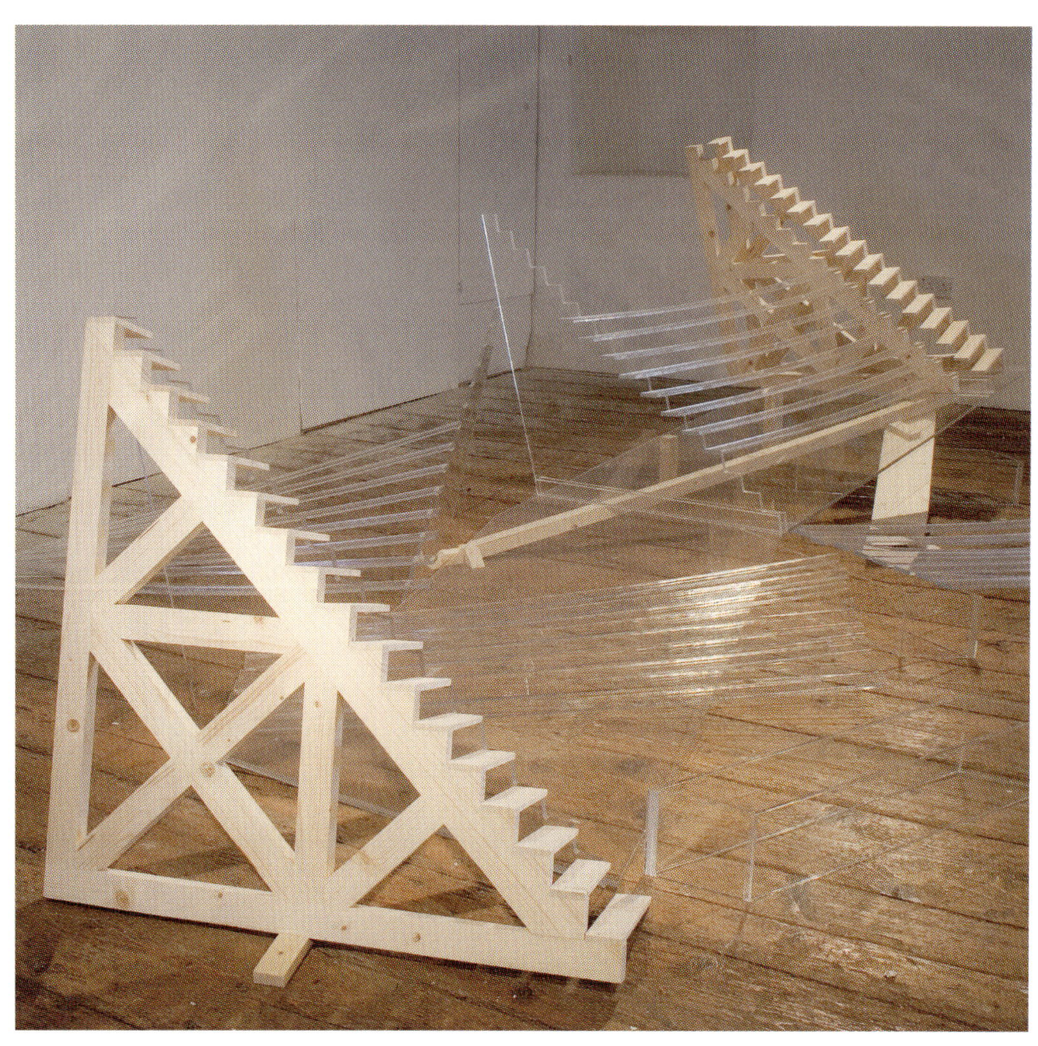

Grandstand, 2004
acrylic, wood
85 x 400 x 200 cms

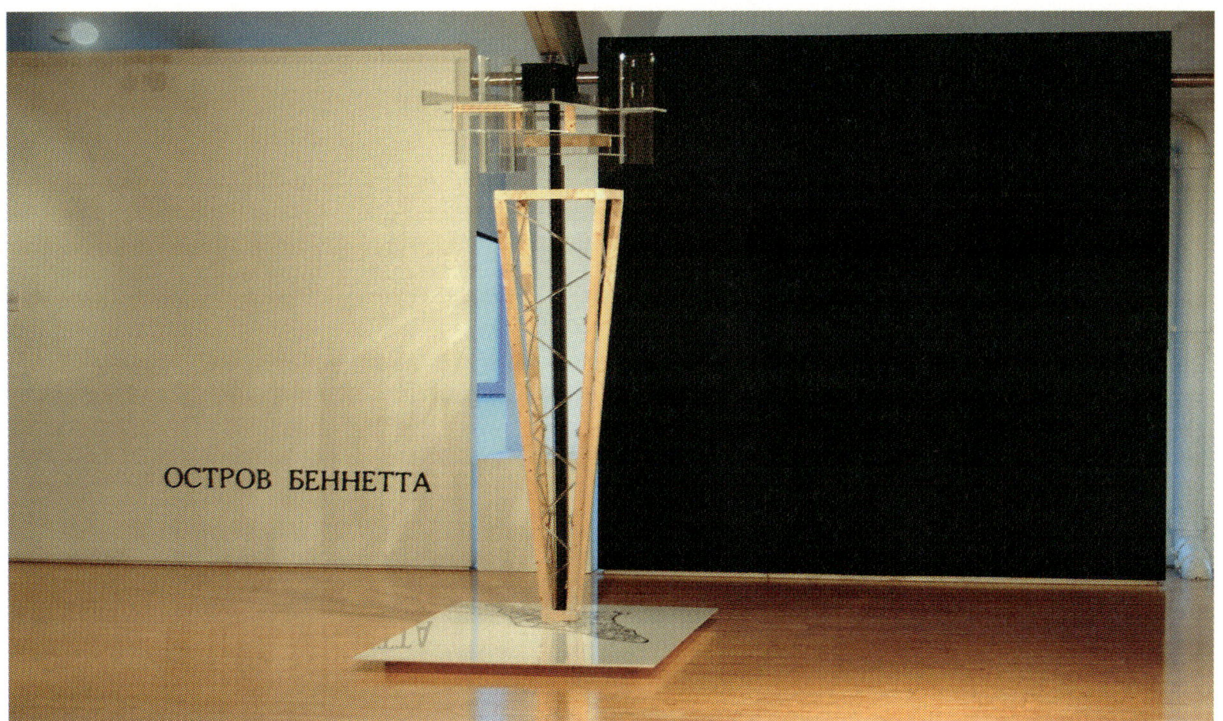


Bennett Island, 2005
acrylic, perspex, wood, metal, paint,
MDF, vinyl adhesive sticker
330 x 95 x 150 cms

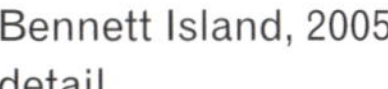

Bennett Island, 2005
detail

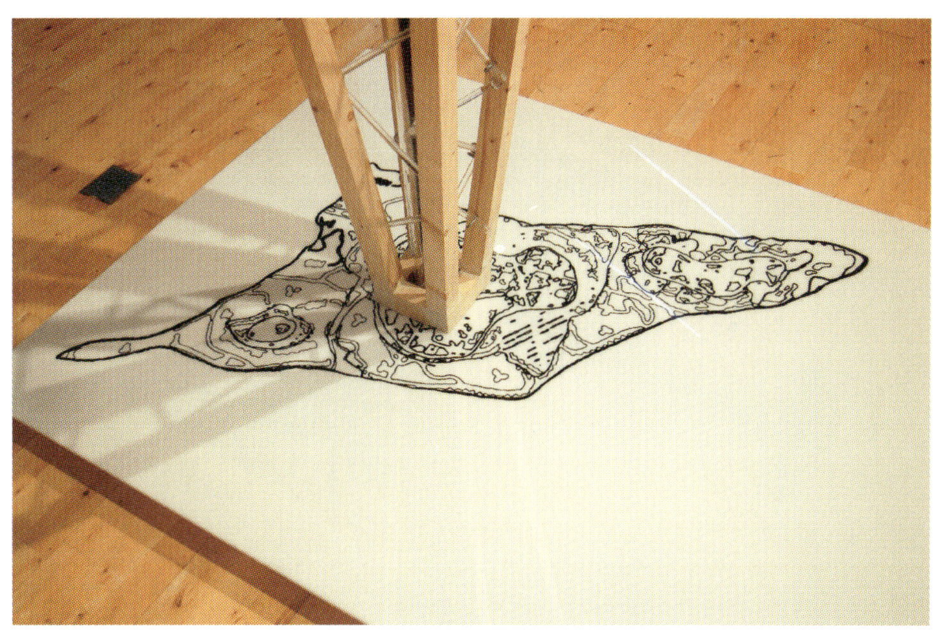

source image for Bald Finch, 2008

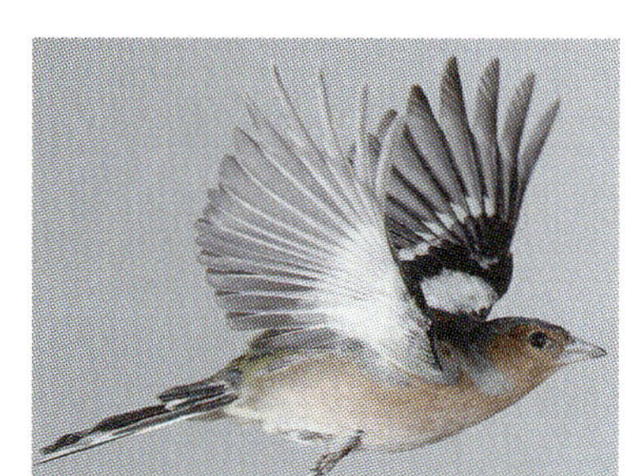

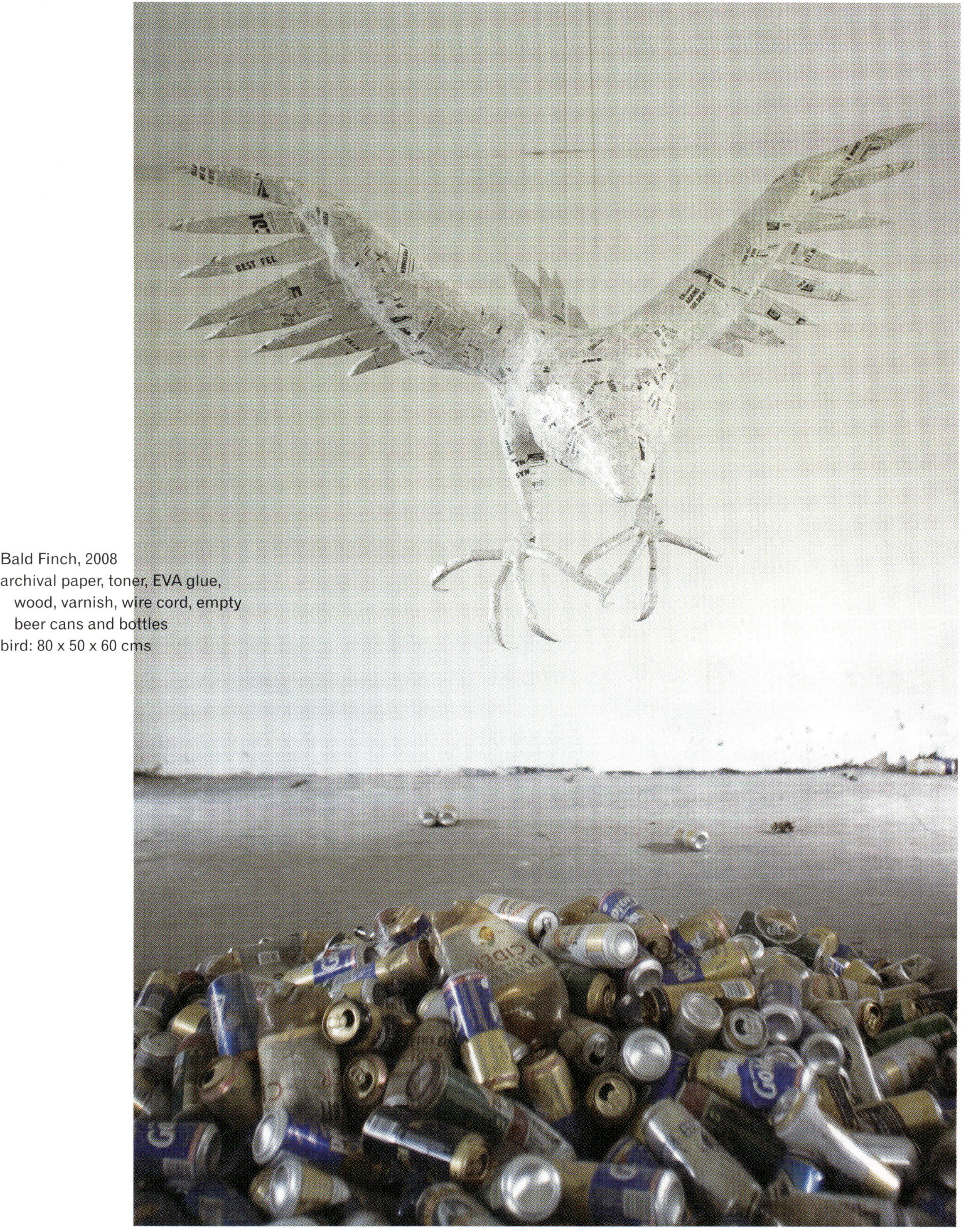

Bald Finch, 2008
archival paper, toner, EVA glue,
wood, varnish, wire cord, empty
beer cans and bottles
bird: 80 x 50 x 60 cms

Pig Protester, 2007
archival paper, toner, EVA glue, aluminium mesh
46 x 57 x 34 cms
(papier-mâché made from articles from Evening Herald, 1971)

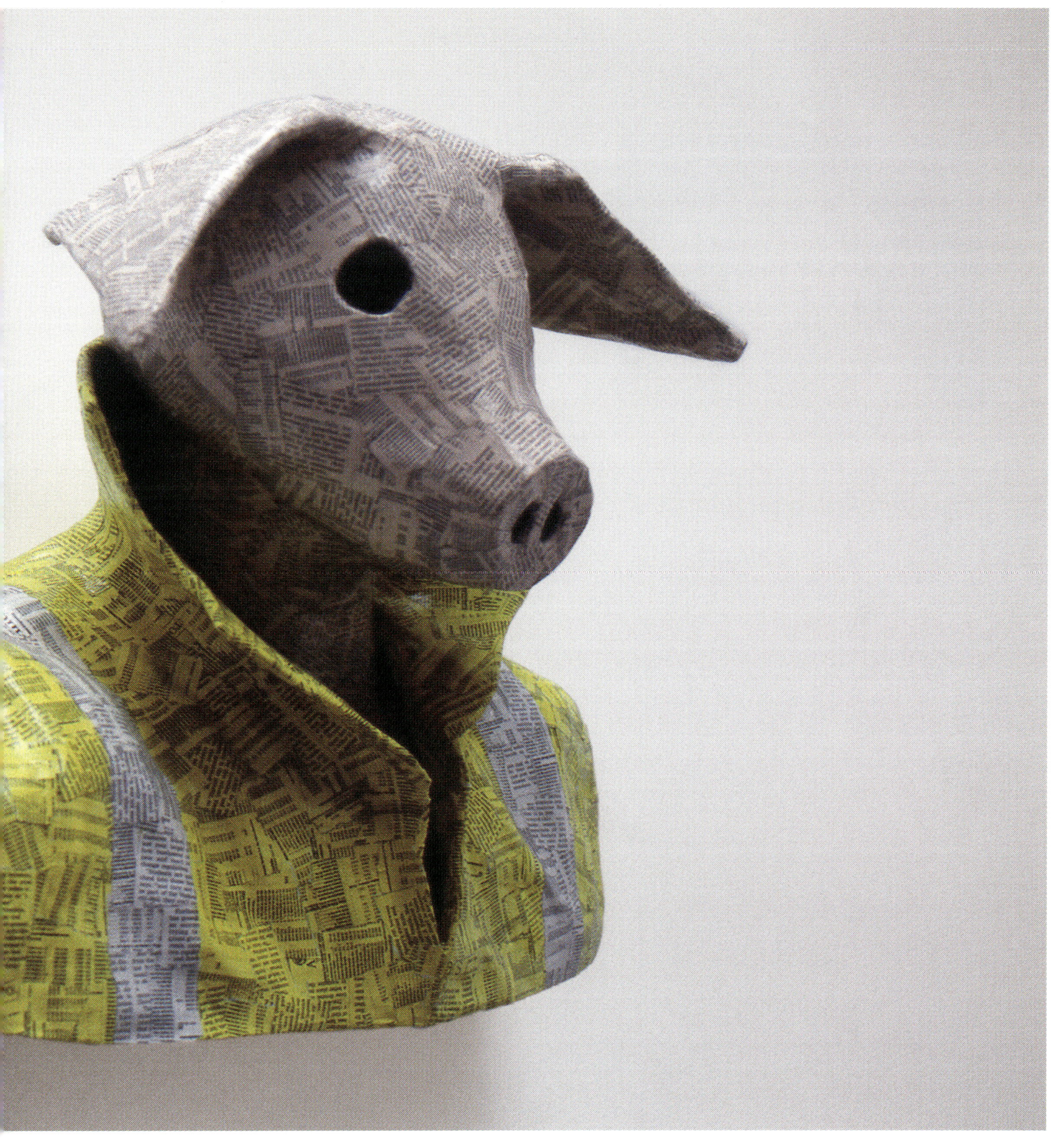

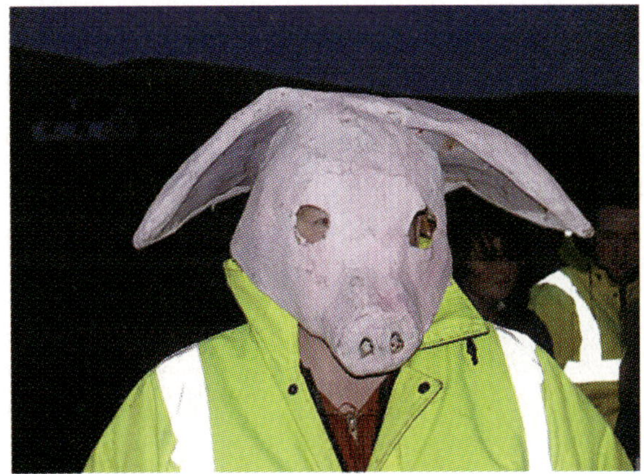

source image for Pig Protester, 2007

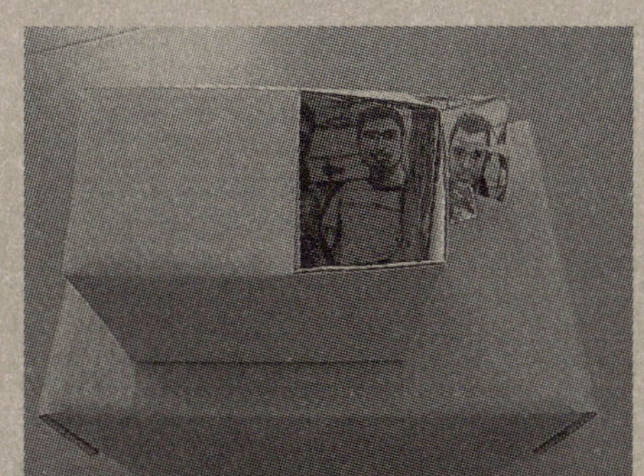

Wrong Box, 2008
die-cut cardboard, poster, glue
17 x 24.5 x 12 cms

does Die Süddeutsche Zeitung Nineteen Eighty-Four the problem with 'militaristic humanism/pacificism' lies not in 'militaristic' but in 'humanism/pacificism' The New York Times the full-scale armed resistance of the Albanians themselves helpless cast off this helplessness they would remain victims perverse Heroine in so far as it remains a victim uncanny The Sun Bild stepping down what would have happened if Lafontaine had not been forced to step down? nothing second there is no second way alternative first and only global capital with a human face

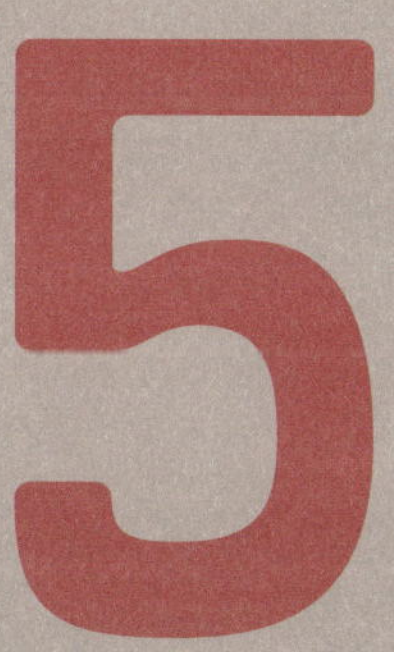

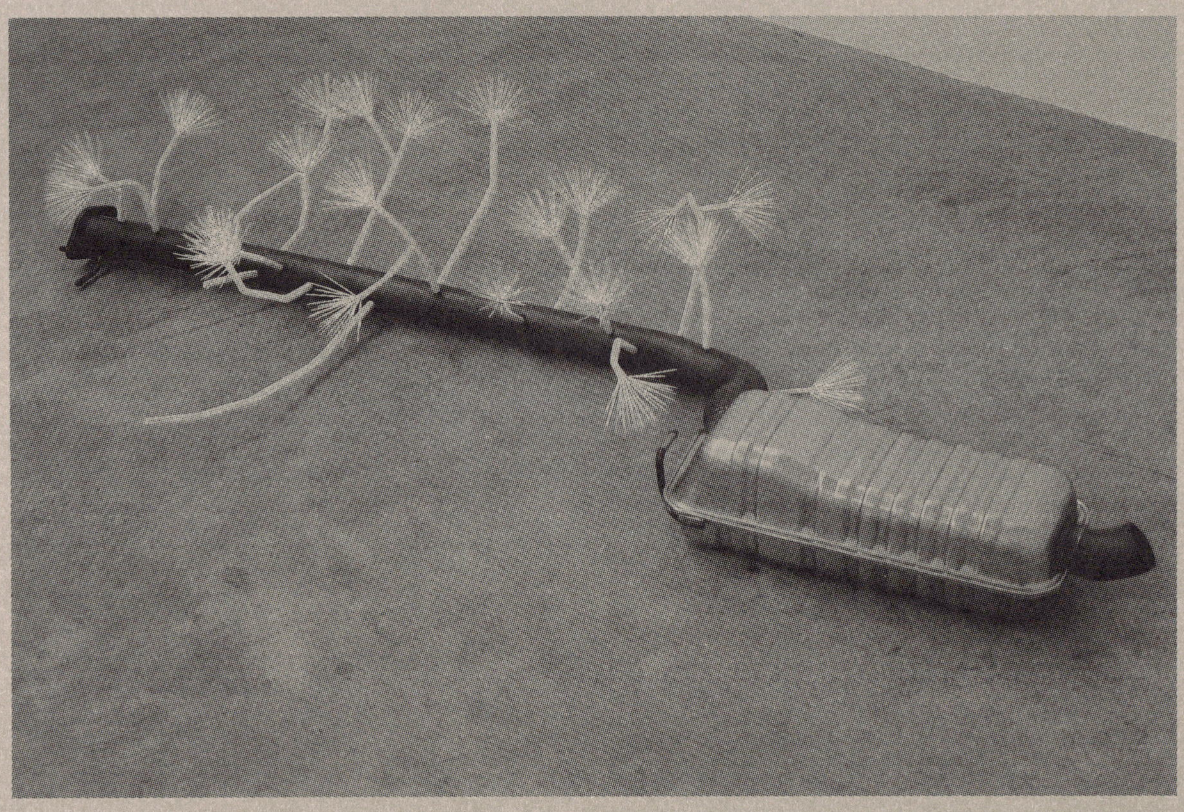

Fino's RS 2 exhaust blended-in as a branch, 2006
metal, balsa wood, cocktail sticks, varnish, paint, polish
25 x 194 x 60 x cms

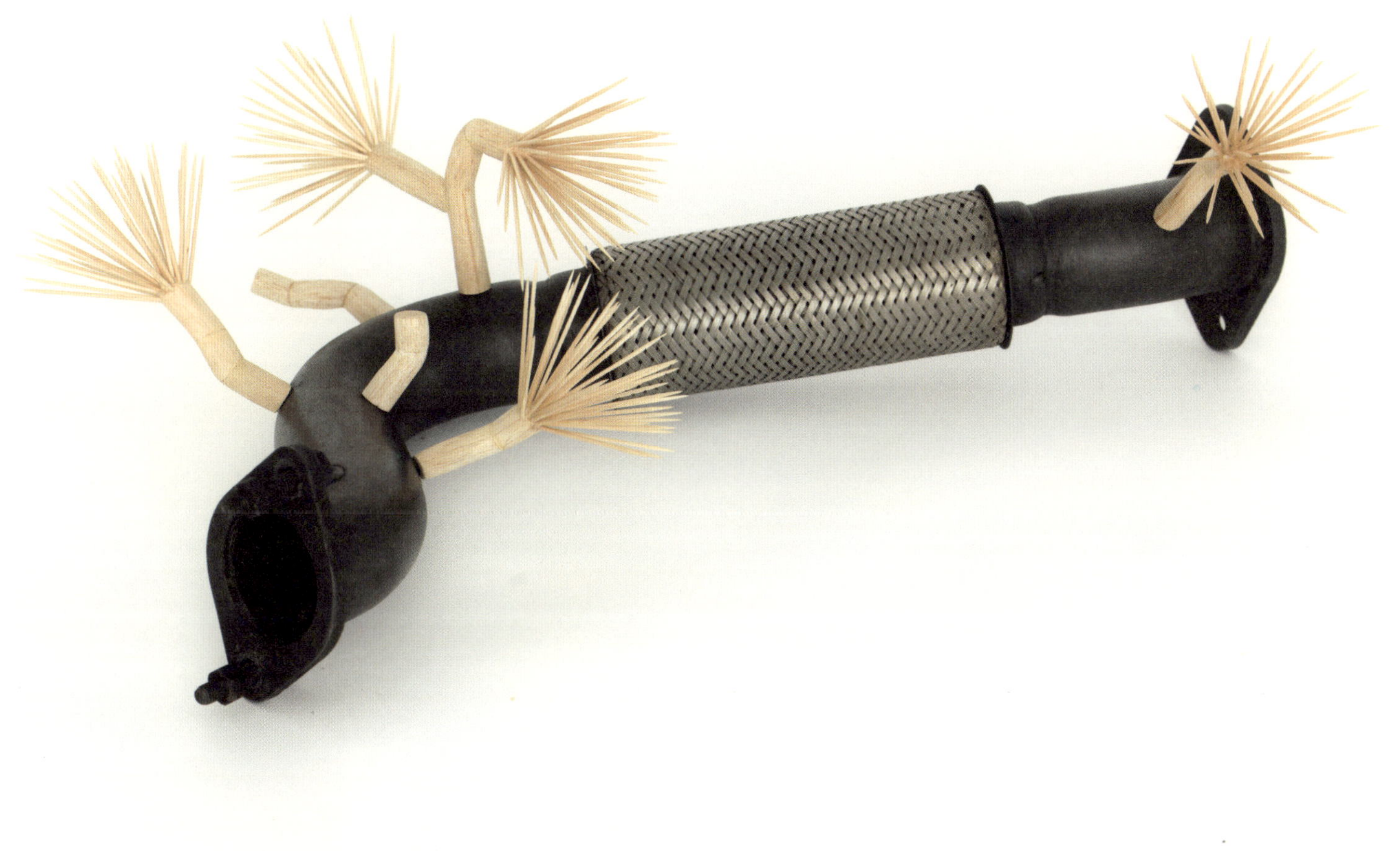

Fino's manifold blended-in as a branch, 2007
metal, balsa wood, cocktail sticks, varnish, paint, polish
25 x 64 x 44 cms

Light Fixture Disguised as a Tree, 2006
plastic, wood, metal
60 x 100 x 50 cms

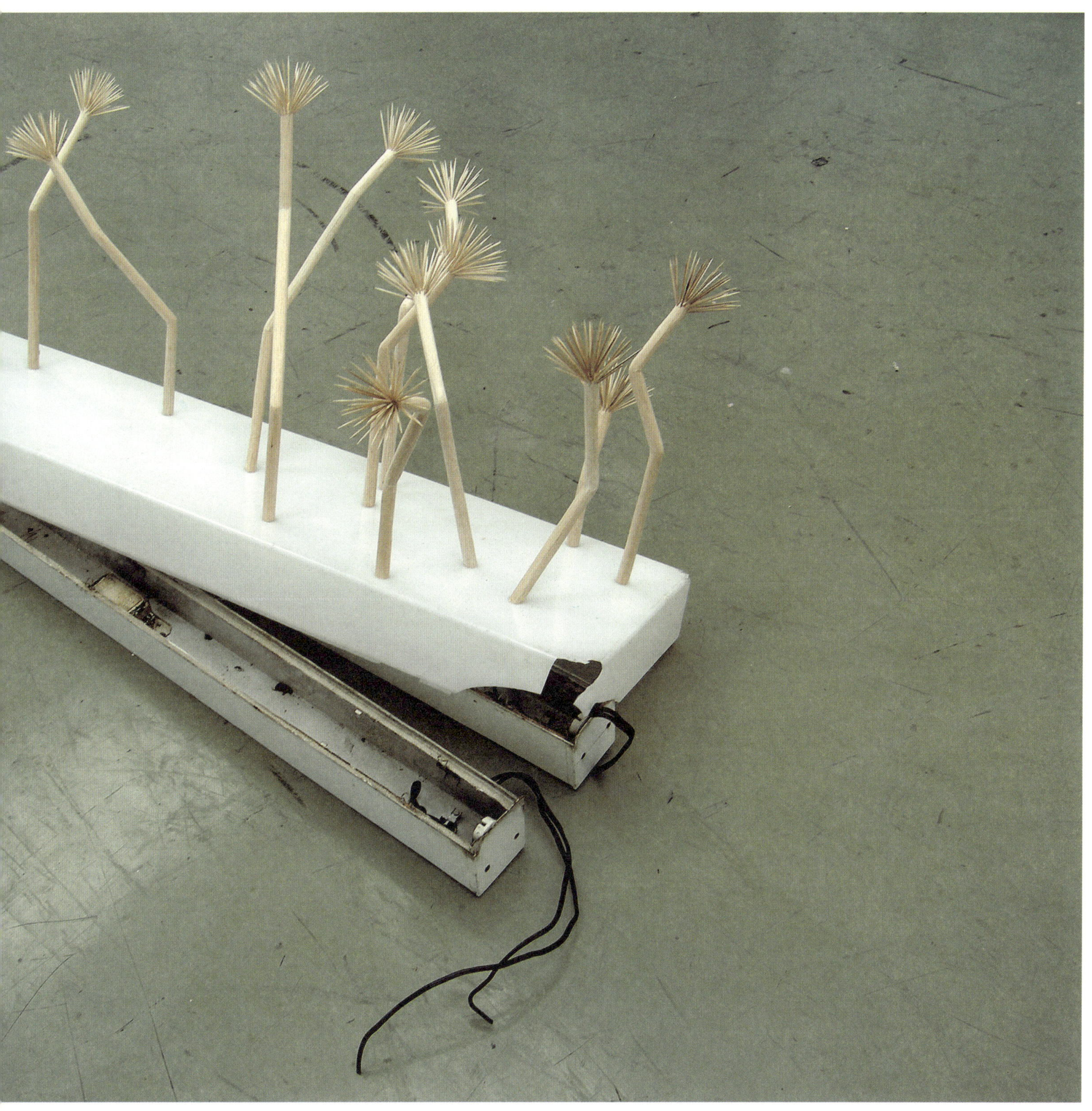

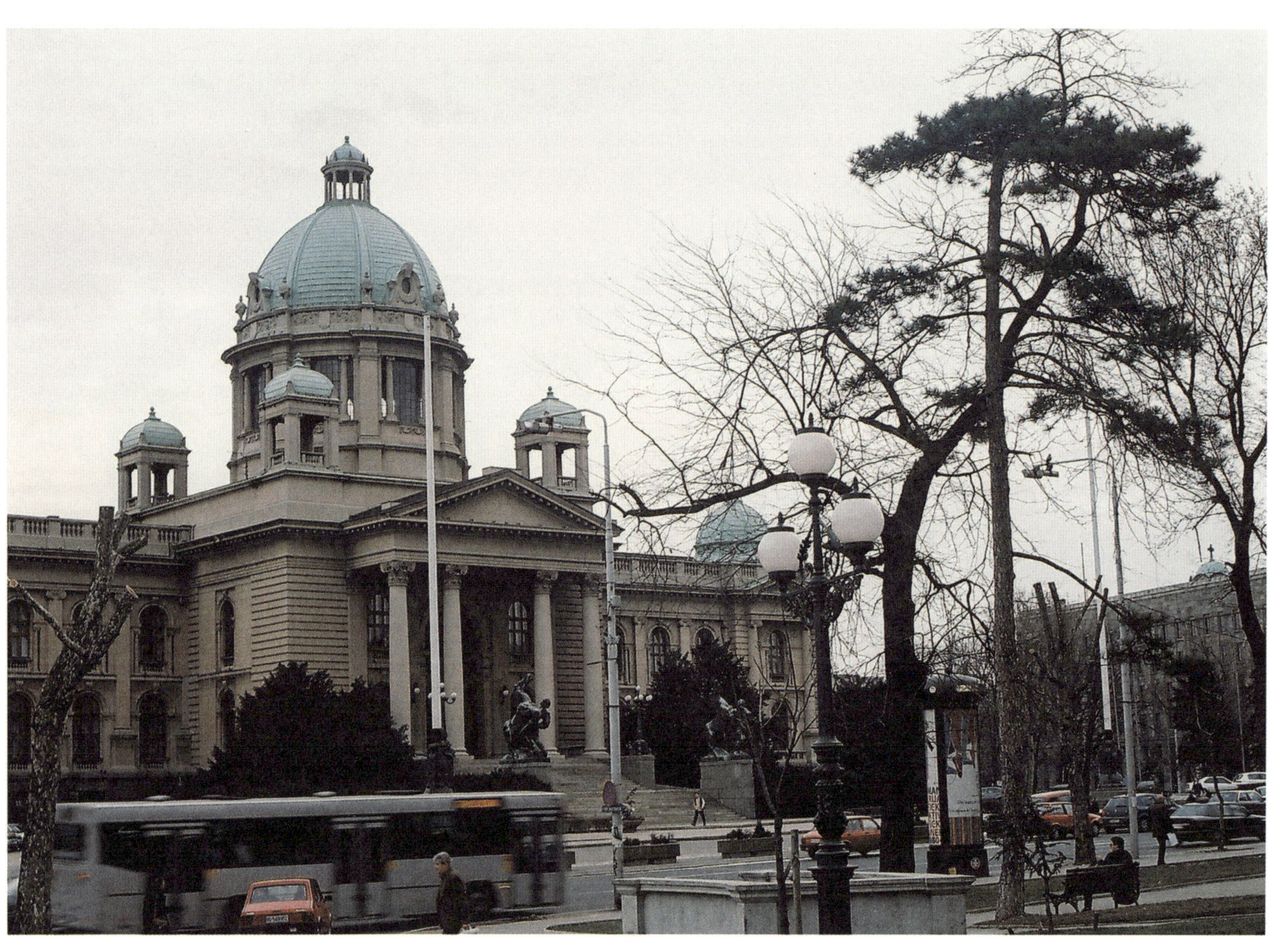

Trees Don't Talk, 2006
vinyl adhesive sticker, c-print
sticker: 300 x 50 cms
print: 23 x 17 cms

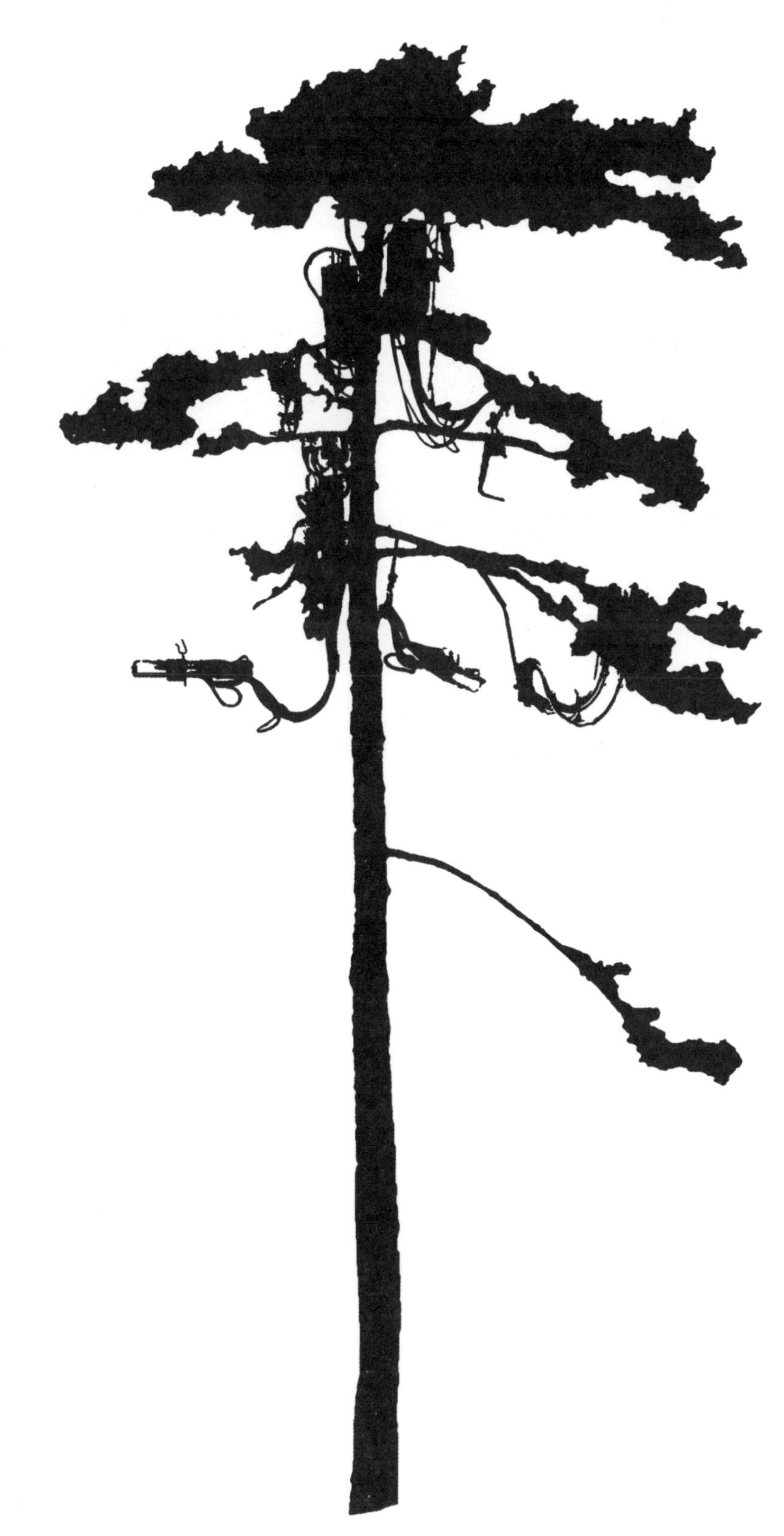

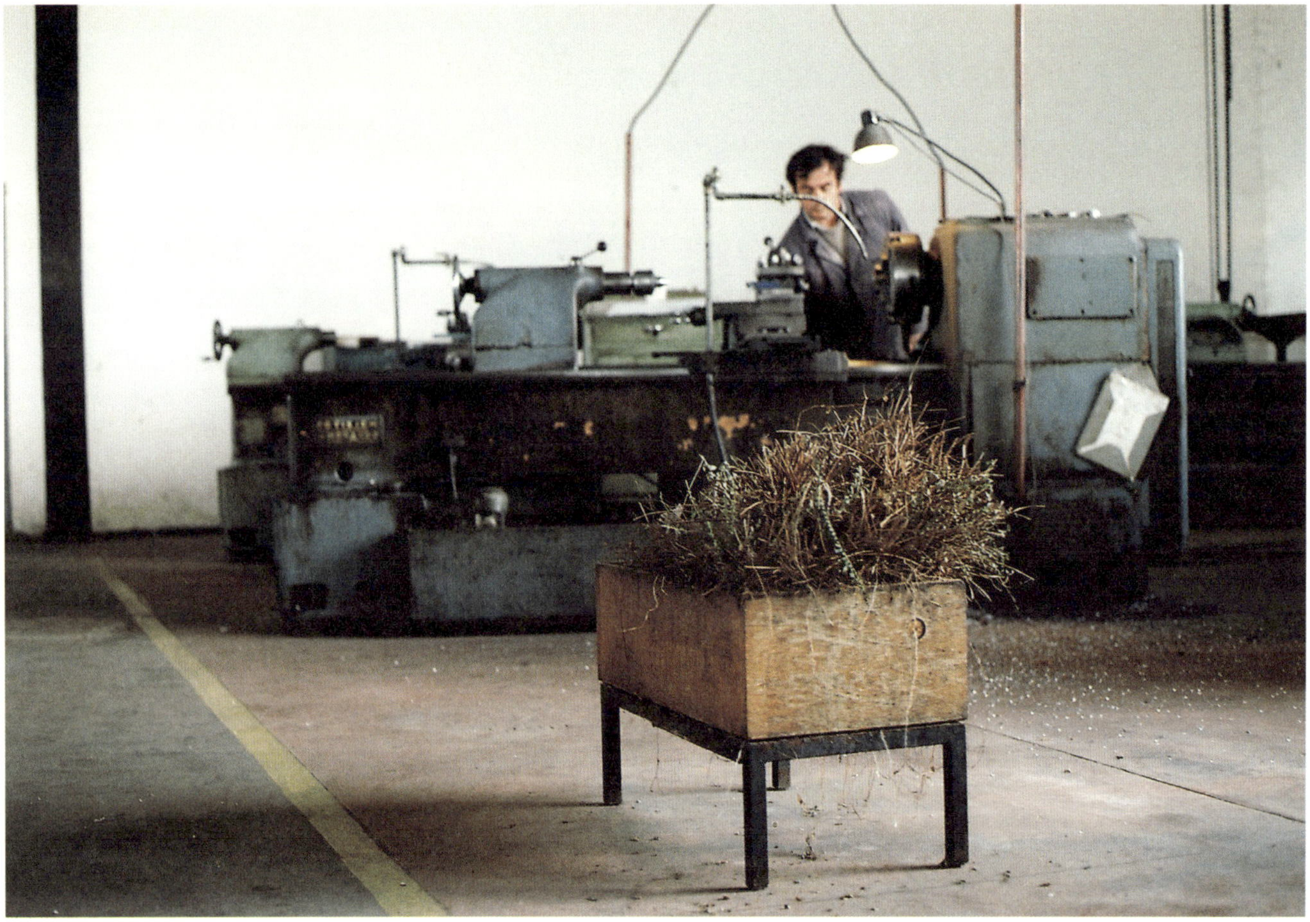

Prototype Laboratory Zastava Factory, 2006
c-print
28 x 20 cms

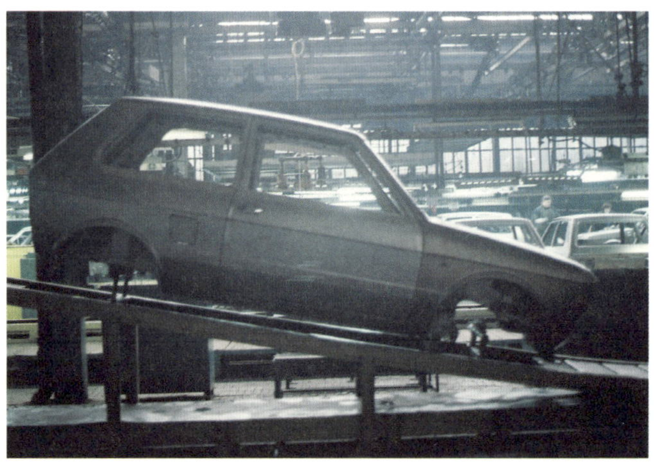

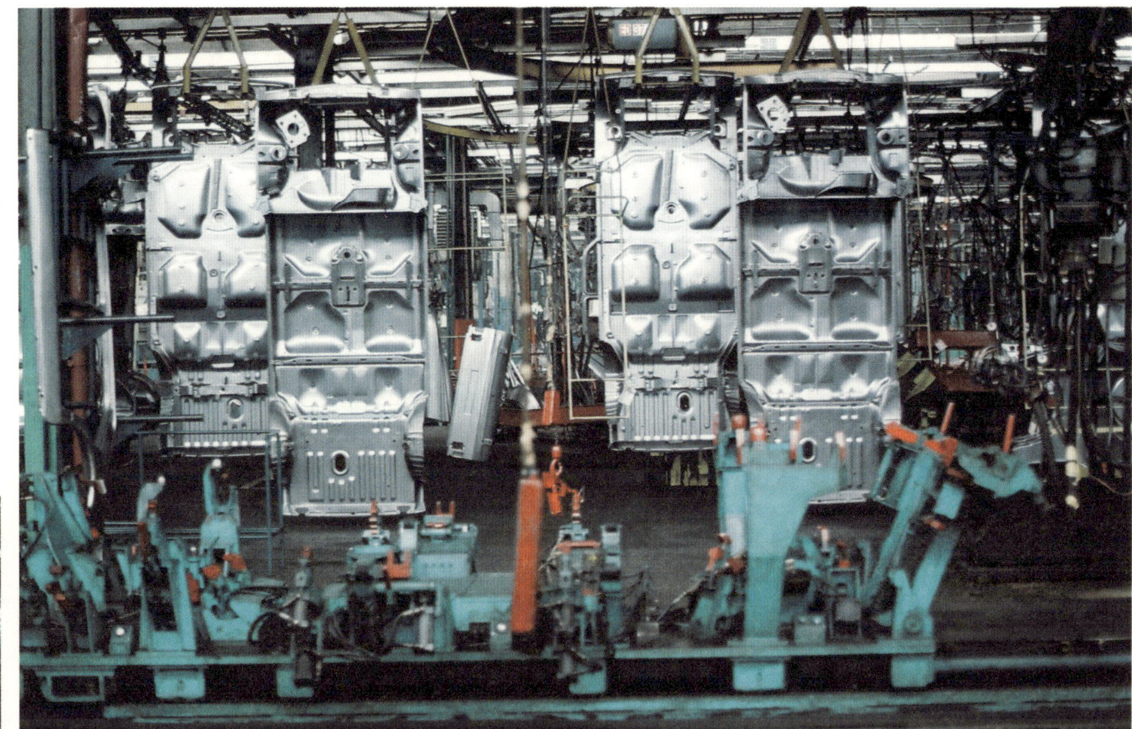

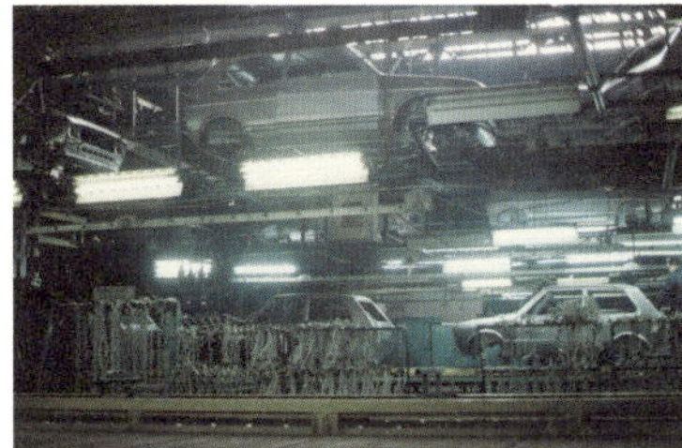

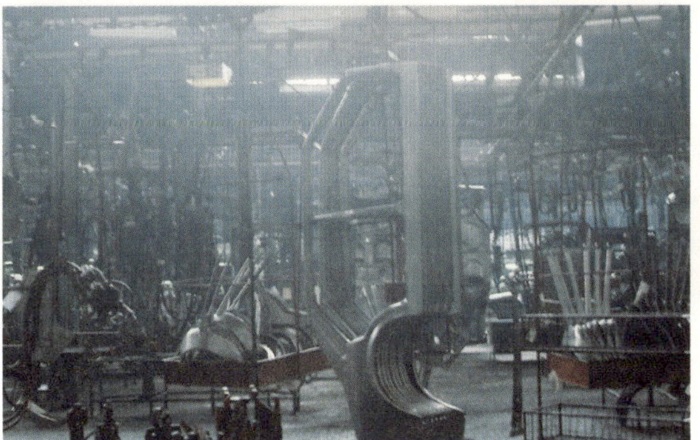

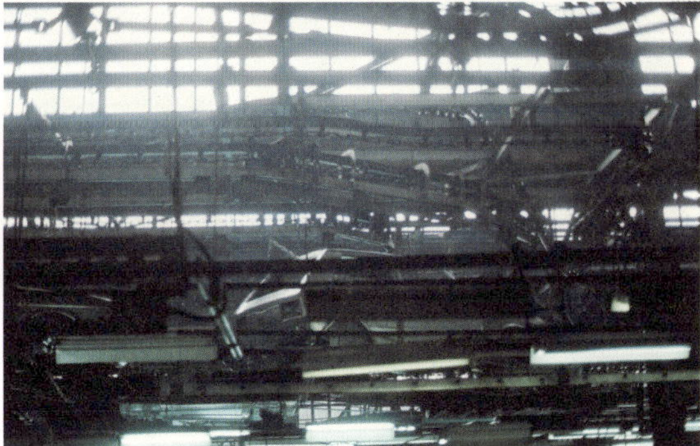

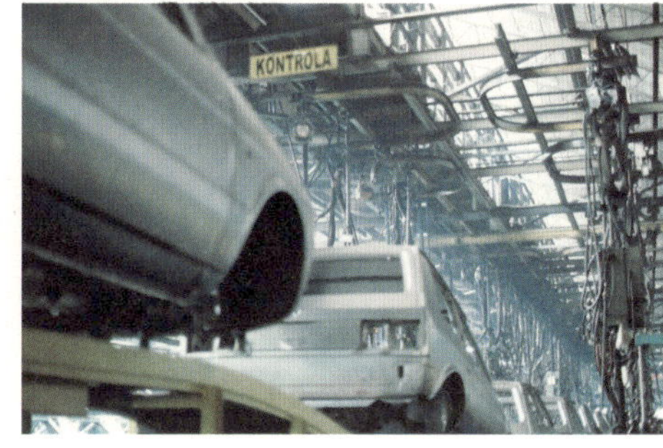


Zastava Factory, Kragujevac, Serbia, 2006

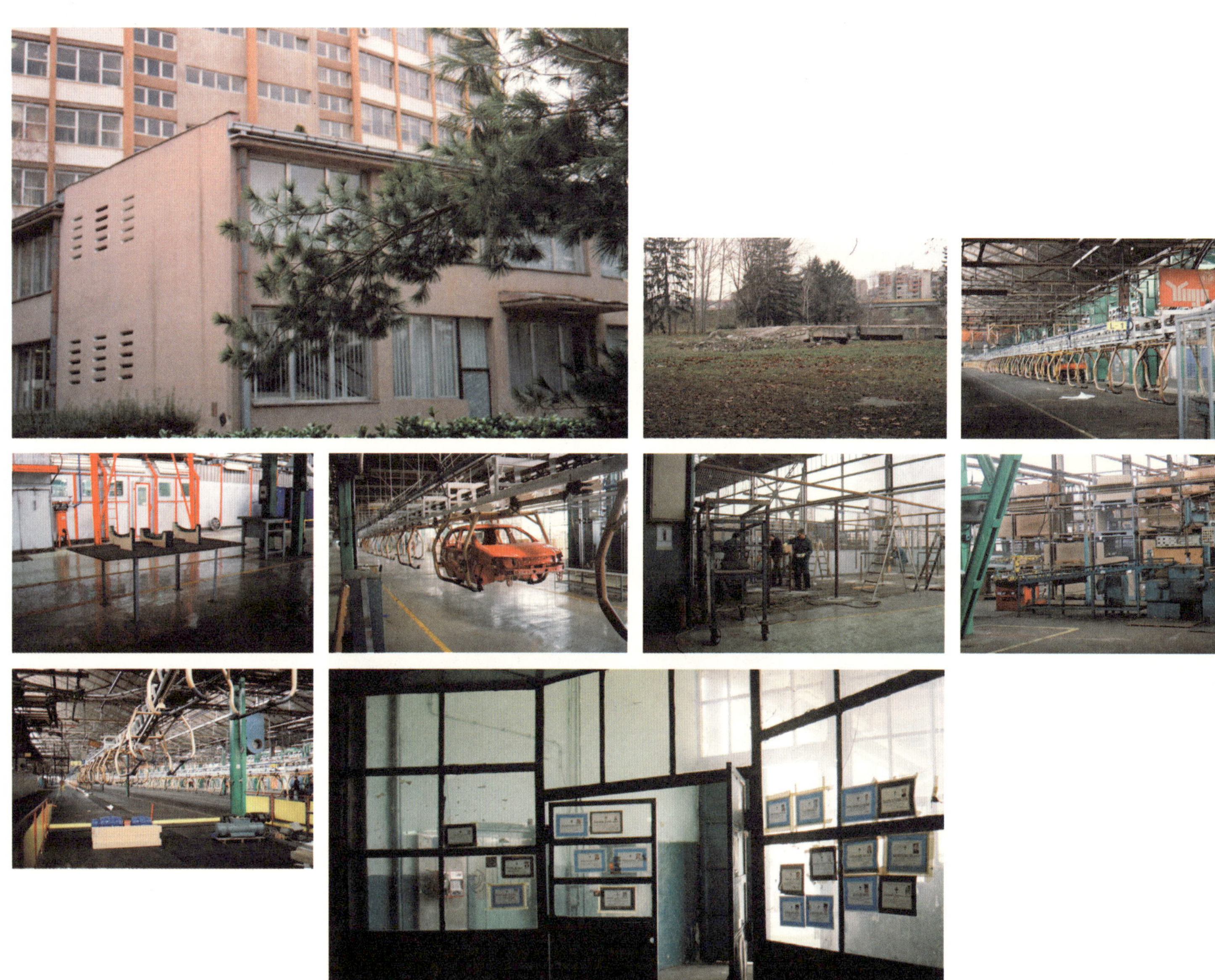

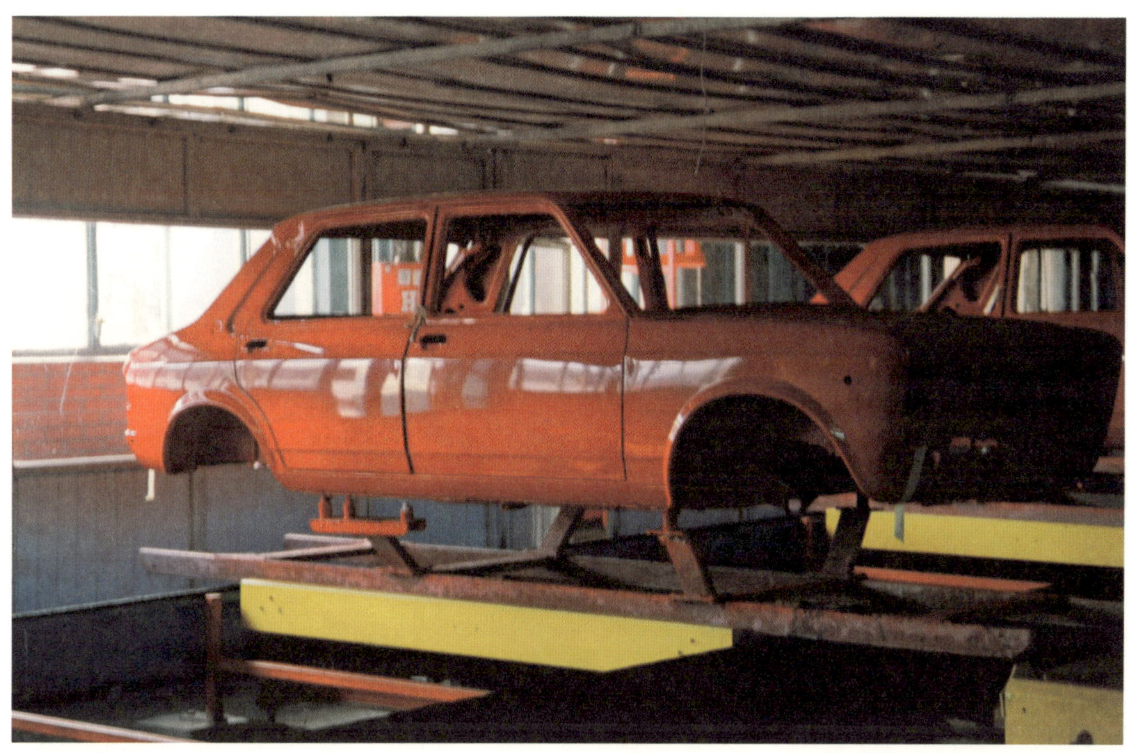

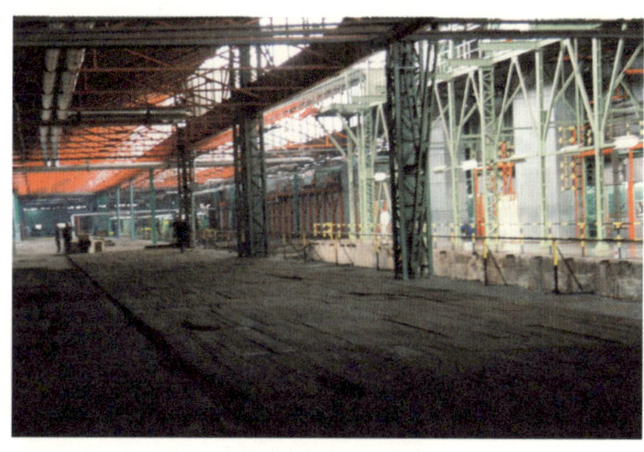

Zastava Factory, Kragujevac, Serbia, 2009

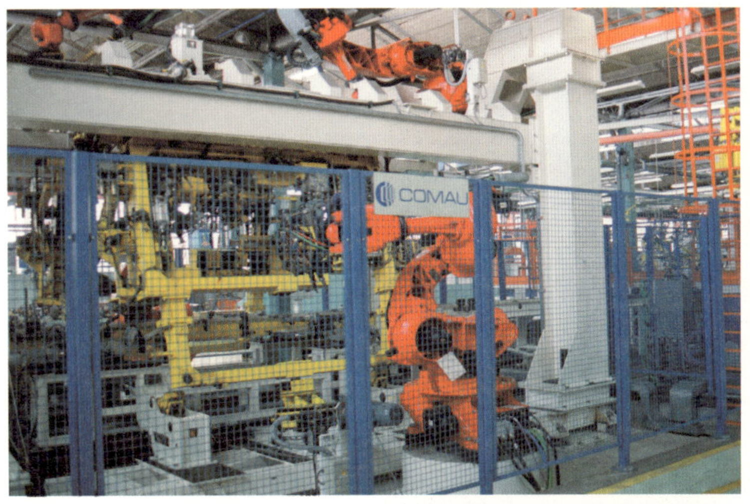


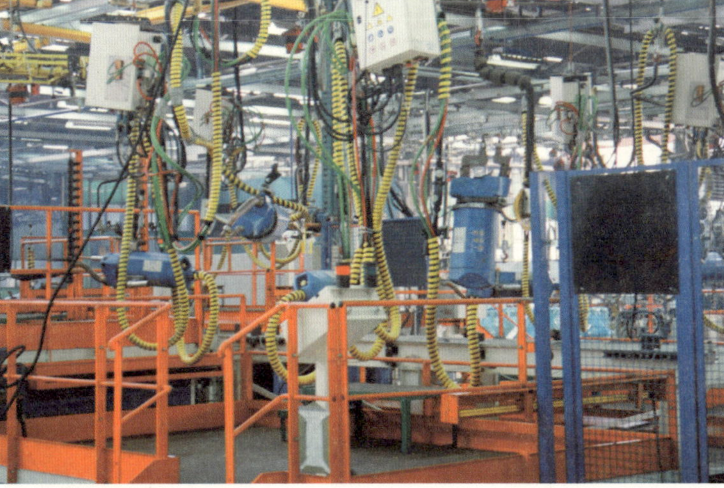

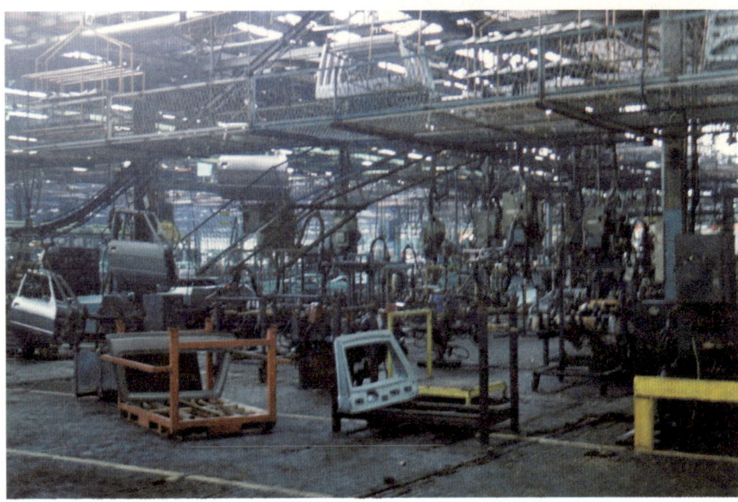

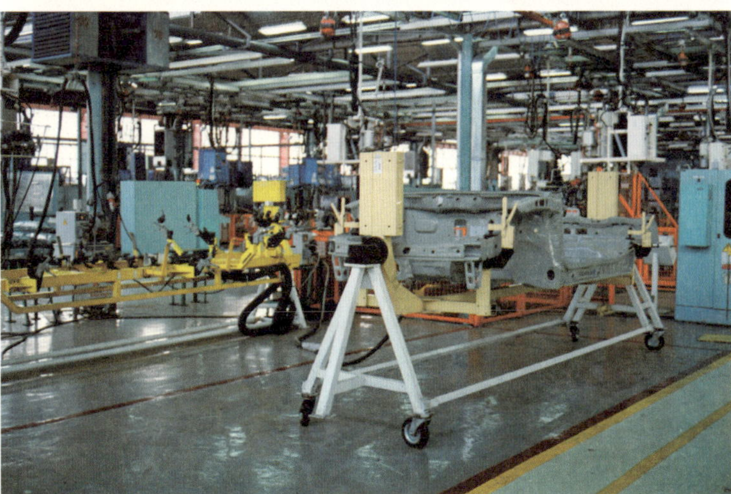

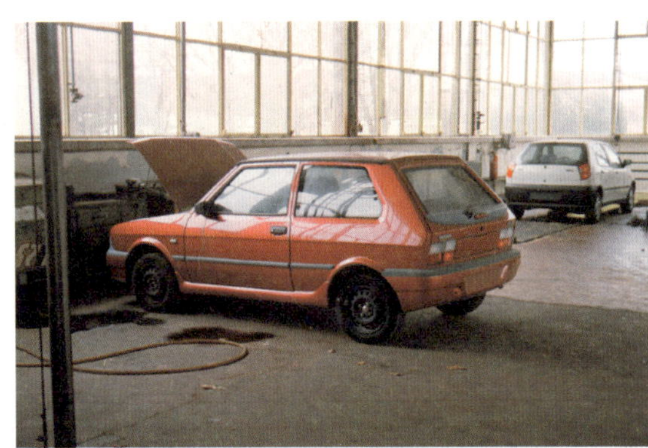

Zastava Factory, Kragujevac, Serbia, 2009

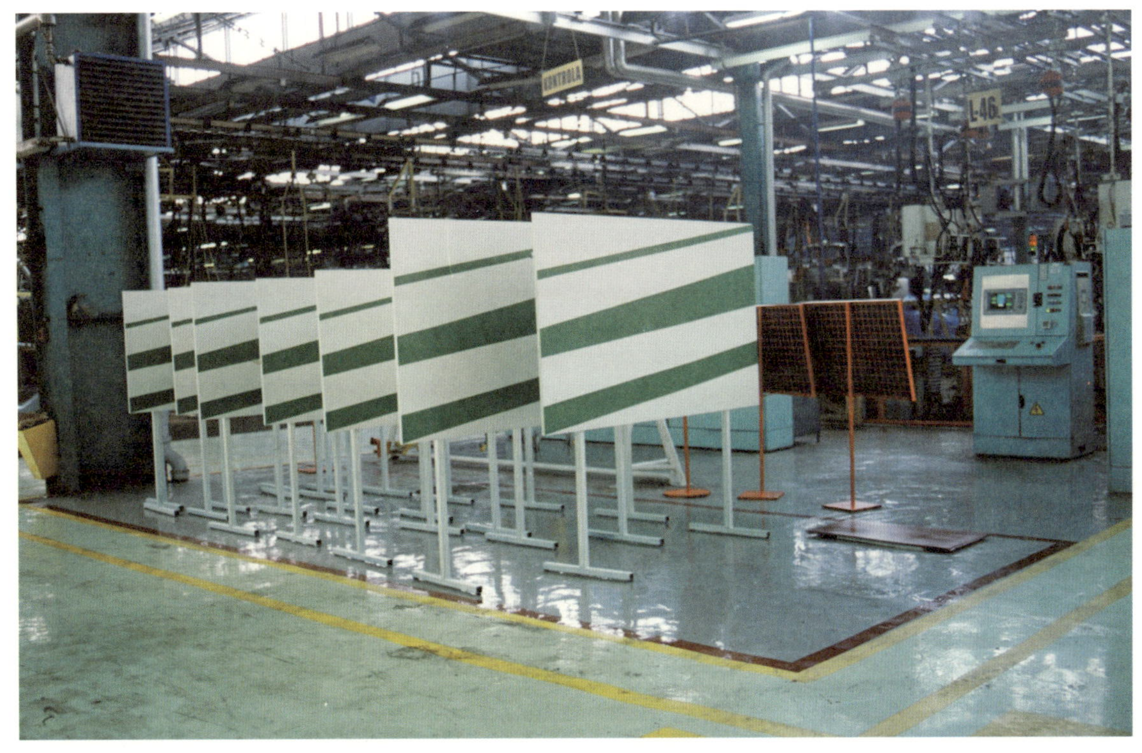
KONTROLA
L-46

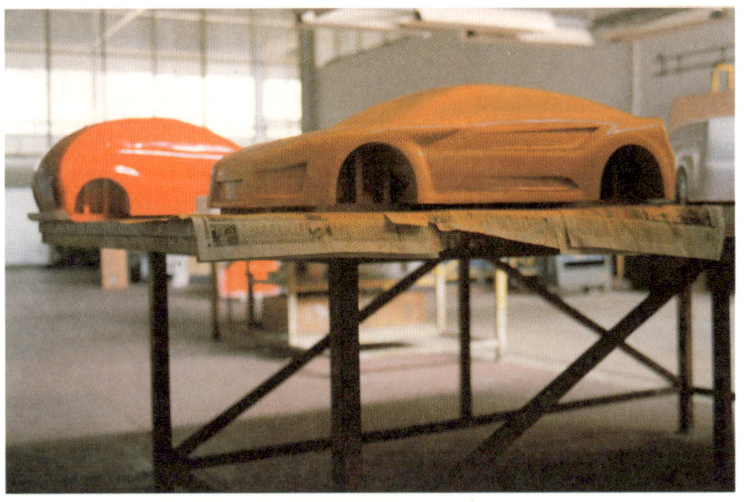

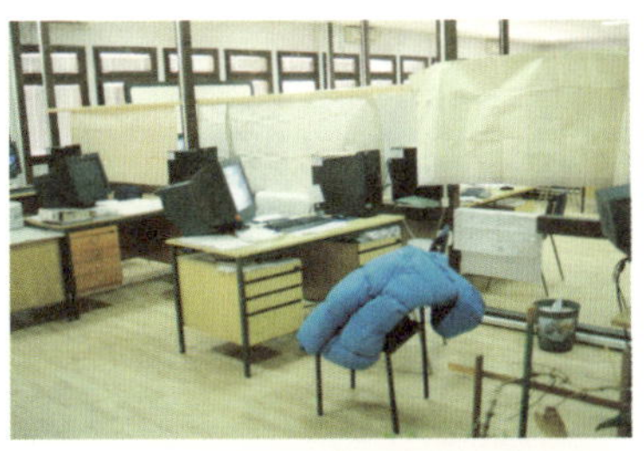

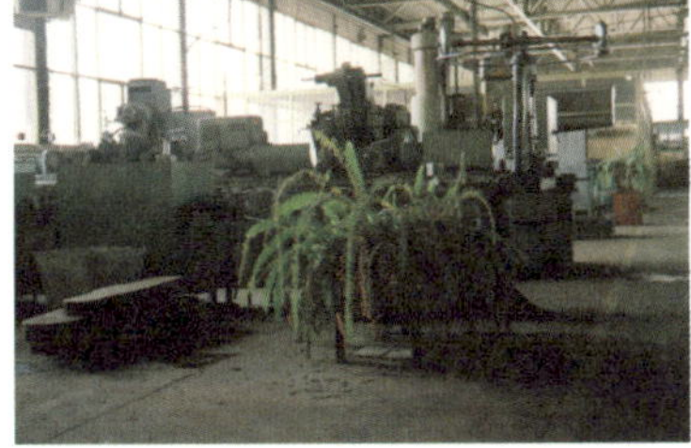

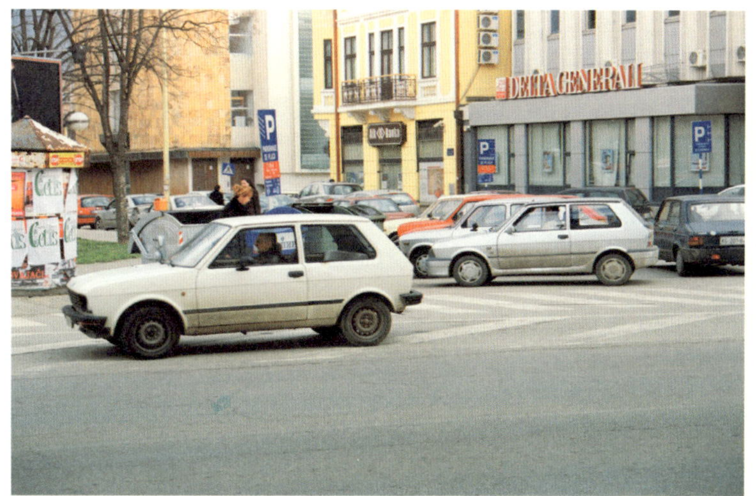
DELTA GENERALI

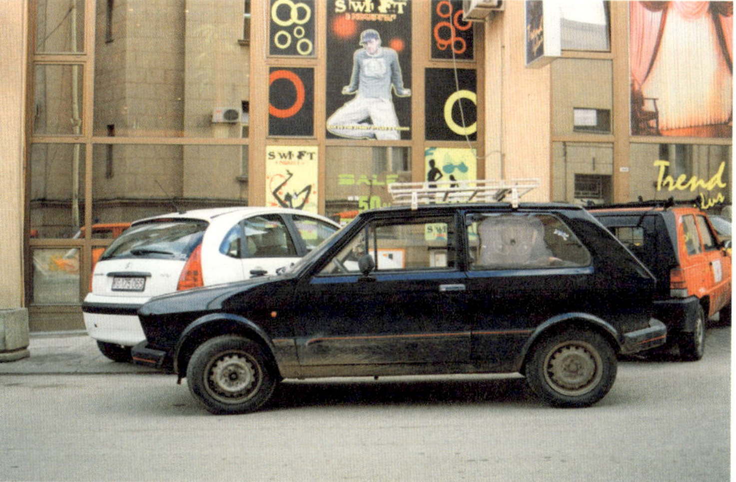
SWIFT
Trend

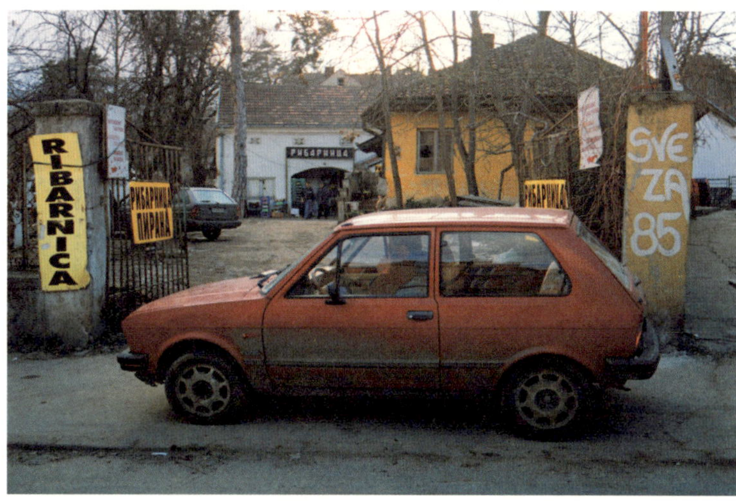
RIBARNICA
SVE
ZA
85

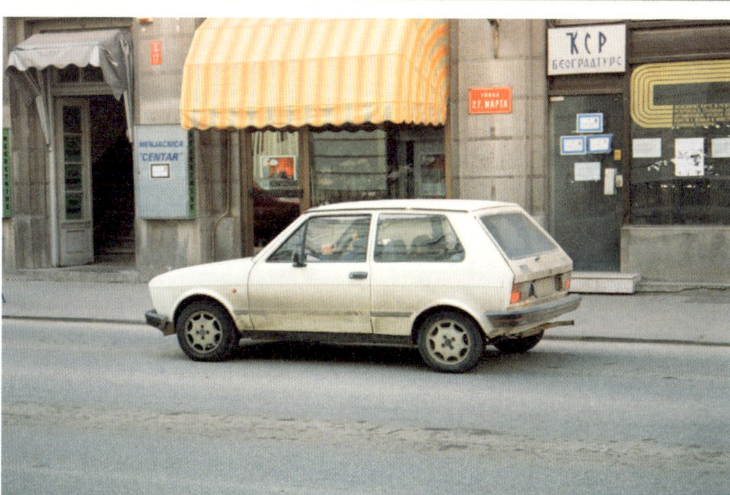
"CENTAR"
КСР
БЕОГРАДТУРС

Zastava cars around Kragujevac, Serbia, 2009

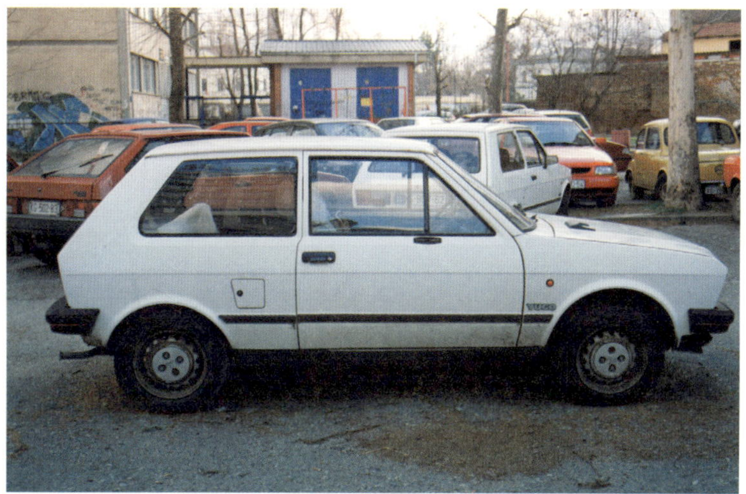

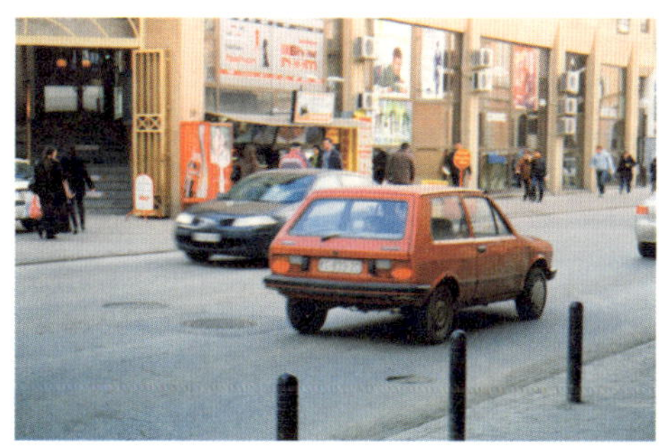

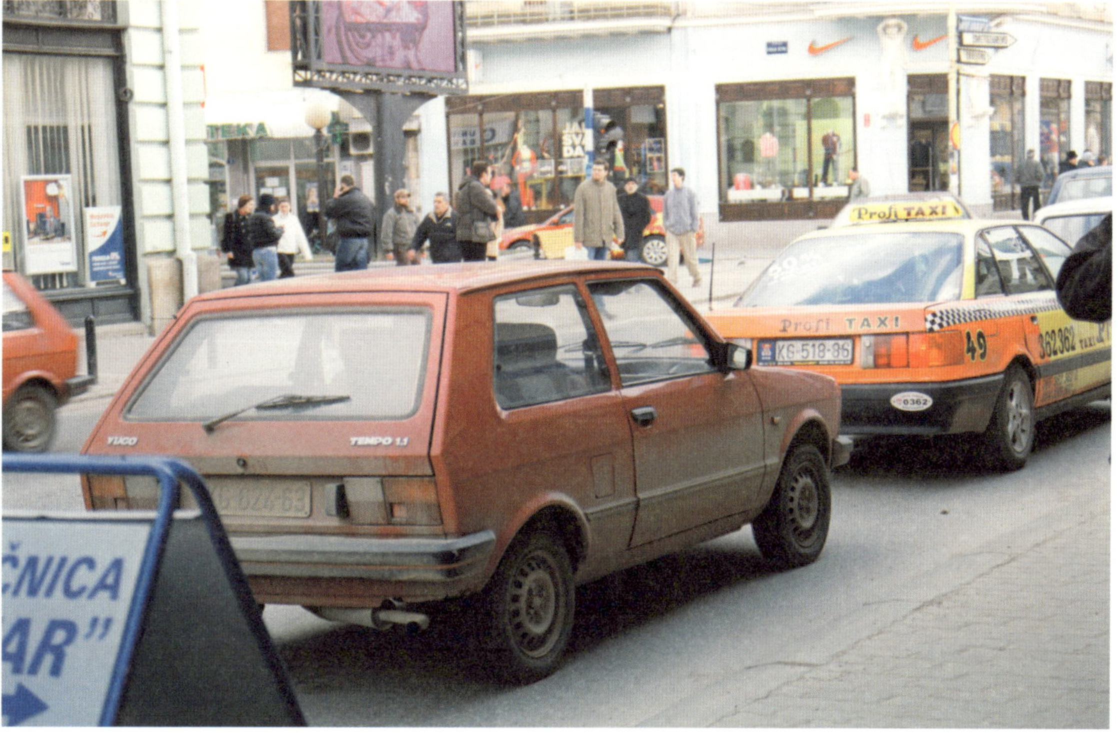

Goran's Stealth Yugo, 2006
diazo print
200 x 450 cms

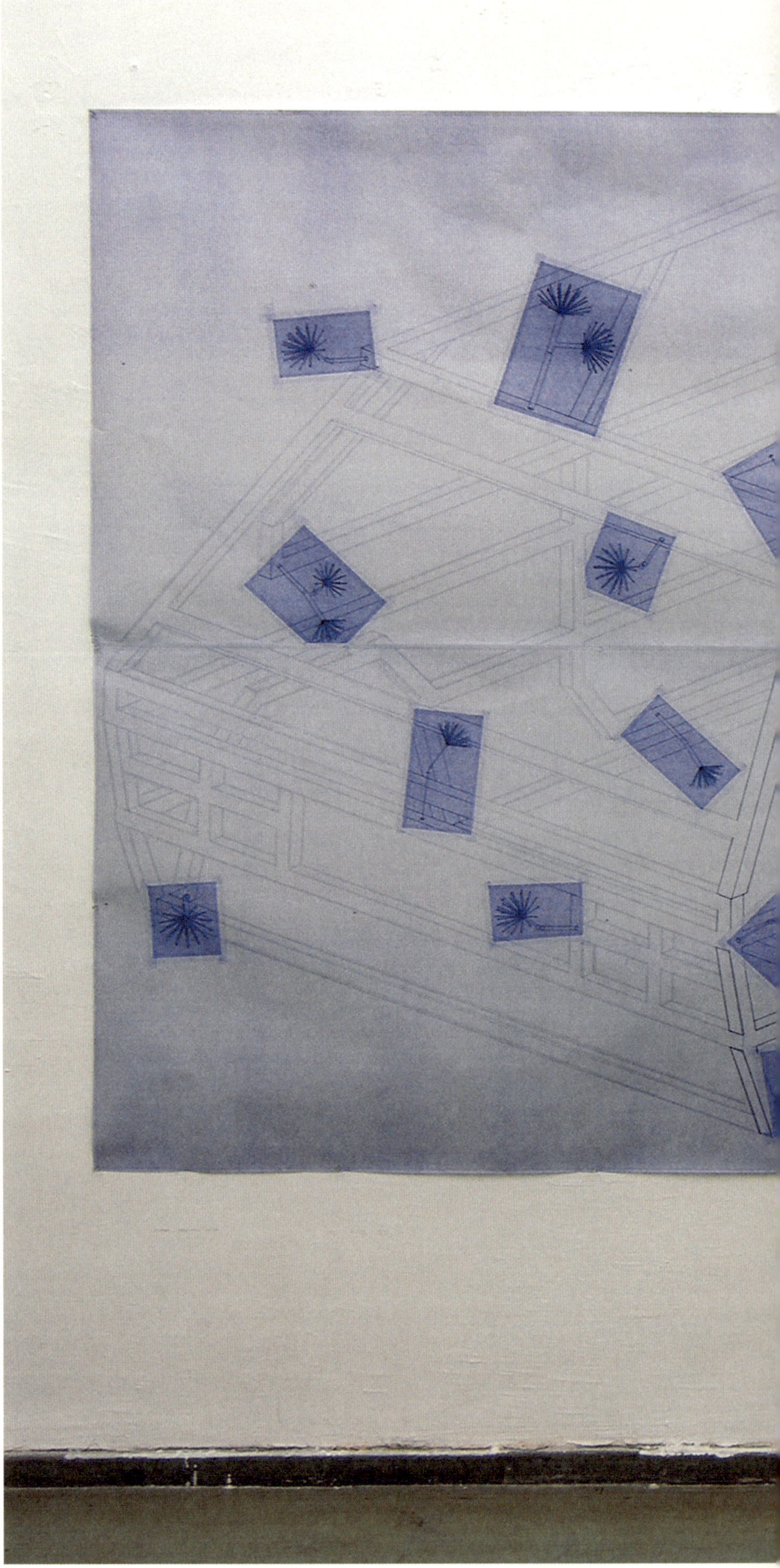

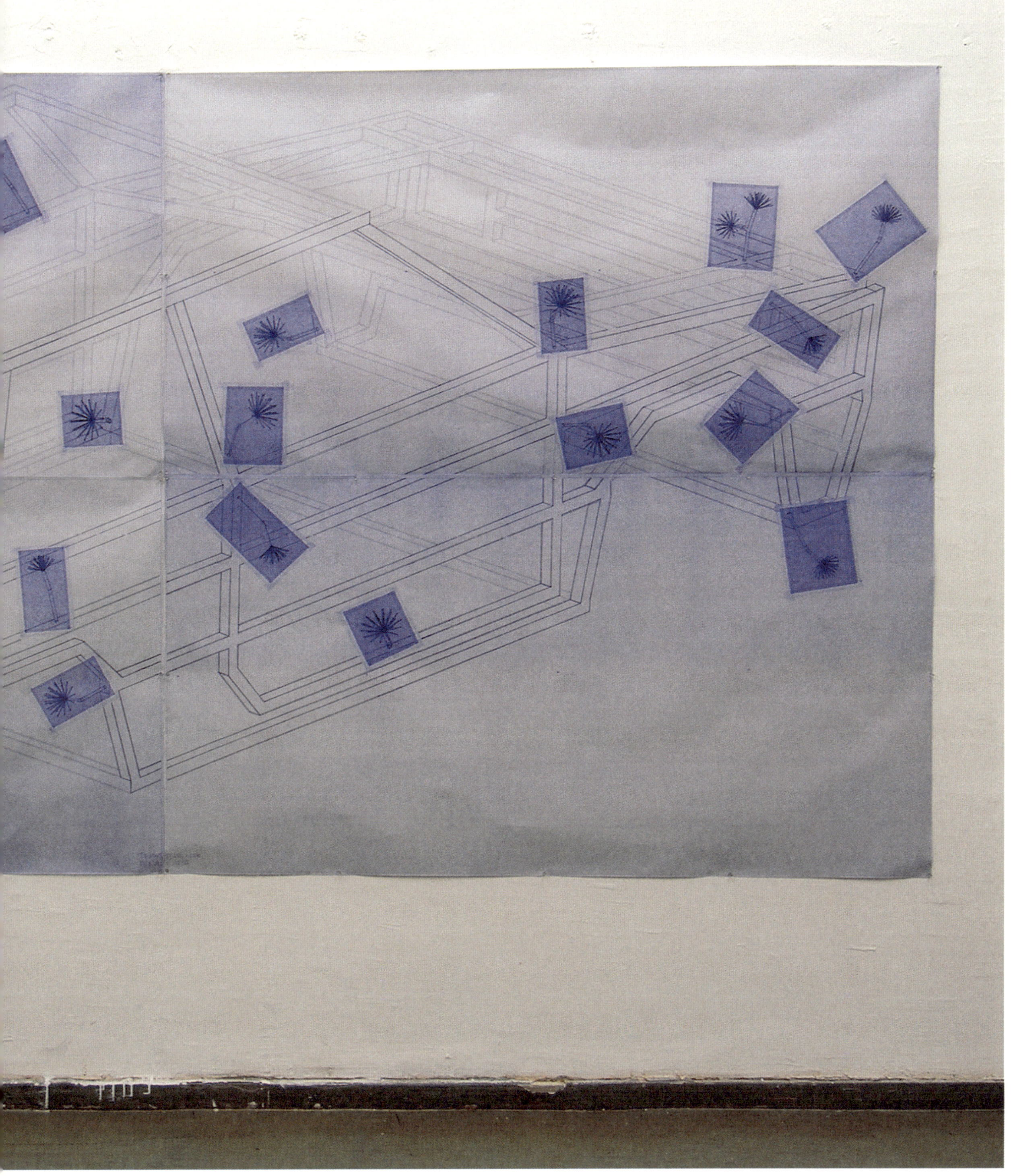

Design plan for Goran's Stealth Yugo
by Goran Krstić, 2008

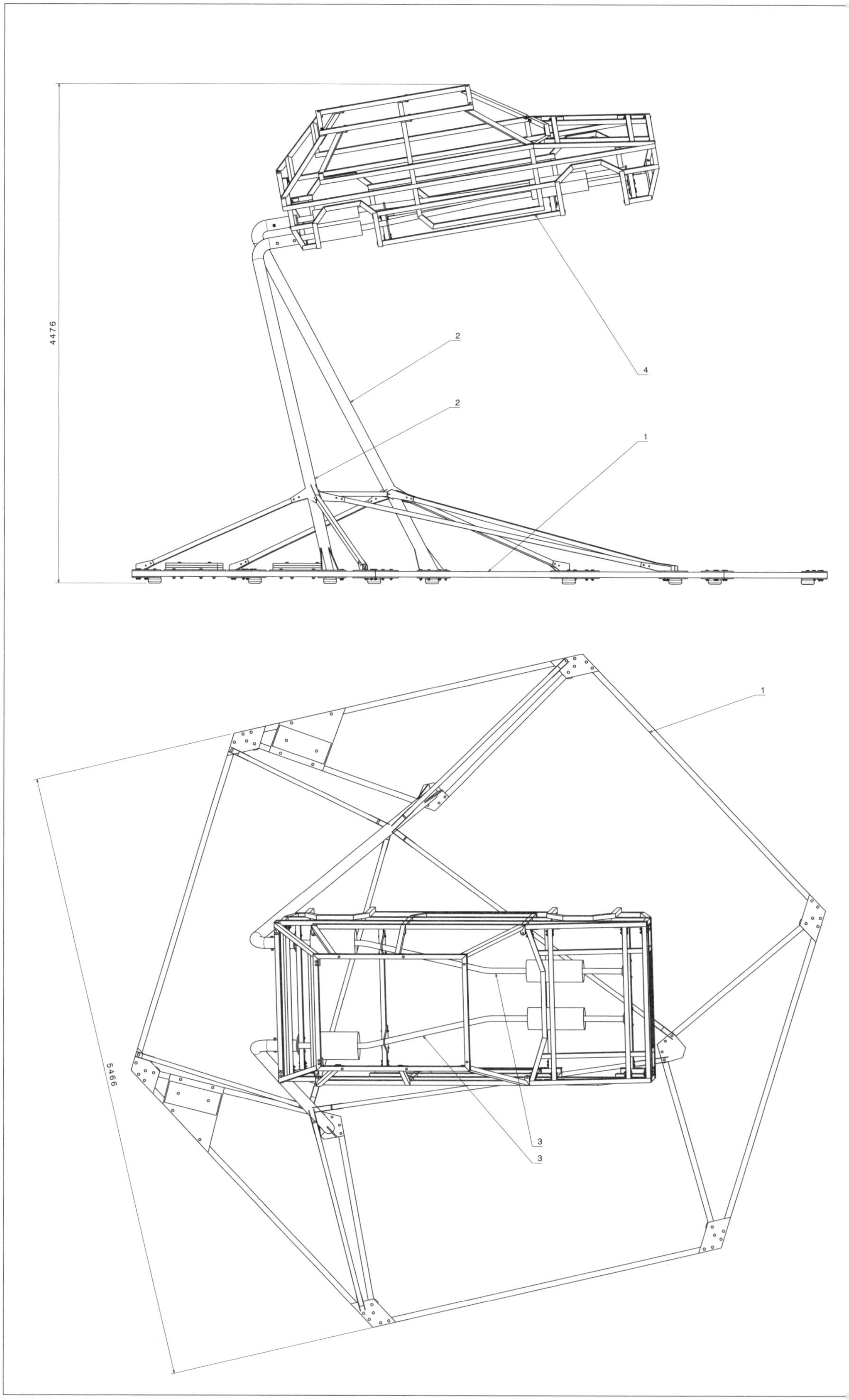

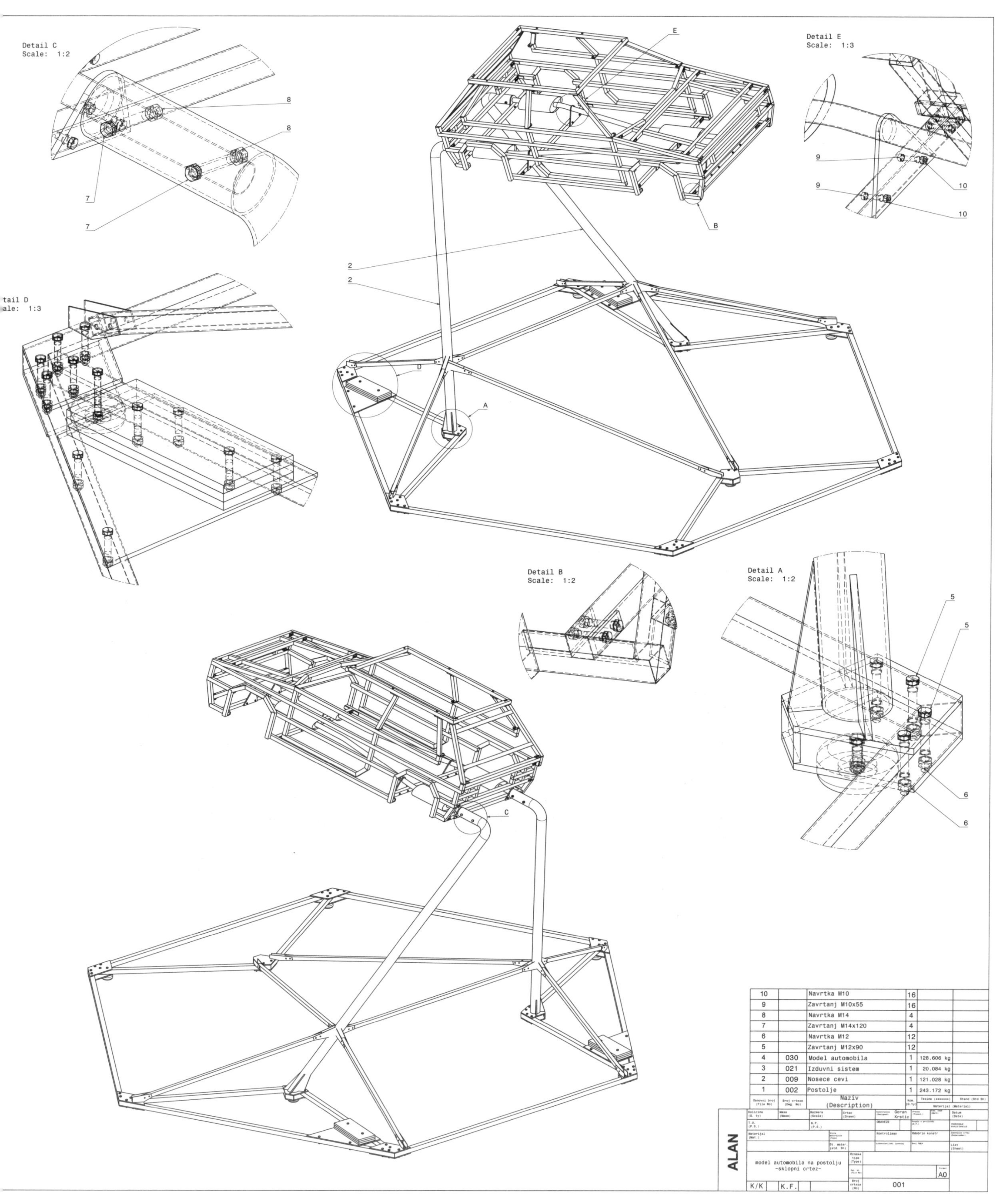
Detail C
Scale: 1:2
8
8
7
7
E
Detail E
Scale: 1:3
9
10
9
10
B
2
2
Detail D
Scale: 1:3
D
A
Detail B
Scale: 1:2
Detail A
Scale: 1:2
5
5
6
6
C
10 Navrtka M10 16
9 Zavrtanj M10x55 16
8 Navrtka M14 4
7 Zavrtanj M14x120 4
6 Navrtka M12 12
5 Zavrtanj M12x90 12
4 030 Model automobila 1 128.606 kg
3 021 Izduvni sistem 1 20.084 kg
2 009 Nosece cevi 1 121.028 kg
1 002 Postolje 1 243.172 kg
Naziv
(Description)
Goran Krstic
ALAN
model automobila na postolju
-sklopni crtez-
A0
K/K
K.F.
001

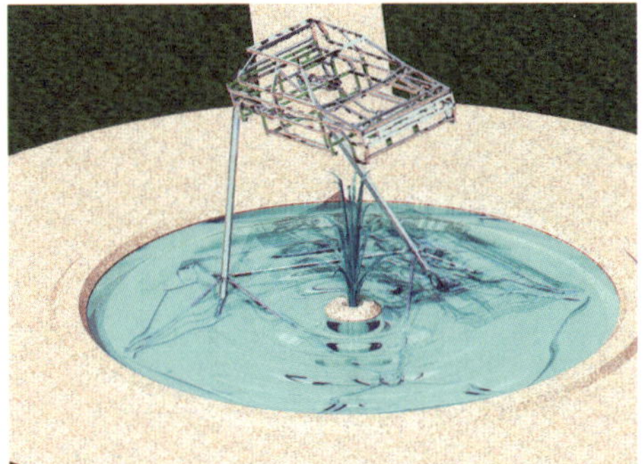

Design plan for Goran's Stealth Yugo
by Goran Krstić, 2008

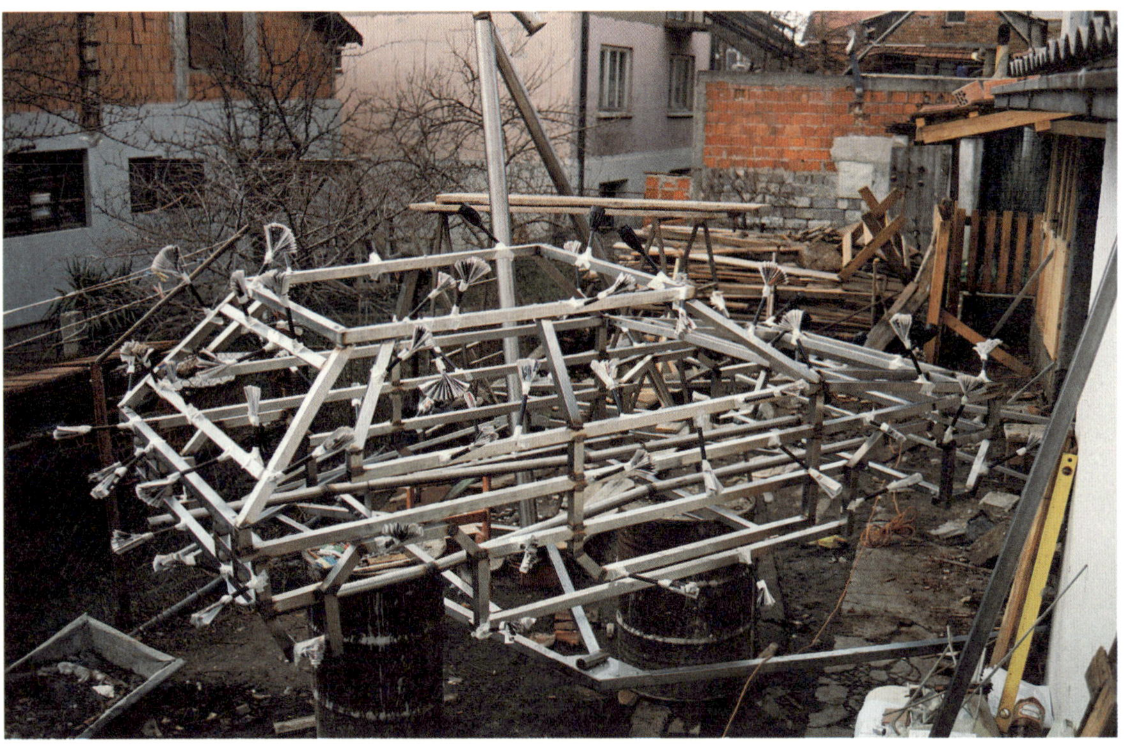

View of Goran's Stealth Yugo during fabrication, March, 2009

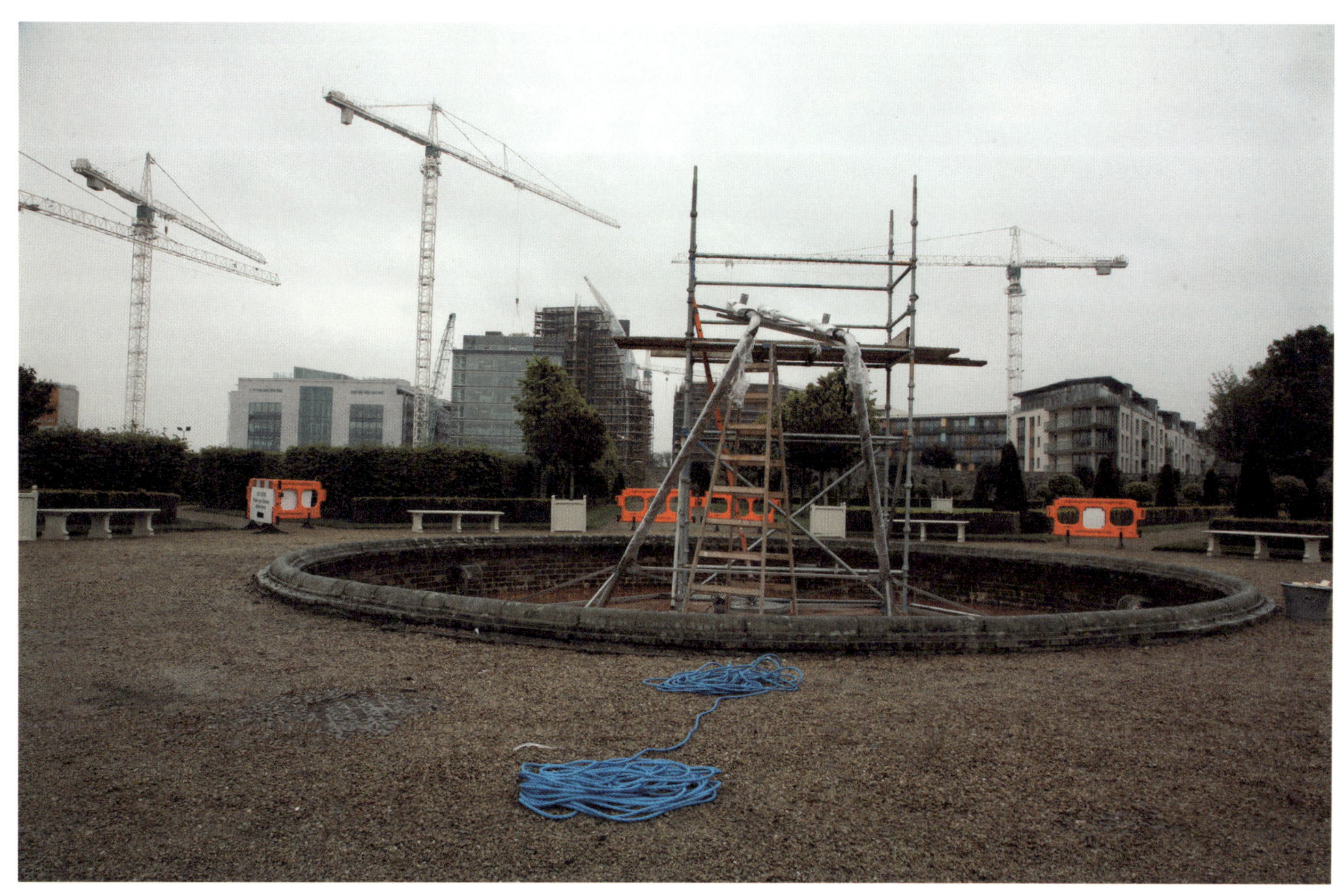

Views of Goran's Stealth Yugo during
installation, April, 2009

Goran's Stealth Yugo, 2009
chrome plated steel, rubber, plastic
450 x 550 x  550 cms

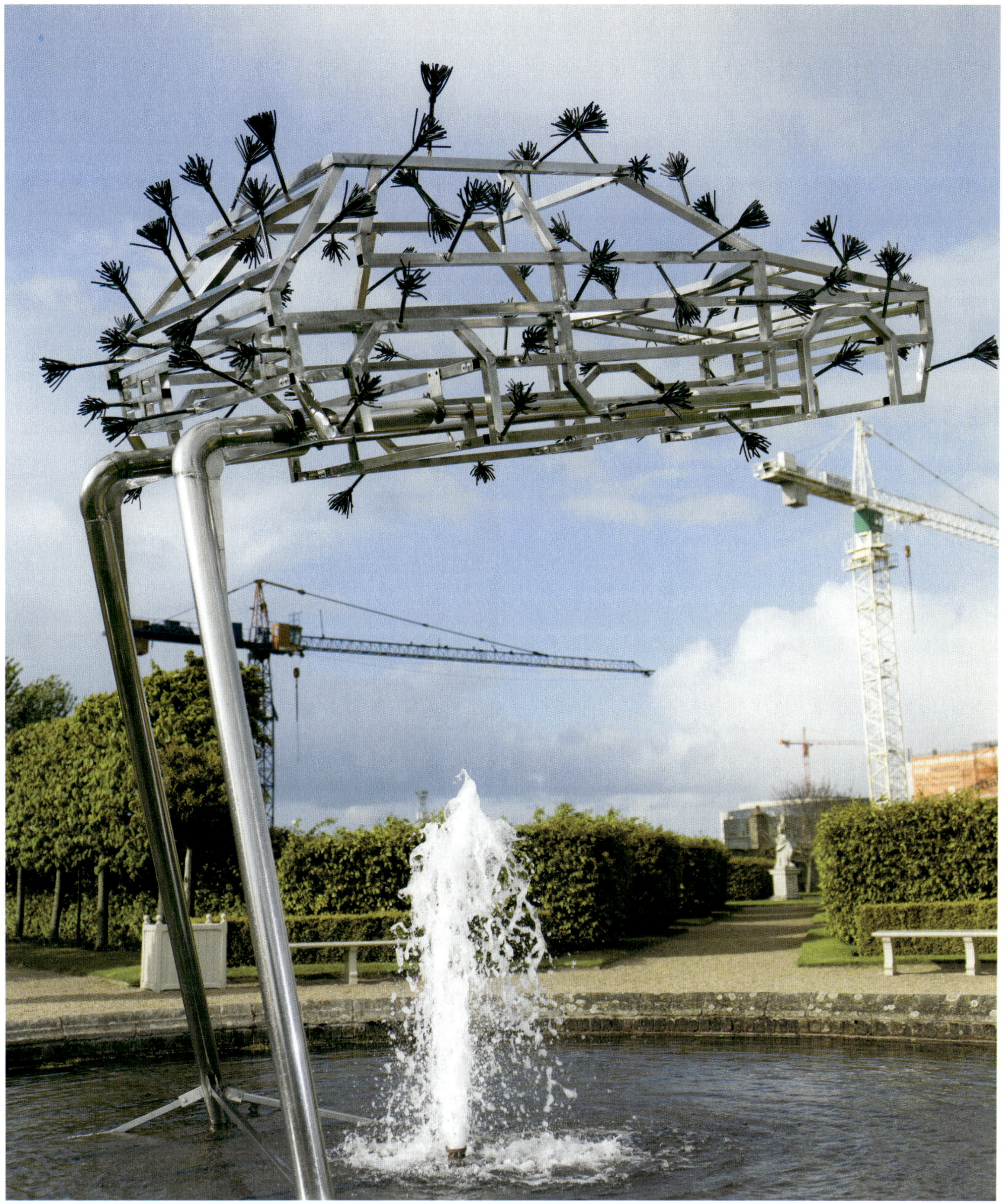

Goran's Stealth Yugo, 2009
chrome plated steel, rubber, plastic
450 x 550 x  550 cms

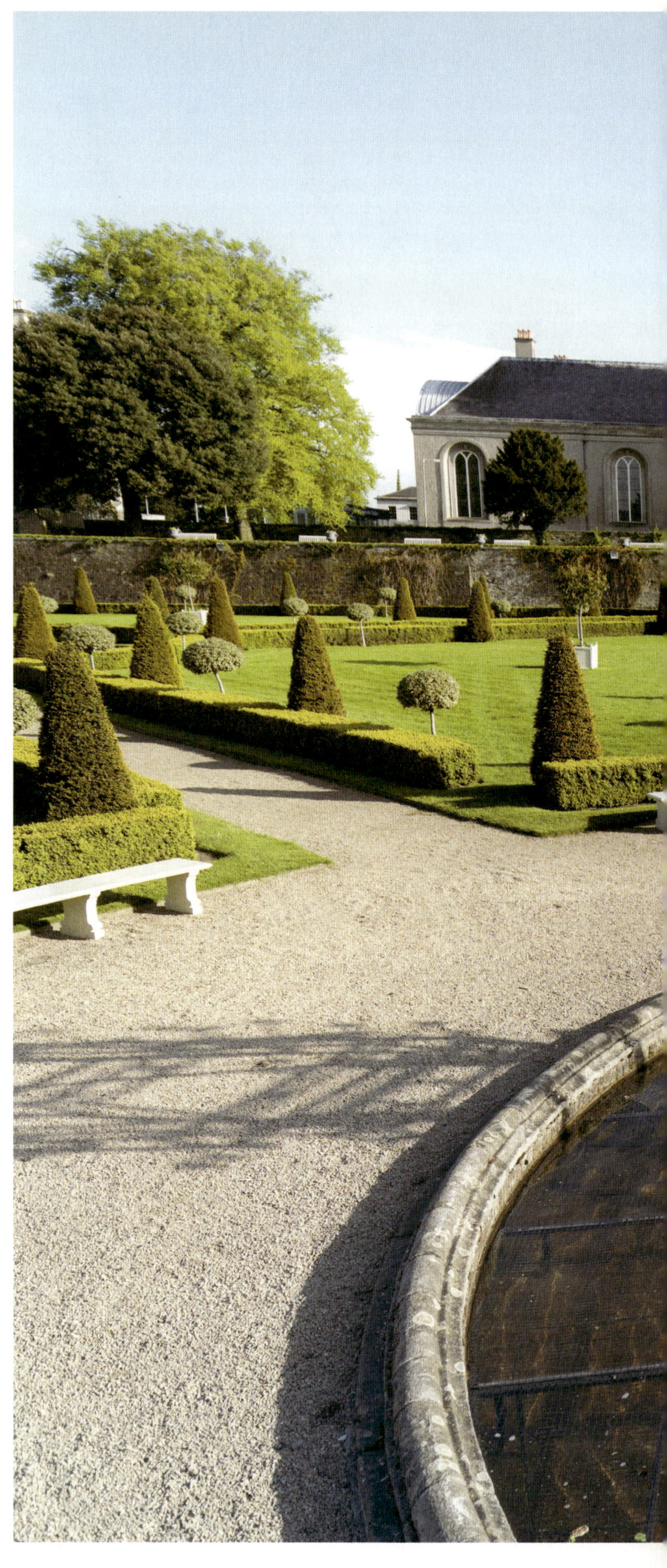

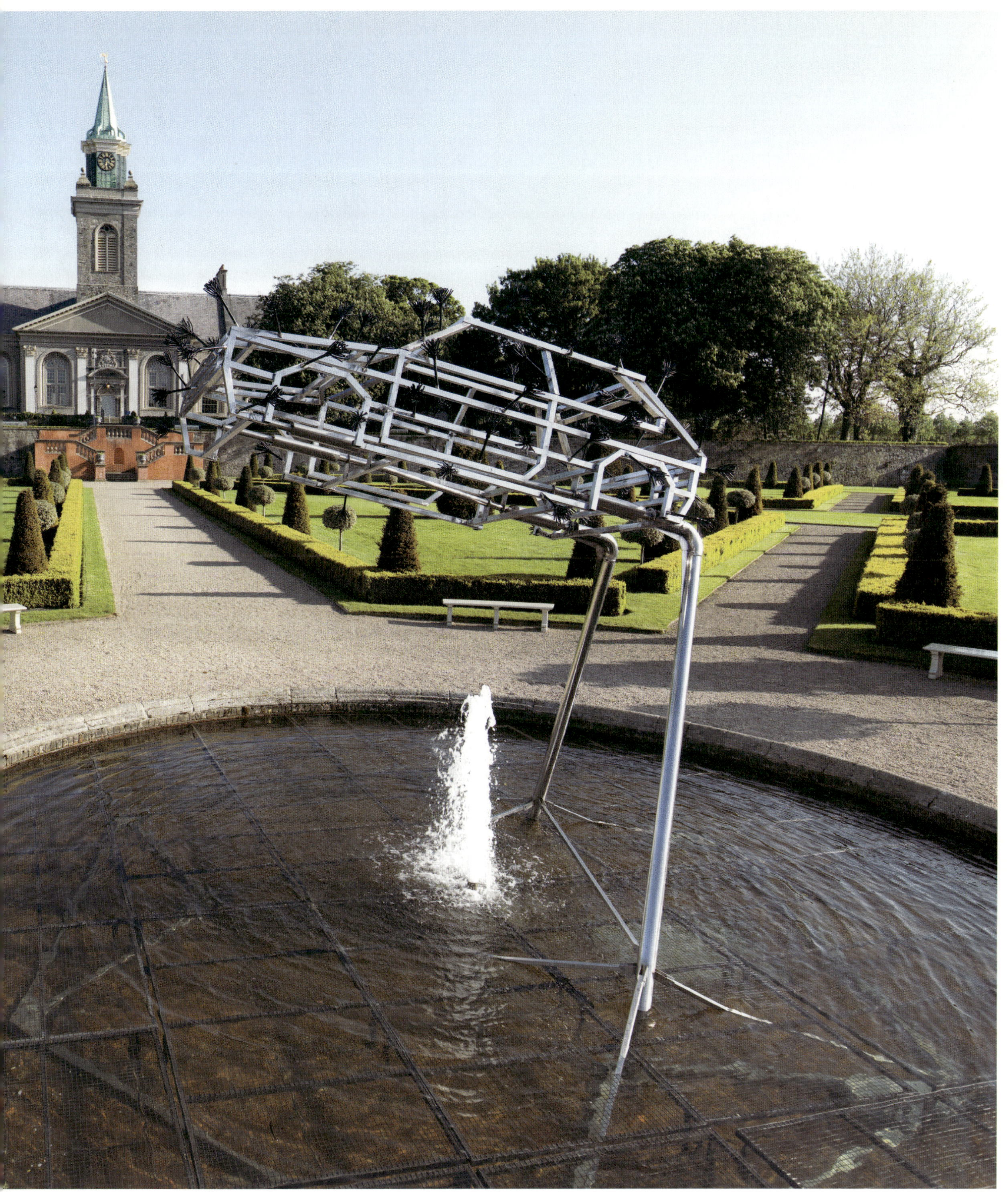

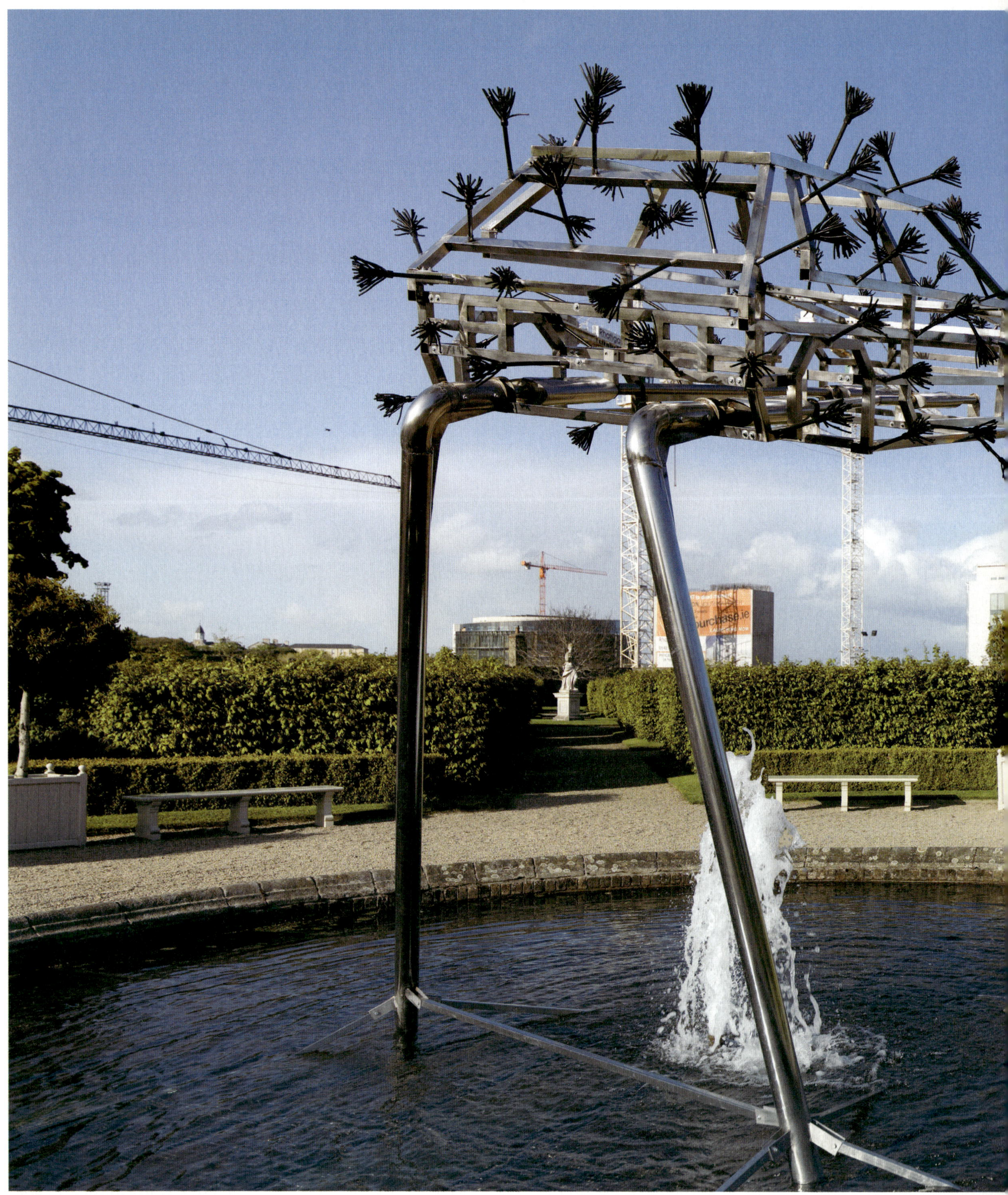

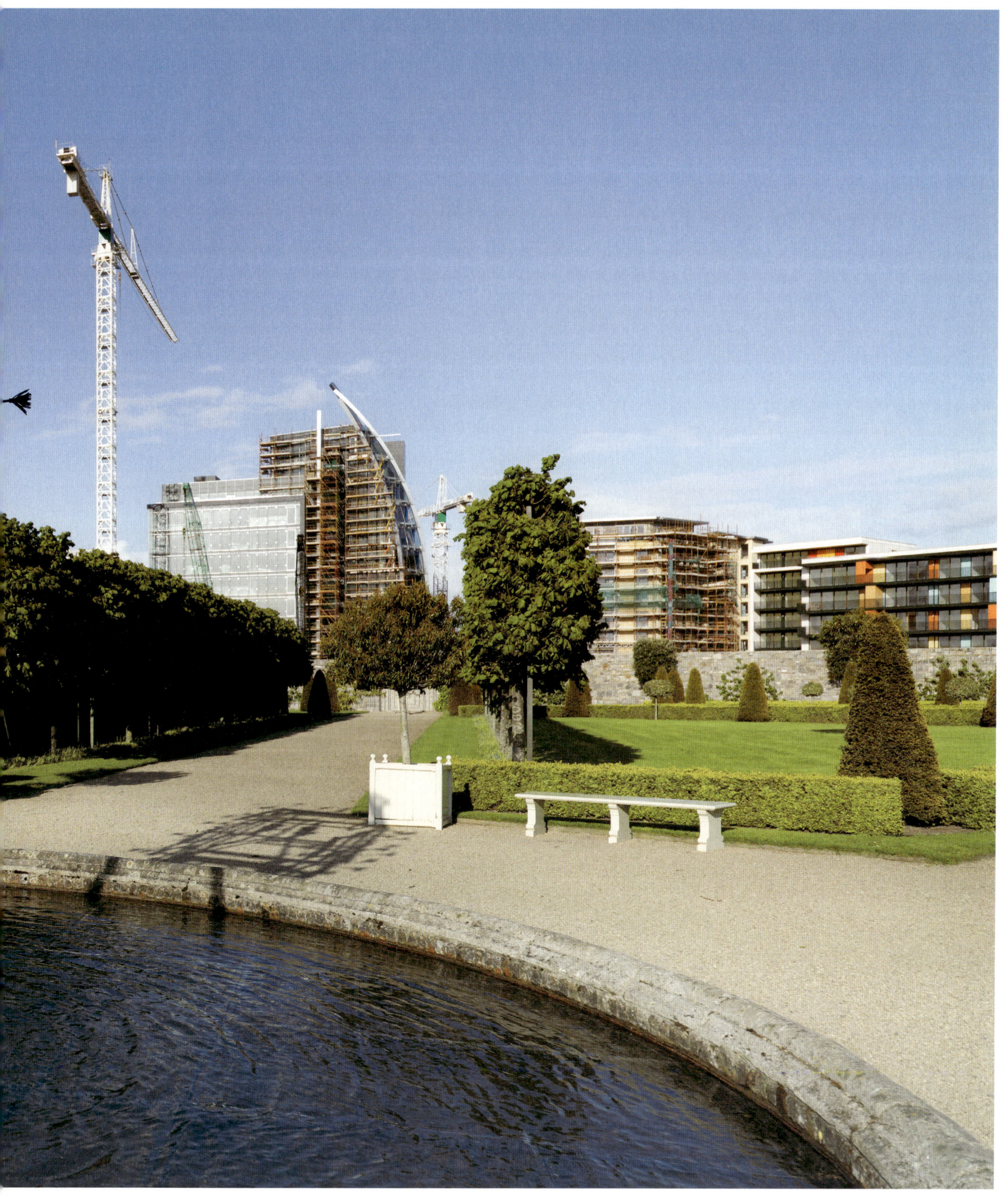

Goran's Stealth Yugo, 2009
chrome plated steel, rubber, plastic
450 x 550 x  550 cms

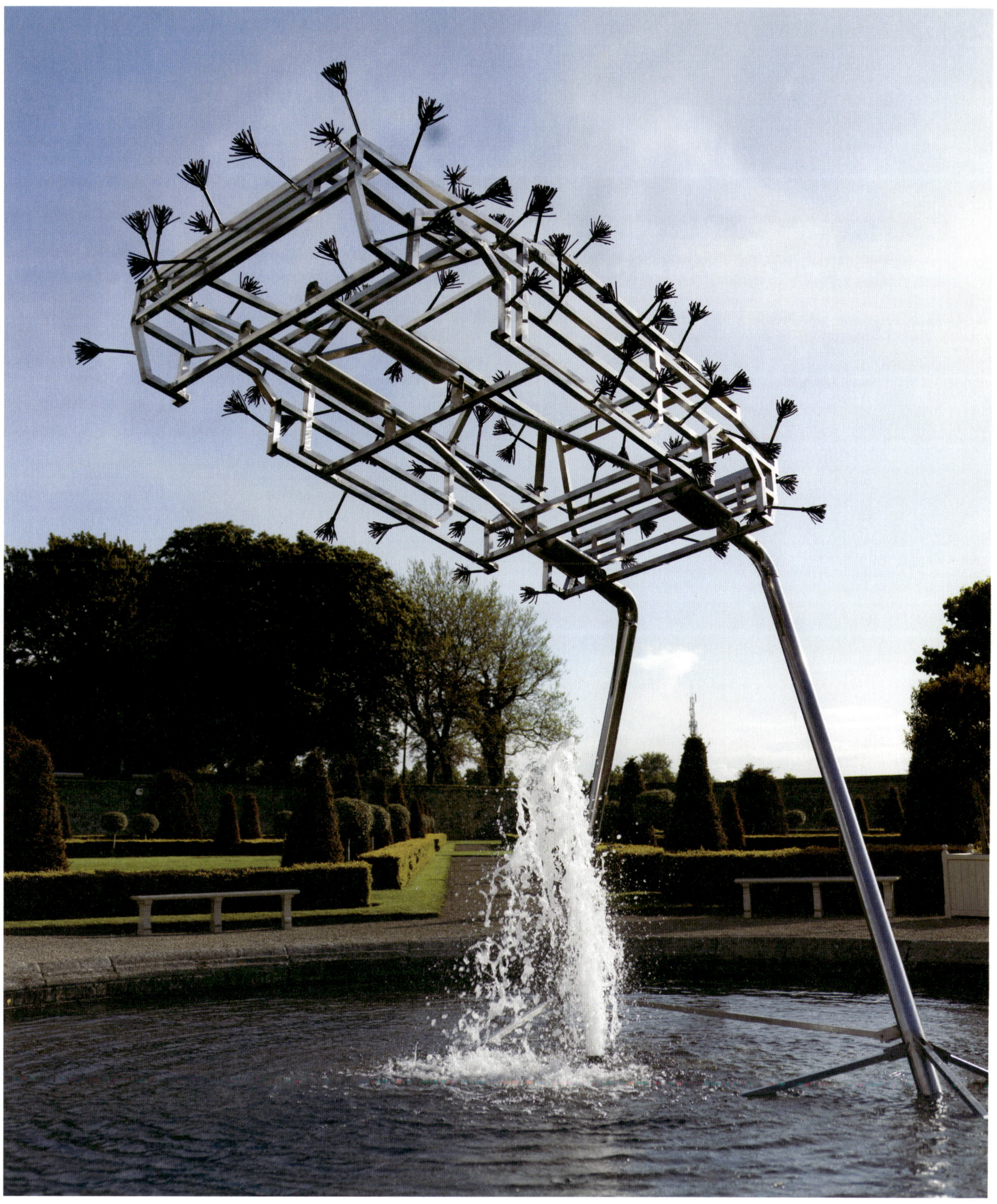

# Can the Subaltern Drive?

Dušan I. Bjelić

"Why does a Yugo have a defroster on the rear window? To keep your hands warm while you push it." Butt of all mechanical jokes, Yugo, the car whose name also denotes in Bosnia a "southern wind" that drives people mad, has recently joined the ranks of legendary cars which are no longer manufactured. The Zastava ("Flag") factory, which produced the notoriously unreliable vehicle, has been taken over by Fiat. And, as the Associate Press reported (November 19, 2008), Zastava workers attached a sign reading "Ćao, nema više" ("Ciao, no more") to the tailgate of the last Yugo to come off the production line. The independent automobile industry begun in the former Yugoslavia, a nonaligned, socialist country, has finally surrendered to the unifying, brute force of global capitalism. With a mechanical construction as precarious as Yugoslavia's multi-ethnic, self-management socialism, the Yugo has for three decades represented an alternative culture of driving. The Yugo demands human power – pushing, waiting, freezing, sweating, swearing-in addition to the engine's horsepower. Though the car has vanished from the global market, it has become the stuff of automotive legend, leaving behind narratives, memories, and crosses along the highways.

In becoming legendary, the Yugo has also inspired various works of art and other creative efforts. A group of Bosnians have placed a video of three Yugos stacked on top of each other on YouTube. Each car has someone in the driver's seat, but the triple-decker assemblage is actually driven by the operator of the car on the bottom http://www.youtube.com/watch?v=XhuQJ4rrZhs), an inventive way of killing time after the time of killing. As this video illustrates, it is precisely the Yugo's idiosyncratic inability to be a "real car" that has extended its life beyond driving and into Yugo-art.

Most of Yugo-inspired art displays the same affectionate, mildly derisive attitude toward its subject as does the Bosnians' video. Alan Phelan's work is an exception. It takes the Yugo very seriously indeed, and succeeds in representing a complex totality of geopolitics, history, industrial production, and aesthetics using the car as a central metaphor. The Yugo's frequent malfunctions disturb the habitual relationship between car and driver. Like Martin Heidegger's broken hammer, with its habitual use unavailable, the referential context of the equipment totality is revealed. Alan Phelan's work discerns this unique quality of Yugo and, expanding on the referential context, "lights up" its setting in the same way that Heidegger's broken hammer "lights up" the workshop.

The setting for "Goran's Stealth Yugo" (designed by Goran Krstić of the Design Institute at Zastava) is IMMA's pond. The Yugo-scupture rises from the water, rooted by its extended tailpipes. What makes this image so striking is the juxtaposition of the fountain (the quintessential bourgeois aesthetic cliché) with the solidly proletarian Yugo. The sculpture also symbolizes a reversal of the dominant East-to-West trajectory of labor-capital relations. Phelan, an Irish artist, has gone to the East in search of his subject. And he himself describes his collaboration with Serb designer Goran Krstić as "reversing the economic flow of labor between recent migratory labor movements from Eastern Europe to Ireland".

The twigs of pine bolted to the car's framework exemplify the technique of "blending-in" artifacts with the natural environment through disguise or camouflage. This is a practice that occurs, for instance, in the telecommunications industry when mobile phone masts are disguised as trees. The technique of "blending-in" as deployed in "Goran's Stealth Yugo" greatly expands the imaginative scope of Phelan's work. The twigs refer to the plants and planters placed throughout the factory complex in Kragujevac where Yugo was manufactured and to the actual pine tree facing the parliament building in Belgrade, the site of many important political events marking the rise and fall of Slobodan Milošević. The exchange of territories by means of "blending-in" allows the story of the Yugo and its country of origin to be told through the sculpture, and to flow as a coherent critique of nationalism.

The break-up of Yugoslavia resulted in the rise of symbolic nationalist sentiment among various ethnic and religious communities and, consequently, the weakening of collective infrastructural bonds whose materials nevertheless remained mute and ready-to-hand. As a machine that bound people of various ethnic and religious communities into a unity of time and things through a common driving experience, the Yugo formed a counterpoint to the symbolic and non-material collectivity of nationalism, which sought to divide people connected through the infrastructural bond it symbolized. Such an entrenched infrastructural bond does not give way easily to political expedience; it has a life of its own. Greek and Turkish Cypriots discovered this after the rush to divide Nikosia had ended, when they realized that the city's sewerage system still mixed their shit, binding them inexorably together despite the political will to separate.

In the case of the Yugo-as-infrastructure, new national borders sliced the temporal unity it had helped to define into national symbolic zones, dividing people along ethnic lines, myths and sentiments. Phelan's work elliptically discerns the political logic of the symbolic infrastructure nested in nationalism, making us aware of how we habitually look upon the history of a region only in terms of symbolic heritage. To take some examples of artists from the Balkans, the work of the art collective NSK (*Neue Slovenische Kunst*) and its intellectual standardbearer, Slavoj Žižek, represents Yugoslavia as a battlefield of symbols; Emir Kusturica's films deploy heavily symbolic magical realism in their portrayal of Yugoslavia; and performance artist Marina Abramović, passionately scrubbing a pile of bones, represents "Balkan Baroque" as geopolitical masochism. Phelan's aesthetics of Yugo-*praxis* bears an implicit critique of the nationalist residue in their work and that of others, juxtaposing the Yugo-machine to nationalist subjectivity and its symbolic heritage. Yugo-*praxis* creates an aesthetic entry into the infrastructural totality of Yugoslavia. In recovering the aesthetics built into the Yugo's production line with an image of the prototype design facility at Zastava Automobili (included in a 2006 exhibition of his new work), Phelan in effect allows the viewer to put on a prosthetic viewing device that enables him or her to *see* the infrastructure of the former Yugoslavia encapsulated and preserved in the nuts and bolts of the refashioned Yugo.

The infrastructure which grew up around the Yugo had its inception in 1978, when the first Zastava Koral (known outside the former Yugoslavia simply as "Yugo" and within it as "Jugo")rolled off the assembly line. Yugo is a subcompact vehicle built by the Zastava corporation in the town of Kragujevac. Zastava was founded in 1853 as a manufacturer of arms to support the Serb national rebellion against centuries-long Ottoman rule. After the First World War, when Serbia emerged as an enlarged, unified nation-state taking in all South Slavs (Yugo-slavia), Zastava joined the Fordist revolution. By the late 1930s, the factory had expanded into automobile production, manufacturing Ford-designed trucks for the Yugoslav Army. After World War II, the company produced Western Jeeps under license from Willys-Overland—and also weapons under license from the Soviets. This dual function of Zastava, producing Western cars by day and Soviet Weapons by night, epitomized the political balancing act of Tito's Yugoslavia. A small country trying to carve out its independence amid the ideologically divided world of superpowers had succeeded with Yugo in asserting its industrial autonomy.

Mechanically, the Zastava was based on the Fiat 127 and Fiat 128 and the body style was a modified version of the Autobianchi A112. It was a harbinger of the Yugoslav working class finding a productive niche in the global market. As an 'authentic' Yugoslav auto, it was one of many industrial products – including "Electronic Industry Niš" televisions, "Rade Končar" refrigerators, "Gorenje" washing machines, and "Elan" skis – raising the standard of living of the working class, a model of independence and modernity to many third world countries. Grateful to Tito for supplying weapons produced by Zastava during the war of national liberation, newly-independent, former European colonies and non-aligned countries – in Africa, the Middle East and Asia – also became importers of other affordable industrial products from Yugoslavia.

The height of the Yugo's commercial success came with its entry into the US market in the 1980s. The former US ambassador to

Yugoslavia, Lawrence Eagleburger, encouraged Slobodan Milošević and Serbian leadership to market the cars in the US in hopes that the Serbs, enjoying profits from overseas markets, would embrace capitalism and end the Yugoslav social experiment. The Yugo was imported into the US under the auspices of Yugo America, a company formed by entrepreneur Malcolm Bricklin, who wanted to introduce a simple, low-cost car to the US market. Over 100,000 Yugo GV's (GV standing for "Great Value") were sold in the US from 1985 to 1991, with the number of units sold in a year peaking at 45,000. The Yugo's entry into the US market also marked its entry into the society of the spectacle. At the Auto Expo show in Los Angeles, the Yugo was promoted by sexy teenage "Yugo-Girls" clad in white T-shirts with YUGO emblazoned across the chest, ultra-short, bright red miniskirts, and 4" high-heeled shoes that matched the car colors." Incredible publicity resulted as the car was promoted with a 10-year /100,000 mile warranty, free maintenance and a price of only $4,500. Front page articles about Yugo appeared in *The Los Angeles Times* (Business Section), *The New York Times*, and *The National Enquirer*.

Along with other Central and Eastern Europe vehicles, the Yugo was subject to harsh criticism in the US. A 1987 *Consumer Reports* review advised that buyers would be "better off buying a good used car than a new Yugo." *Car & Driver* magazine reported that shifting the Yugo's gears was "like trying to shift a baseball bat stuck inside a barrel full of coconuts." There is no doubt as to the Yugo's mechanical shortcomings, but the context of Cold War politics and the Reagan revolution should also be taken into account when considering its reception in the US. The mechanical and aesthetic modesty of the Yugo became a counterpoint to the development of the SUV, a new concept that reflected the politics of the Reagan administration, mechanically fusing civil comfort with a dominant, imposing exterior.

Western popular culture has presented the Yugo as a dangerous car that only strange people drive. For instance, the Hollywood movie "Drowning Mona" directed by Nick Gomez and released in 2000, is a murder mystery which portrays a small town in New York State. The town is inhabited by weird people, every one of whom drives a Yugo. At the end of the film, the mysterious killer is revealed to be...the Yugo itself! With its demonization of the Serb-manufactured car, the film is reminiscent of the 1942 Hollywood movie "Cat People," about a Serb woman in New York City who turns into a killer cat and murders innocent Americans.

In 1968, Elvis Presley recorded a song called "In the Ghetto," with lyrics by Mac Davis. It is a melodramatic social commentary about a black boy shot in a ghetto in front of his crying mother. Paul Shanklin, a conservative political satirist, parodies the song as "In a Yugo." Shanklin's parody tells the story of a liberal, environmentally-conscious couple who die in their Yugo: "And their knees on their chest/They're gonna save enough gas/For all of the rest." They swerve to avoid hitting a duck, lose control, and get squashed beneath a produce truck: "And as the crowds drive past a little flat car/ You know they saved a lot of gas/But they didn't get far/In a Yugo/ And as they're trapped inside/At a used car lot on the other side of town/A liberal guy and a liberal gal/Buy a Yugo/ And they drive with pride..." We might improvise our own ending: "... and we had to bomb this technological ghetto Yugo-Zastava and transport the criminal Milošević in our SUV to the airport to take a plane to the Hague."

The Yugo also has become a cultural signifier in the land of its origin. As such, it makes an appearance in the film *Cabaret Balkan* (*Bure Baruta*, 1998), directed by Goran Paskaljević. *Cabaret Balkan* is set in Belgrade and introduces the social dynamics of the internal split among Serbs in the 1990s, when Serbia was under embargo, excluded diplomatically and culturally from the global community. Paskaljević effectively uses cars, space, time and speed to illustrate those dynamics. Since Henry Ford's customization of the car, it has become the chief means of social connectedness in industrialized countries. In the modernized Balkans and elsewhere the social grid constructed around time and speed has also introduced new forms of conflict – car crashes, drag racing, road rage, etc. Cutting off is very common in Belgrade traffic, and it is directly related to the global economy of time. It is a form of primitive accumulation of temporal capital – a force that produces relations, personal trajectories, and conflicts as well as synchronicities. The cab driver from the opening scene in *Cabaret Balkan* is enraged by being suddenly cut off in his white Mercedes by a punk in a yellow Yugo. The makes of the cars instantly establish social and political hierarchy: Mercedes, the West; Yugo, the East. The cabdriver follows the punk to the first stoplight and demands aggressively, "Who gave you a driver's license?" This is enough to spark an explosion in the (junior) wild Balkan man. The punk gives him the finger and speeds up, cutting off the cab left and right and forcing it to slow down, with obvious pleasure in stealing somebody else's time by means of speed, as if saying "West is the West but we are the best!"

By the late 1980s, Yugoslavia was falling apart, malfunctioning as drastically as a Yugo engine. Just as the Yugo turned out to be "an assembled bag of nuts and bolts" so Yugoslavia turned out to be an assembly of ethnic groups, and the country's implosion was the catalyst that ended export of the Yugo to the US. As a result of the forthcoming breakup of Yugoslavia, Zastava and the Yugo, as well as the Yugoslav military, became a Serbian asset. Because of Serb aggression against other Yugoslav republics and the anticipated civil war, Zastava became more focused on the production of weapons and less on the manufacture of parts for the Yugo. This did not bode well for the lavish 100,000-mile warranty offered to purchasers of the car in the US. Export to the US ended in 1991. Though manufacture of the car continued until 2008, the best years were during the 1980s. During that time Zastava had assembled around 230,000 cars a year and sold those cars in 70 countries. The international heyday of the Yugo ended with the fall of Yugoslavia.

Tito's Yugoslavia had operated on the mechanical principle of maintaining a balance of forces – both among ethnic groups inside the country and, externally, between the West and the East. Production of the Yugo by Zastava, a factory licensed to produce both Soviet weapons and "Jeeps", was emblematic of how the Titoist political machine maintained its independence in the post-World II climate of ideological polarization. But the Yugo, and the country that produced it, seemed able to exist only within a divided world. Unification of Germany, and of Europe, destabilized a Yugoslavia that was put in place after World War I to provide a bulwark against German influence in the Balkans. Once the technological revolution had changed the balance of forces and erased the politics of détente, Tito's political machinery fell apart, leaving the Yugo in a world without its political referent.

The preparation for the collapse of the Soviet bloc marked the political landscape which the Yugo had to negotiate. In the same way that the Yugo was relegated to the bottom of the automotive food-chain on US and West European roads, so had ethnic minorities in Yugoslavia found the same undesirable position in relation to the dominant majorities. And just as the Yugo became the undesirable minority to the SUVs, driven by the war criminals and Serb politicians inside Serbia during the Milošević regime, so Bosniaks became the Yugo to the Serb military as Milošević's killing machine was unleashed, equipped with BMWs, AUDI's, and Hummers.

Back home in Serbia – now a pariah state – the Yugo lost its global significance and morphed into a parochial signifier. When Vojislav Koštunica assumed the first post-Milošević presidency of Serbia and Montenegro in the Fall of 2000, he ran on a platform of honesty in order to underscore how different he was from Milošević. The evidence of his *bona fides*? He drove a Yugo. But as soon as the new political elite took over the fleet of BMW's, the Yugo lost its ethical capital. I recall, on July 4, 2005, just a few years after the fall of Milošević, I was driving two of my NGO friends up the exclusive Dedinje hill in Belgrade to a party organized by the US ambassador at his residence. Members of the Serbian new political elite arrayed in silk and jewels formed the majority of the guest list, and a line almost a kilometer long stretched along the sidewalk. As I pulled up in front of the ambassador's residence, a tsunami of disapproving gazes washed over us and our vehicle. This a*rriviste* crowd were not pleased to be reminded of their humble origins as Yugo drivers, and they welcomed the reminder about as much as a Christian fundamentalist would have welcomed being confronted with direct evidence of the human-ape link.

The Yugo may not have made as long lasting a contribution to global transportation as other popular, nationally-identified cars like VW or Ford, yet no other car ran on so little fuel and so much trust and hope. In contrast, the comfort, reliability, and predictability of Western cars isolate the driver within the grid of global capitalism to allow him or her to meet productive responsibilities within global time. Moreover, the hearse-like comfort of these cars suppresses the competitive instinct, and their drivers move passively in a funereal traffic flow. Fans of the Yugo delight in pointing out the advantages of the Yugo in relation to Western cars: "This is driving in its most natural form. You feel every bump, squeak and jolt, and one can enjoy the sweet smell of gasoline and exhaust fumes. No car can replace it." Here is where the history of human transportation becomes transparent. Driving a Yugo is like riding or driving a horse. It presumes cooperation of human and machine in the course of time.

As I was finishing this essay on Christmas Eve, news was breaking of the official demise of the SUV. A story in *The New York Times* proclaimed, "With Plants Shutting, the S.U.V. Lumbers to the End of the Line." "Ćao, nema više" ("Ciao, no more"), the sign tailgated on the last Yugo car, could have been borrowed for the Detroit Big Three. And, coincidentally, *Time Magazine* declares the Tesla Roadster, an electrical car, as the best technological accomplishment of 2008. Tesla, the "man who invented the twentieth century", came from the same subaltern space as the Yugo; he was a Serb born in Croatia who regarded himself as a Yugoslav.

The title of this essay paraphrases the title of Gayatry Chakravorty Spivak's groundbreaking essay, "Can the Subaltern Speak?" In other words, can the marginalized, excluded peoples of the world find their own voice and escape hegemonic representation? Alan Phelan answers the question in the affirmative by revealing Europe's subaltern in the Yugo's infrastructural materiality. His art allows industrial materials, machines, blueprints, trees, tools, to tell their version of history and so seriously challenge post-Yugoslav aesthetics grounded in the hegemony of the symbolic of the national subject. Phelan's infrastructural aesthetics also affirms Heidegger's guerrilla metaphysics of *zu-handen-heit*, ready-to-hand-ness, and the artist as a tool-based Being in the world. In the manner of Antonio Gramsci's "organic intellectual" he relates to the social totality of the Yugo from within the actual conditions of material production. Committed to recovering the Yugo-*praxis* (as opposed to the Yugo symbolic) Phelan lends a voice to the mute industrial artifact in order to tell us its version of history.

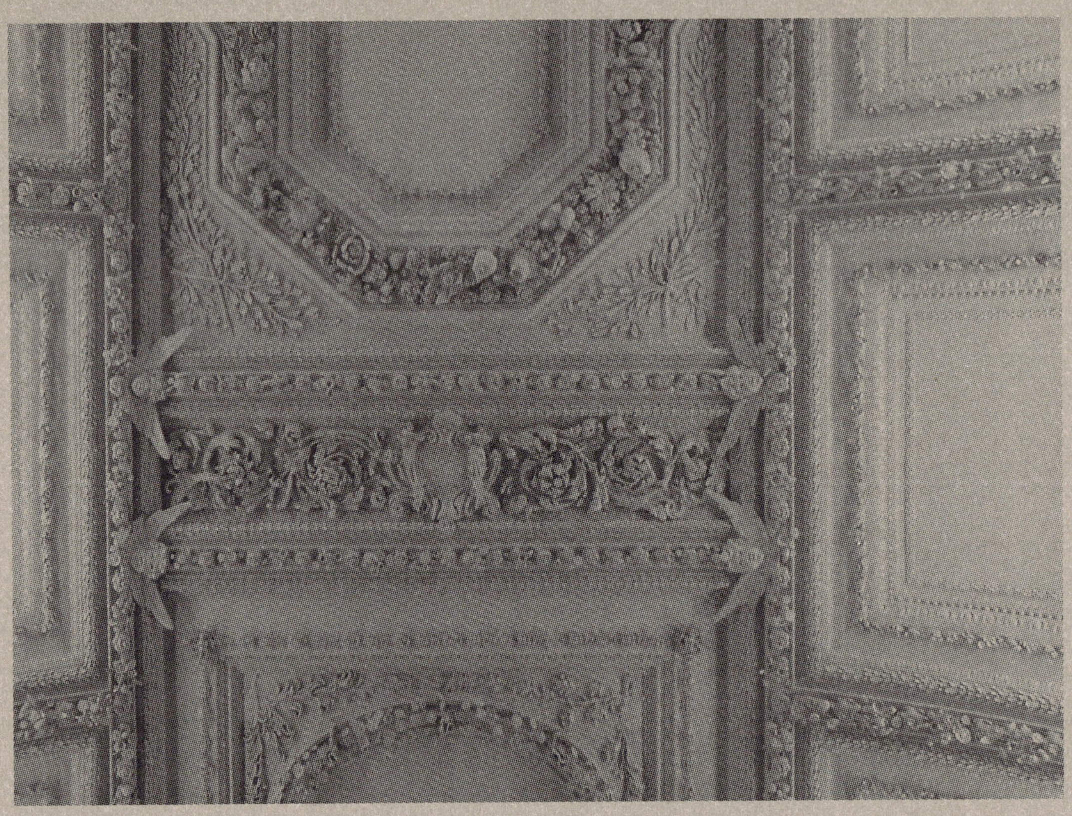

Chapel ceiling at Royal Hospital Kilmainham

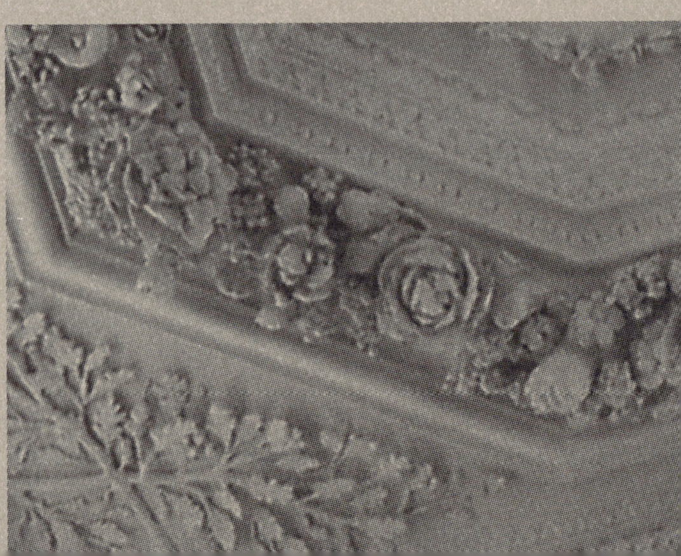

not its own symbolic history 'spectral', fantasmatic history Moses and Monotheism Encore not not more real than reality logos The Woman and the Ape Blade Runner unbearable ideal couple of a male ape copulating with a female cyborg My Best Friend's Wedding they performing a fake appearance sublime shine through Dr. Caligari Woman in the Window The Strange Affair of Uncle Harry All-Movie Guide Woman in the Window, Uncle Harry engages we were

6

p.108

Cabbage, 2008
archival paper, toner, EVA glue, polystyrene
24 x 11 x 24 cms

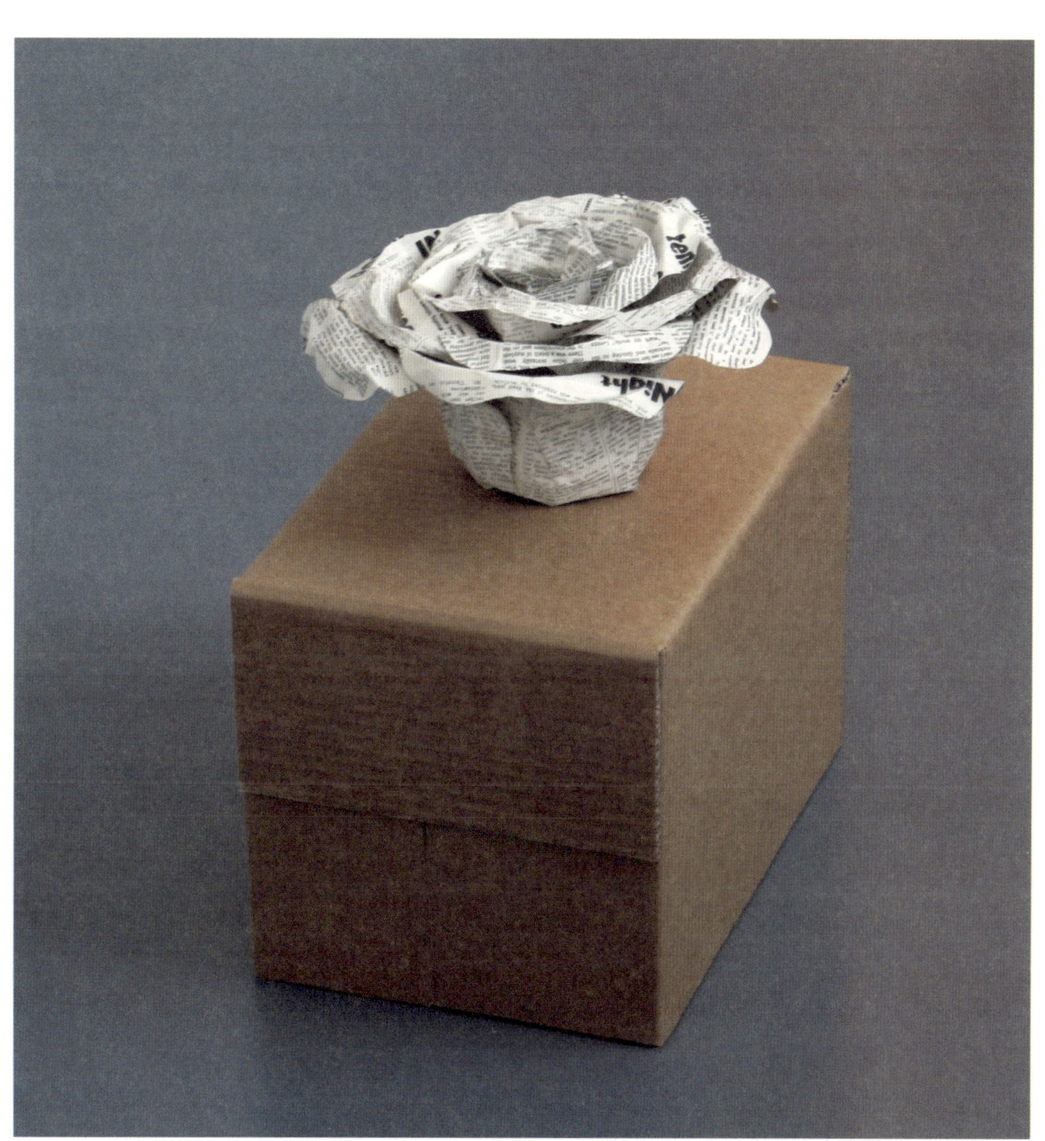

Proposed layout for
Cabbage (symbolic history 'spectral' fantasmatic history), 2009
archival paper, toner, EVA glue, polystyrene

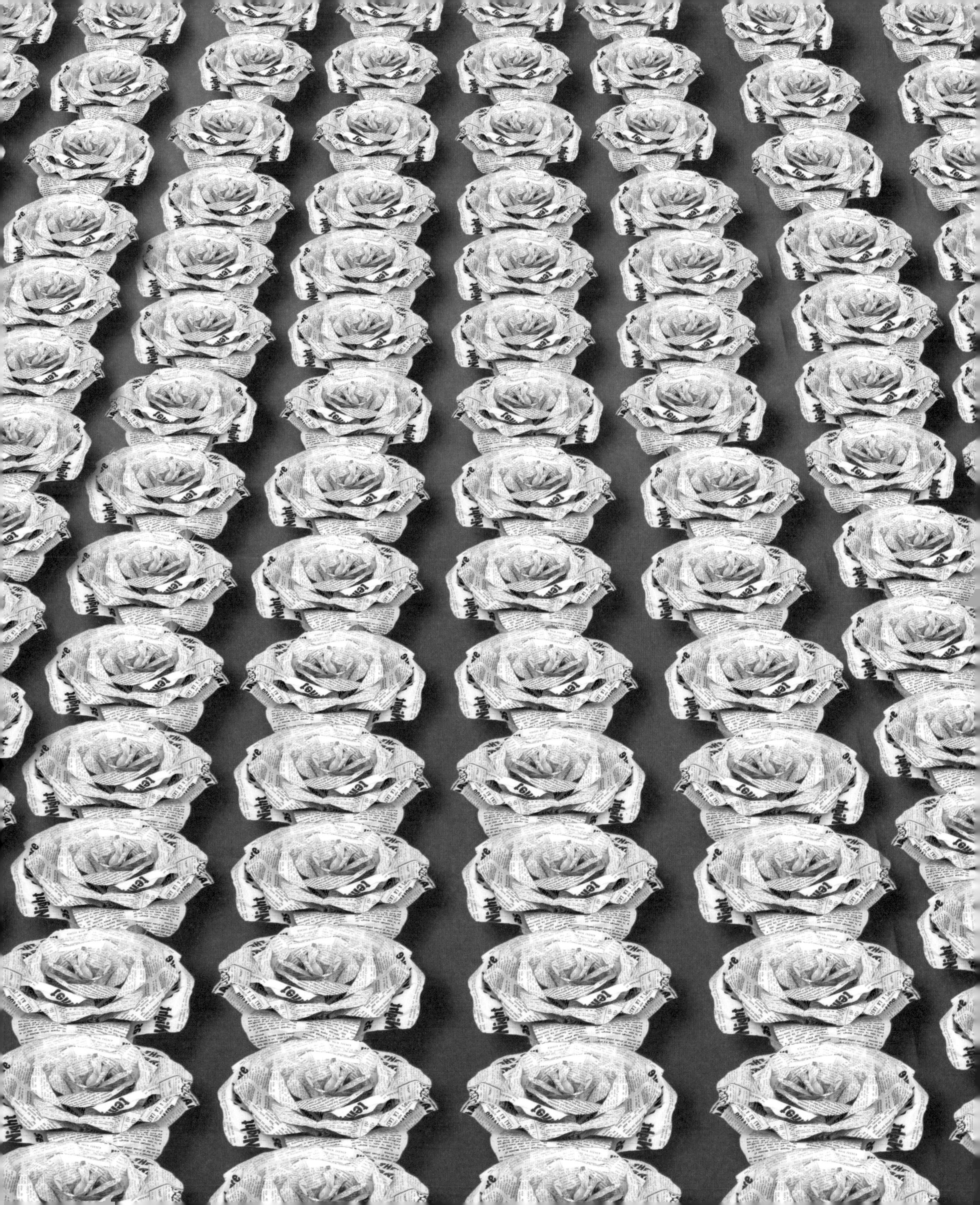

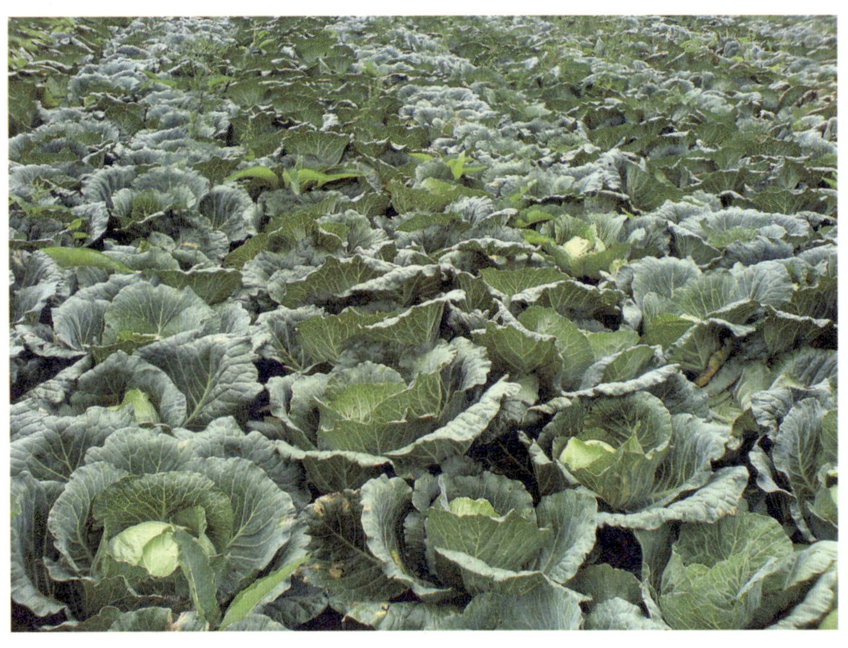

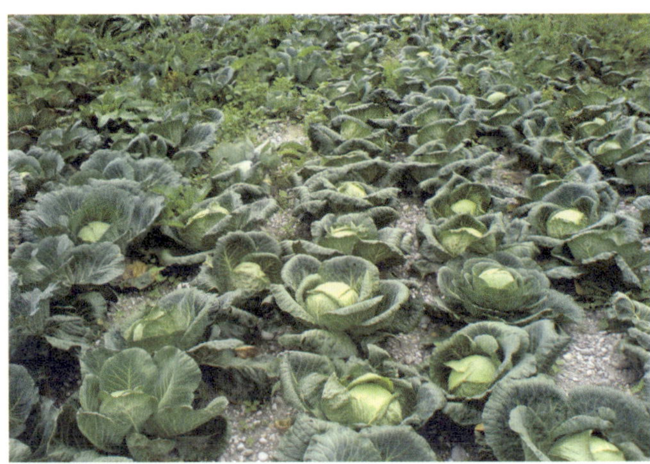

Cabbages, Dolsko, Slovenia, 2008

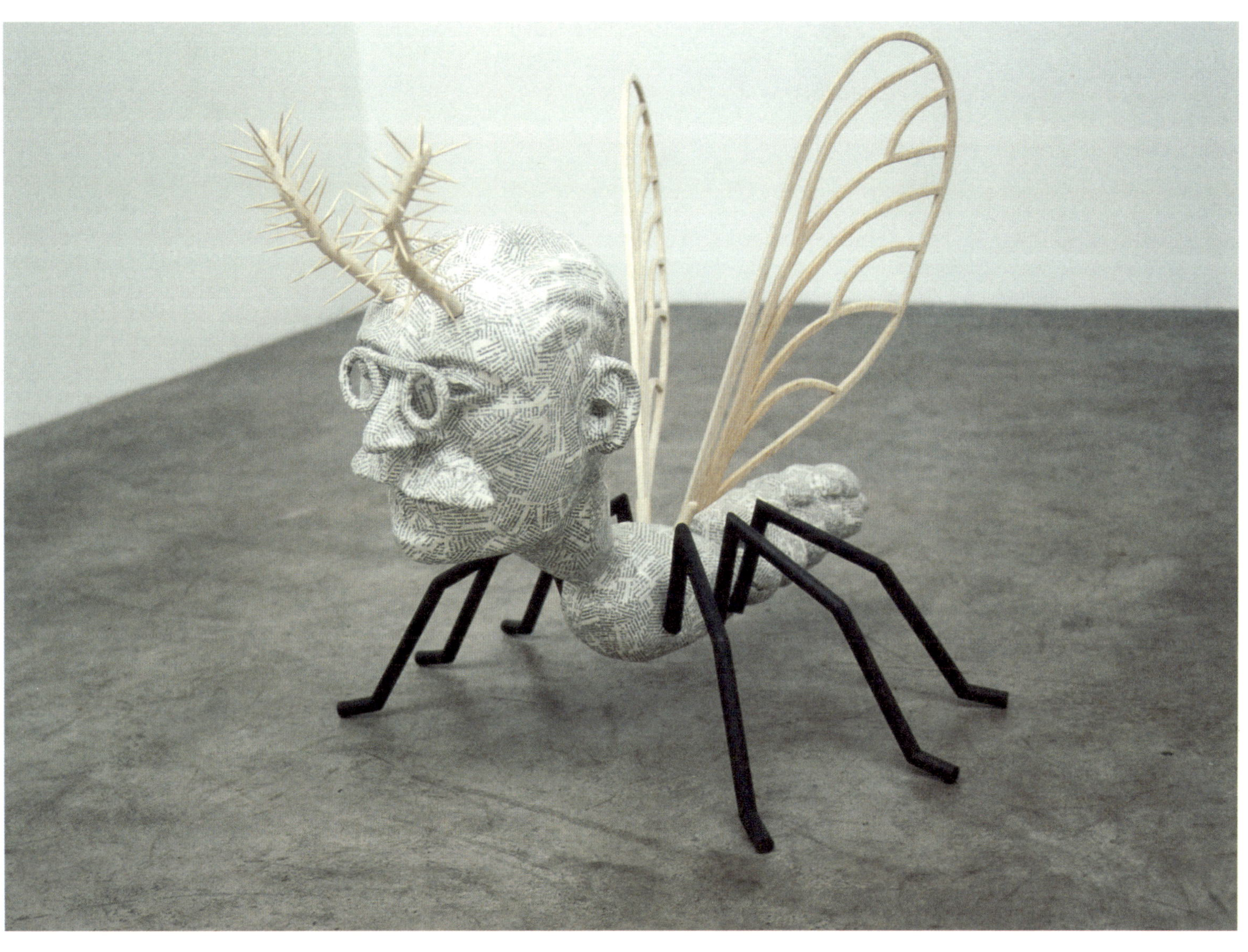

Mosquito Man Arthur, 2007
archival paper, toner, EVA glue, balsa wood, cocktail sticks,
aluminium, plaster, metal pipe, plastic
82 x 80 x 80 cms
(papier-mâché made from articles from the Daily Telegraph)

Roger should have stayed in the jungle, 2006
archival paper, toner, EVA glue, balsa wood, rubber car tyre, terracotta pot
34 x 27 x 27 cms, with pot 54 x 67 x 58 cms
(papier-mâché made from articles from the Daily Telegraph)

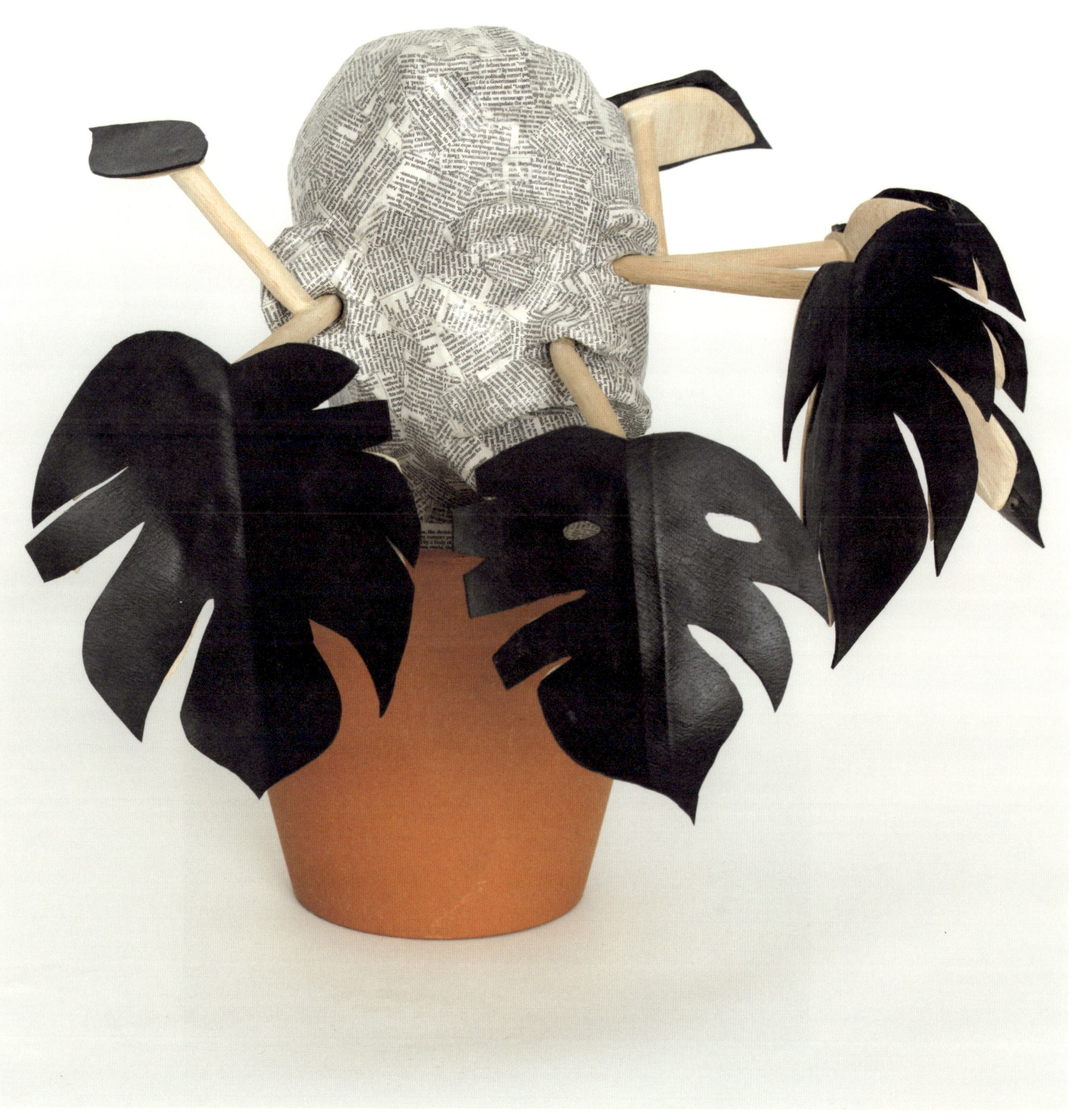

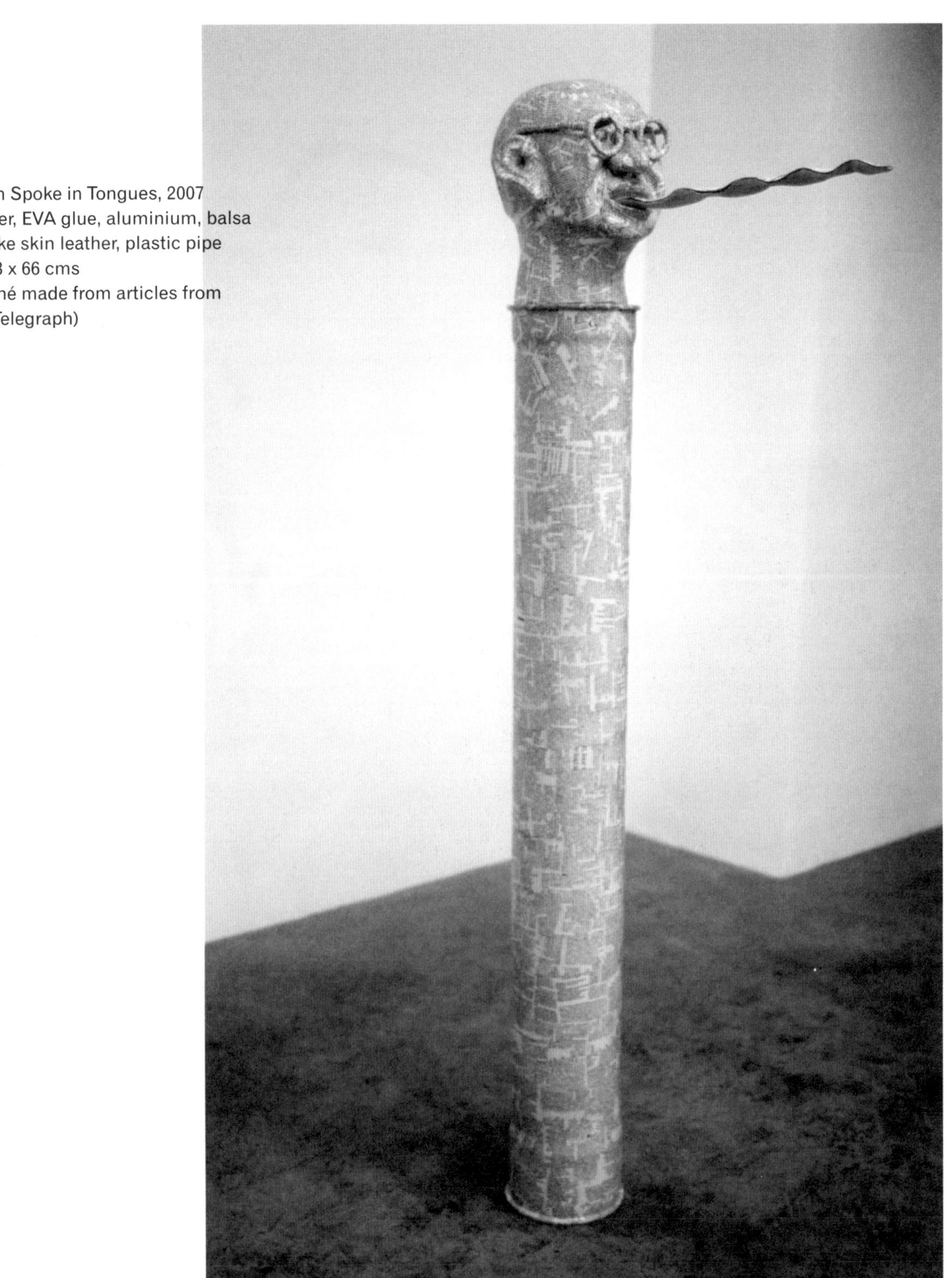

Eamon Often Spoke in Tongues, 2007
archival paper, EVA glue, aluminium, balsa wood, snake skin leather, plastic pipe
head: 29 x 23 x 66 cms
(papier-mâché made from articles from the Daily Telegraph)

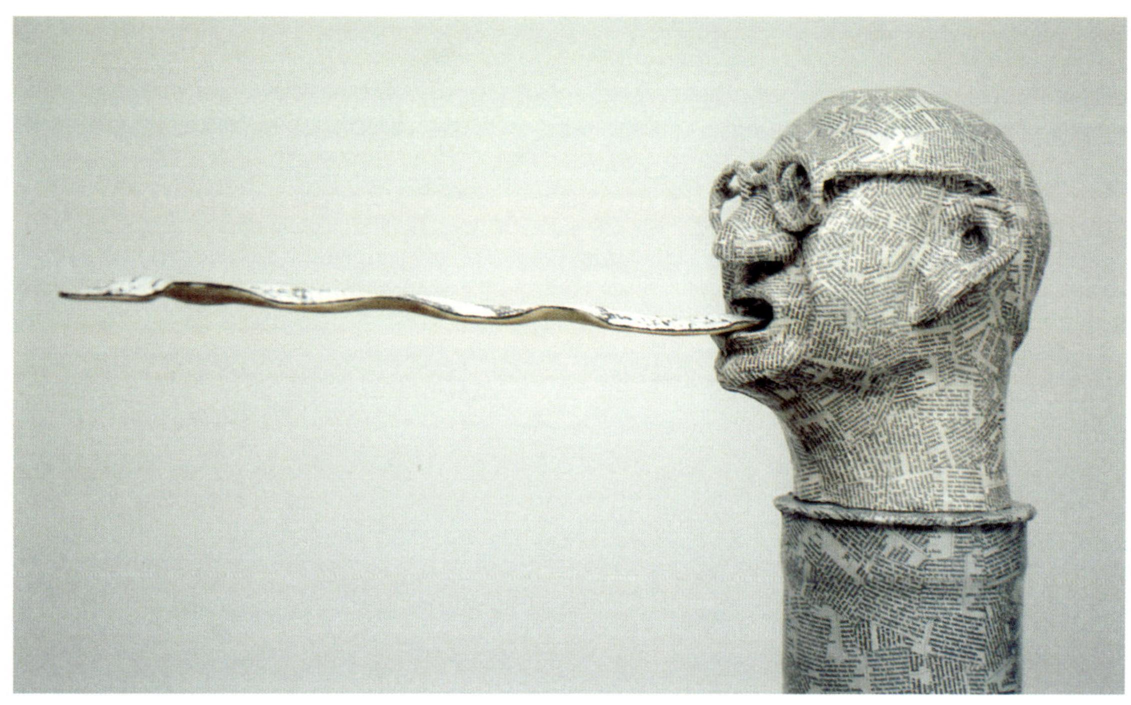

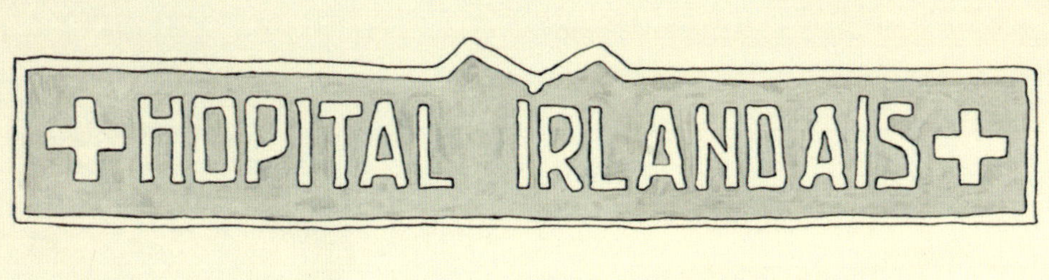


Hopital Irlandais, 2007
silver and black ink on paper
57.5 x 76.5 cms

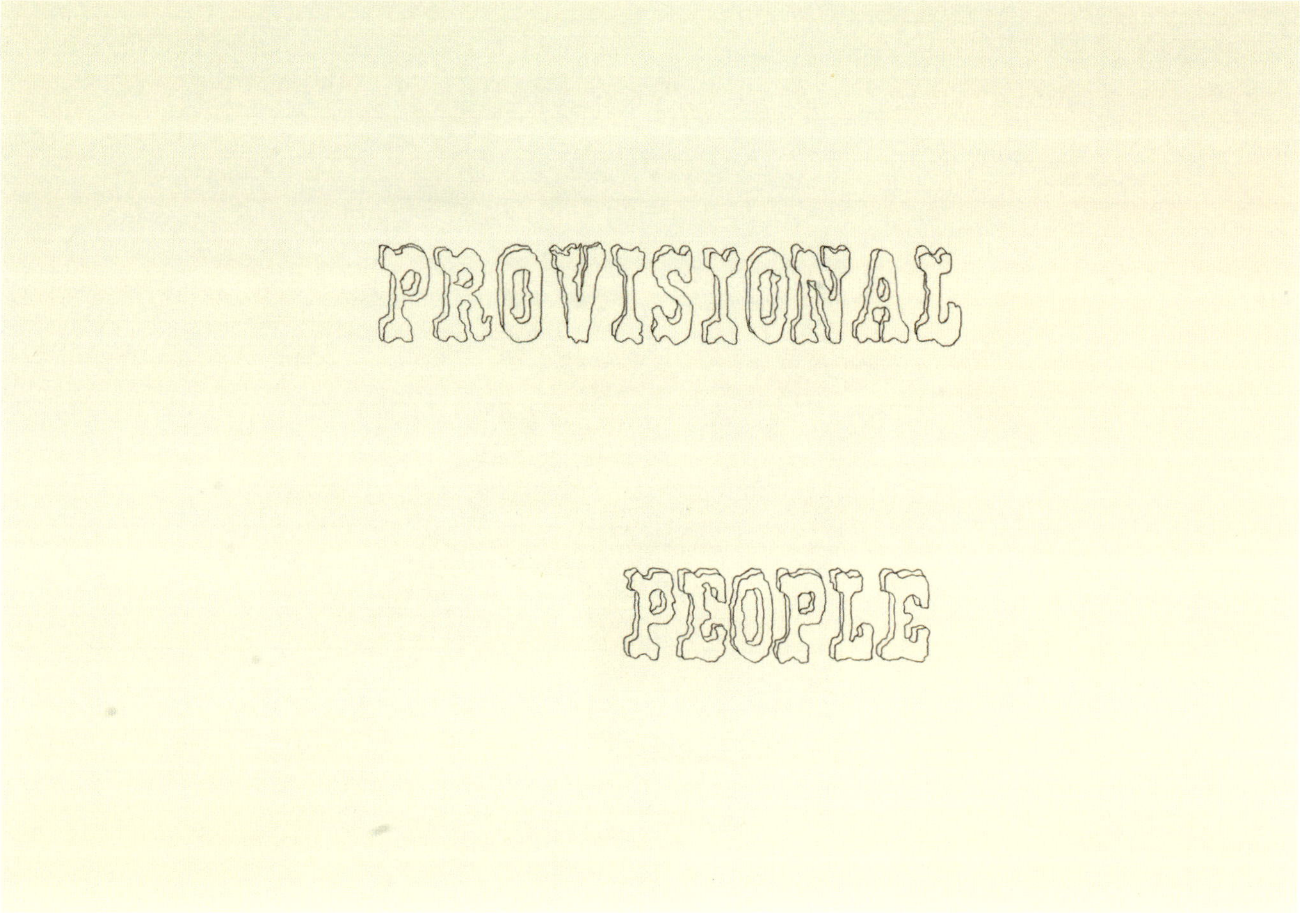

Provisional People, 2007
ink on paper
57.5 x 76.5 cms

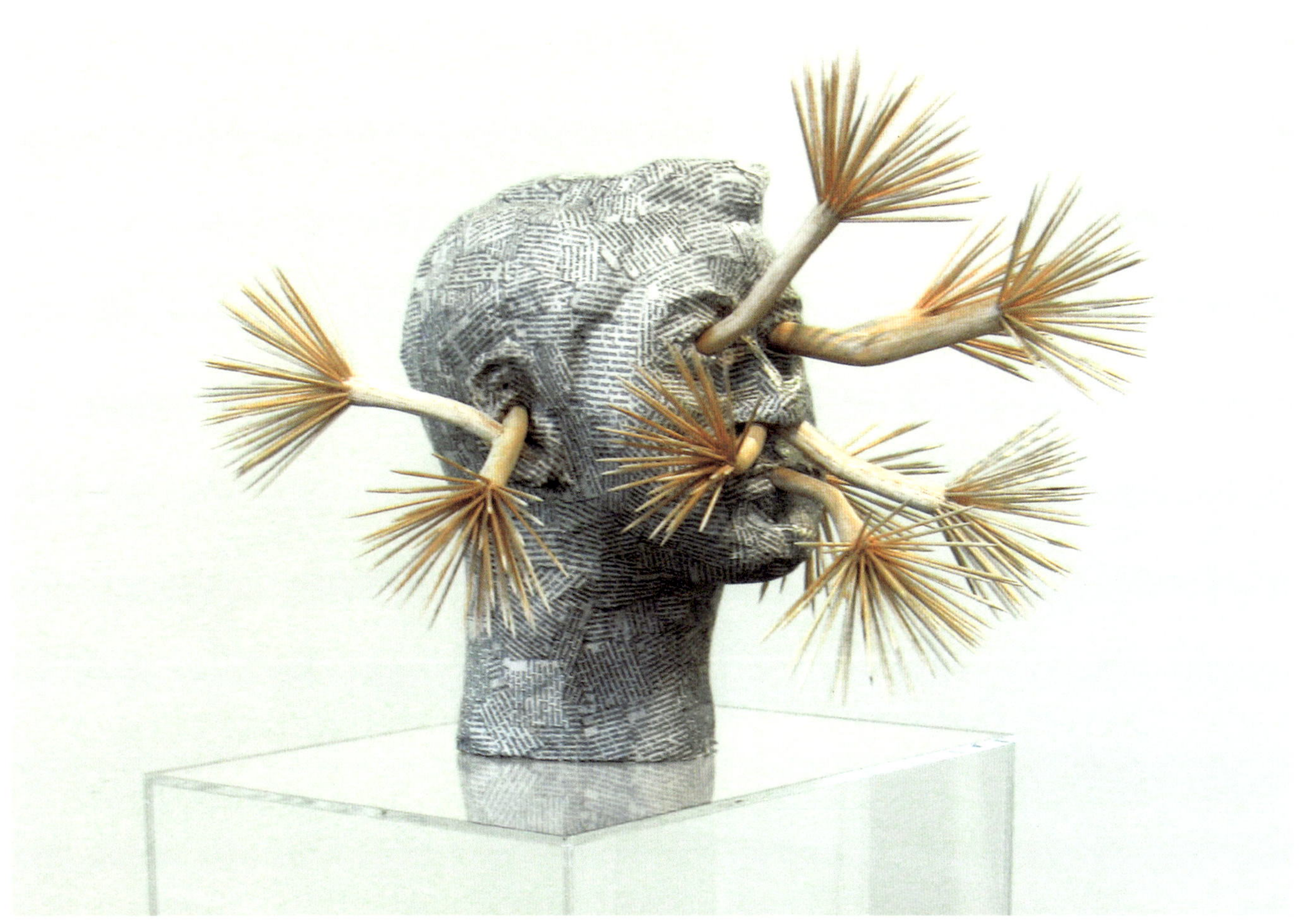

p.121

Michael should have learned to blend-in better, 2006
newspaper, PVA, balsa wood, cocktail sticks
32 x 20.5 x 25 cms
(papier-mâché made from articles from the Daily Telegraph)

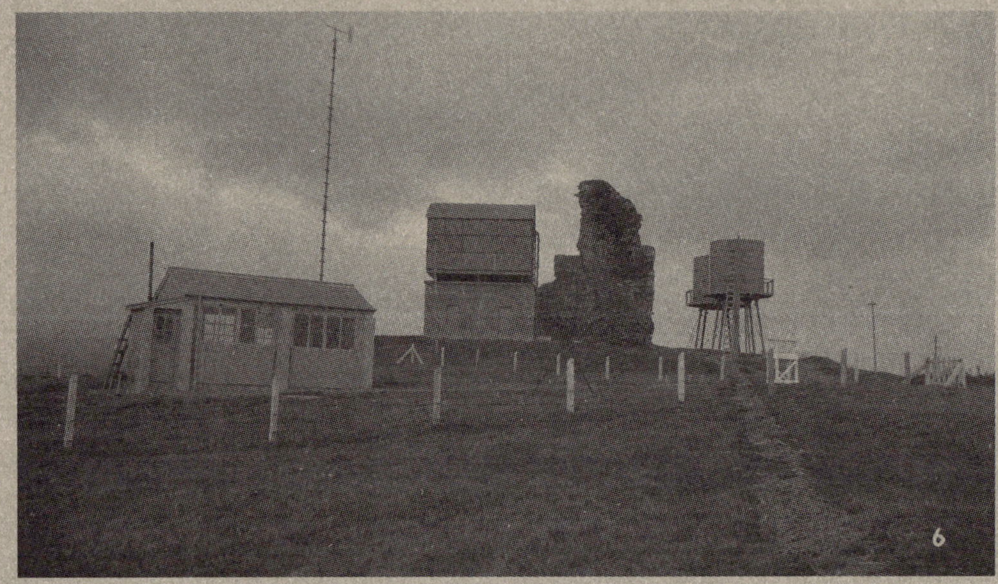


Ralph Gifford
Buildings on Whiddy Island, Ireland, 1910-1919
scan from nitrate negative

reality did excess logos
act Weltalter Weltalter
logos Weltalter mythos
logos act Ent-Scheidung
Weltalter Ent-Scheidung the
highest Deed of my self-positing Weltalter
logos logos Ent-Scheidung
Life is Beautiful Celebration jouisseur
Celebration Urvater
Celebration Fragments jouissance
somewhere there is full, unconstrained enjoyment?
suspend the agency of the symbolic
Law/Prohibition outside the constraints of the (symbolic)
Law desire guilty anxiety
not Festen Life is Beautiful
against Urvater this
Grund act? 'the kind of error
adequatio adequatio
adequatio this modi qua
qua feign to feign lie in the
guise of truth itself not and
lethe derangement [Ver-rückhung]
ontological Treatise on Human Freedom
ontological madness sine qua non

7

**p.124**

The Other Hand of Victory, Hebei version (ontological madness), 2009
marble
40 x 40 x 60 cms

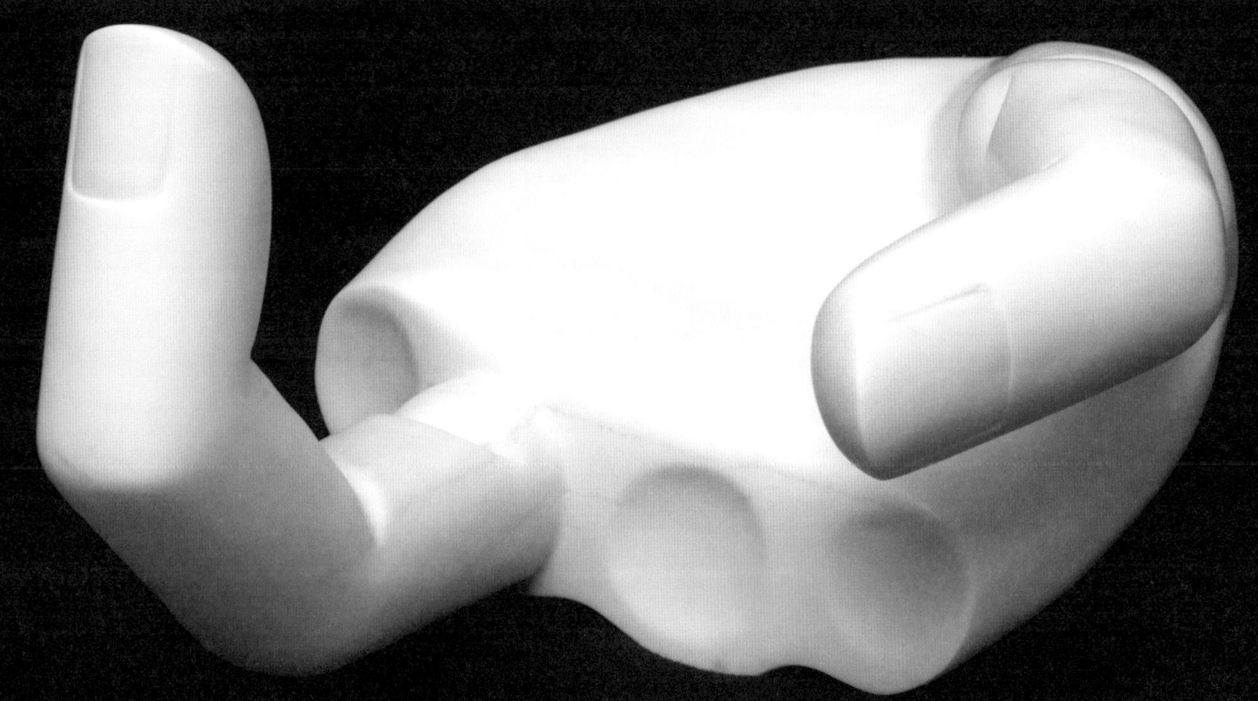

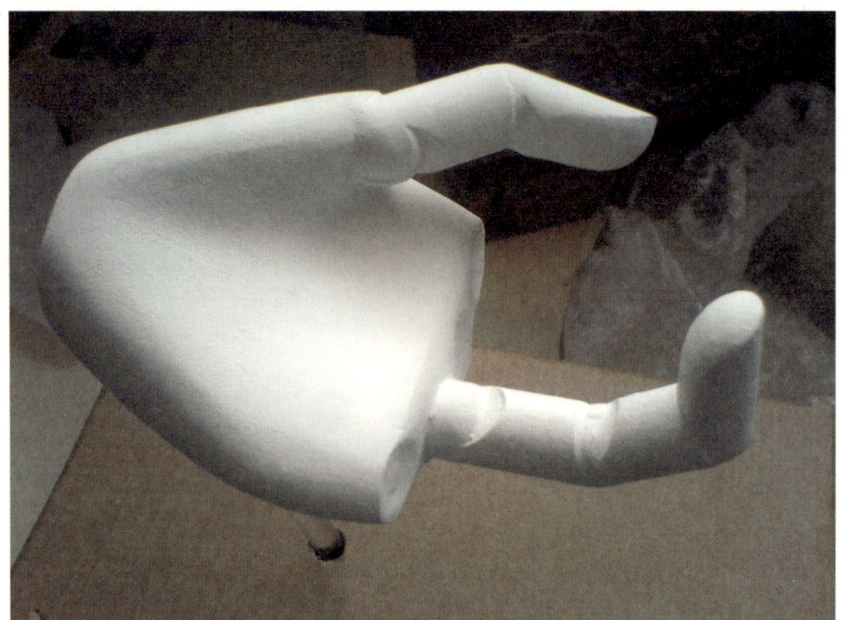

The Other Hand of Victory, 2008
Lidl wooden hand, filler, glue, paint, acrylic rod
10 x 8 x 15 cms

View of sculpture in stone carver's yard, Shijiazhuang, Hebei, China, 2008

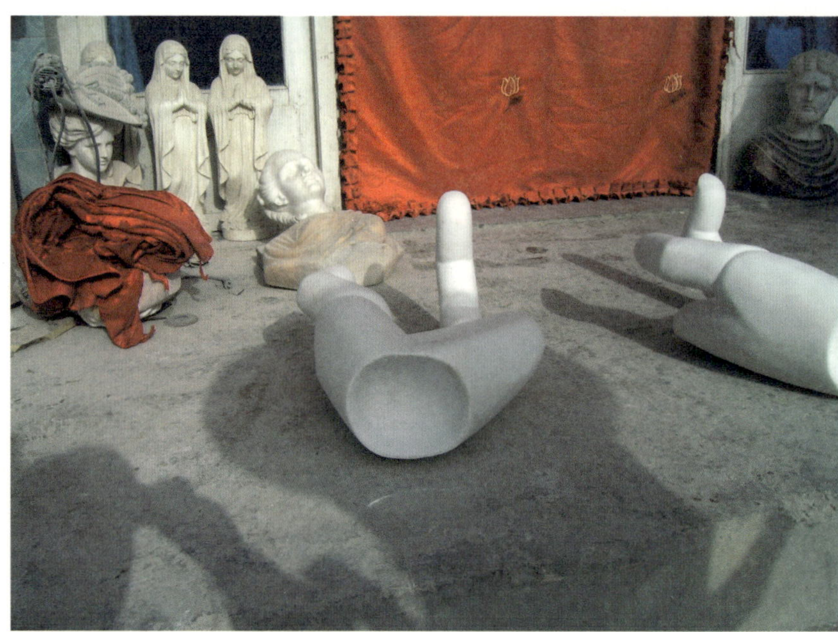

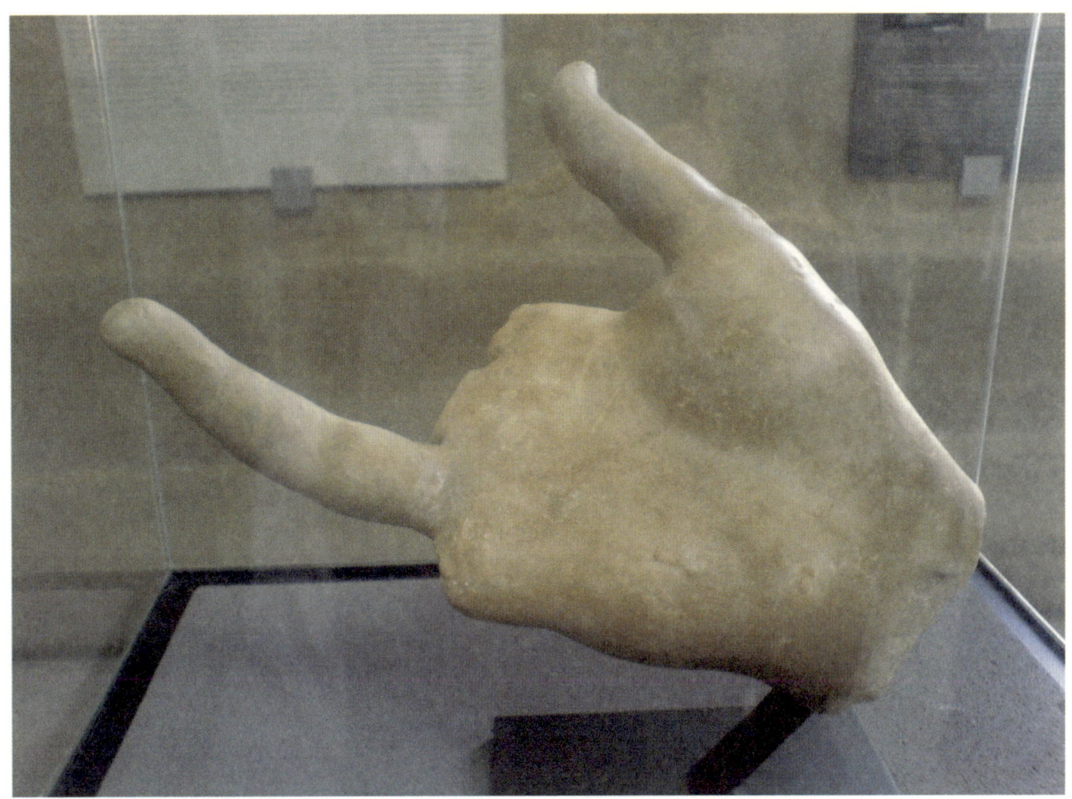

Hand from the Winged Victory (main droite de la Victoire de Samothrace, marbre blanc de Paros), Louvre, Paris, 2008

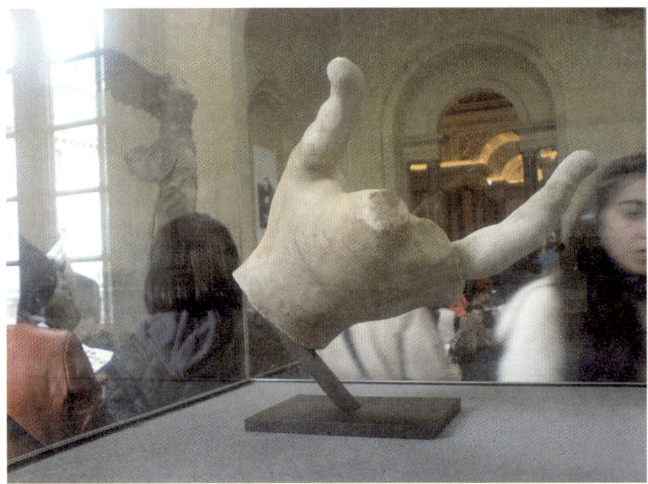

Hand from the Winged Victory (main droite de la Victoire de Samothrace, marbre blanc de Paros),

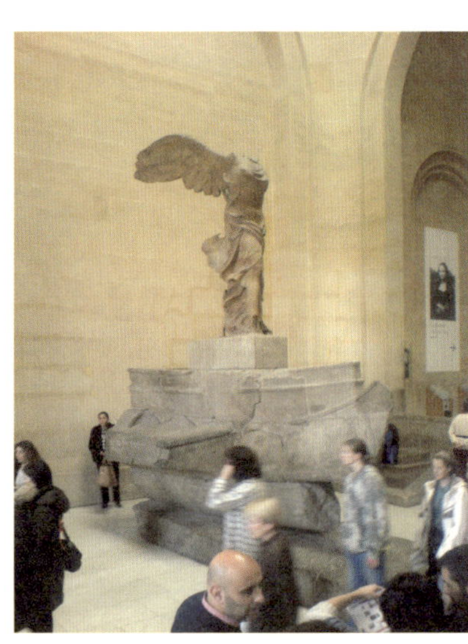

Winged Victory (Victoire de Samothrace, marbre blanc de Paros), Louvre, Paris, 2008

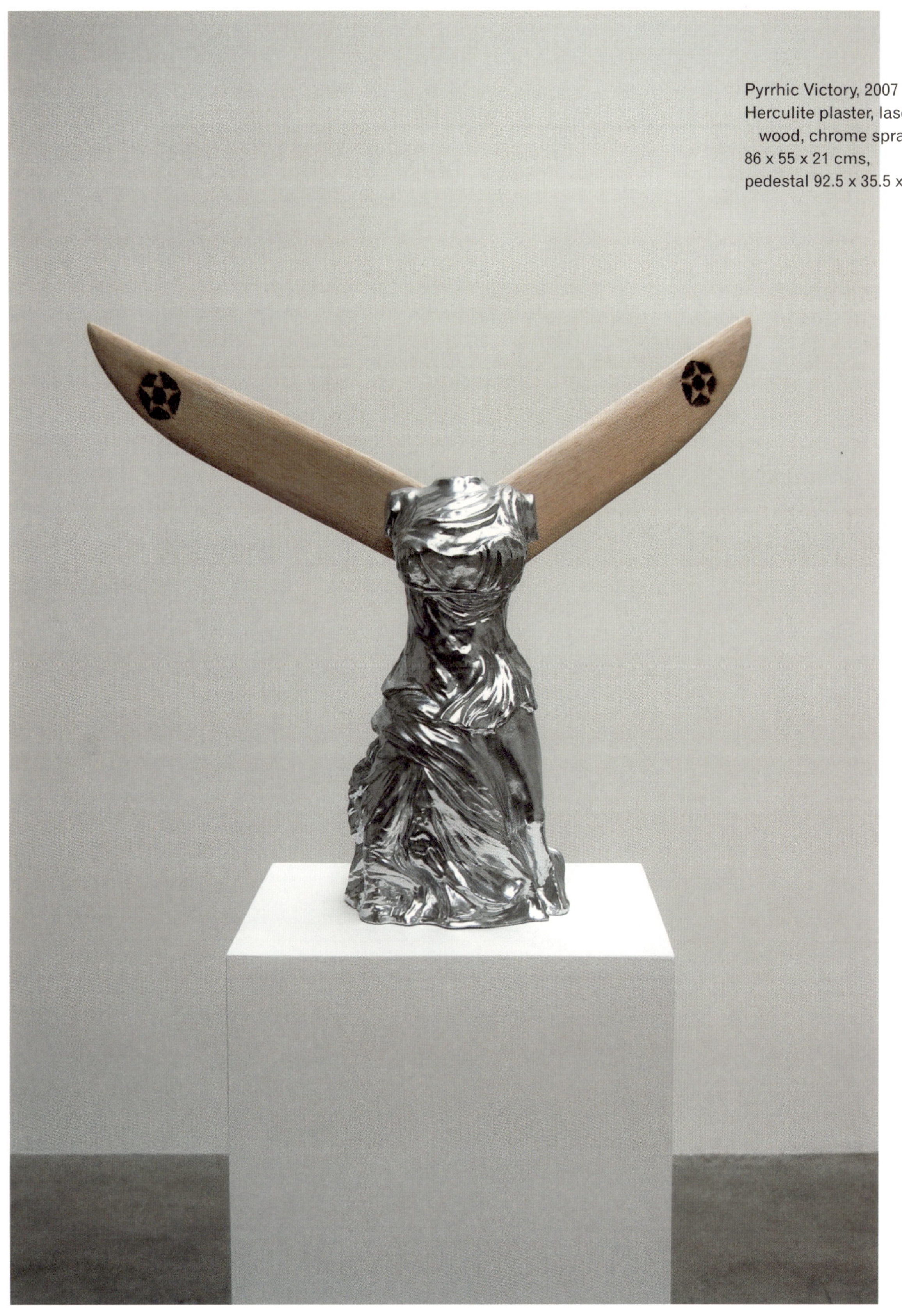

Pyrrhic Victory, 2007
Herculite plaster, laser cut balsa
wood, chrome spray paint
86 x 55 x 21 cms,
pedestal 92.5 x 35.5 x 35.5 cms

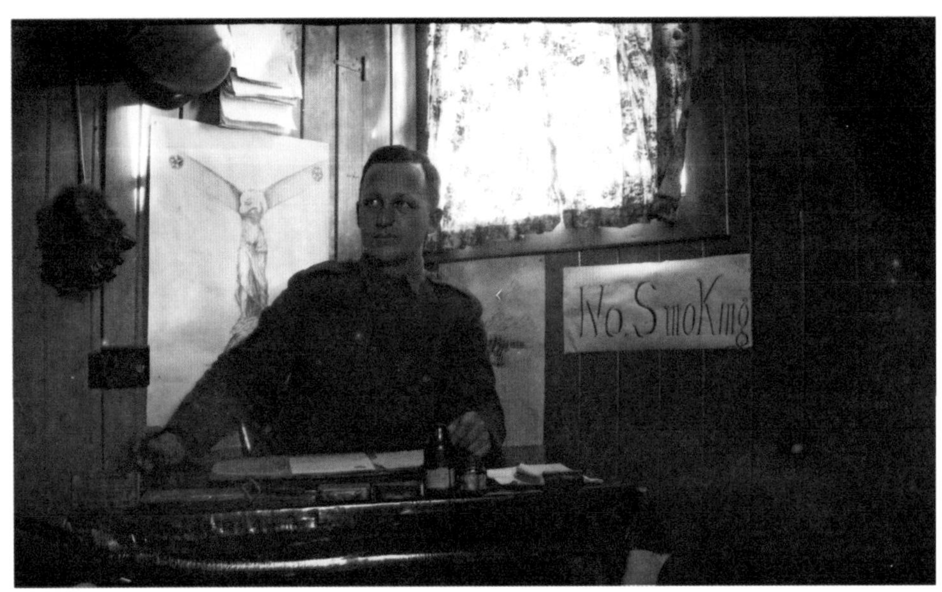

Ralph Gifford
Soldier, 1910-1919
scan from nitrate negative

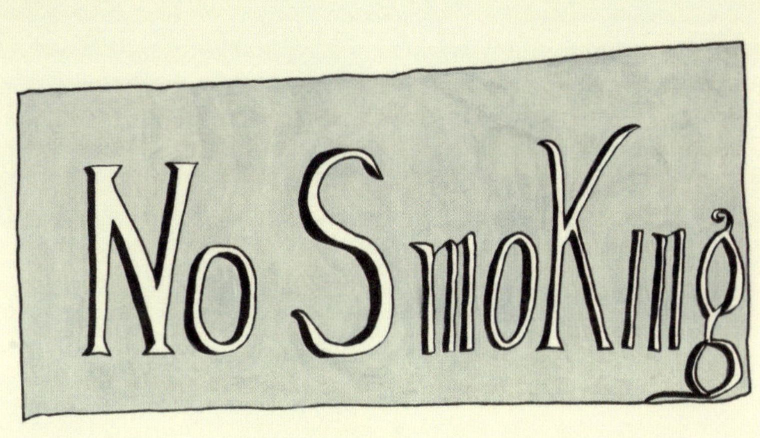


No Smoking, 2007
silver and black ink on paper
64 x 81 cms

p.133

p.135

derangement Letter on Humanism proton pseudos has lethe alethia fantasy he is not aware how Jews really seem to him? this is not how things really seem to you phenomenal inaccessible inaccessible phenomenal empty, non-phenomenal subject phenomena that remain inaccessible to the subject phenomenon monstrosity grounds sustains The Fundamental Concepts of Metaphysics are logos logos Naturphilosophie Satyricon Gemeinschaft Gesellschaft historical historical the present itself ourselves

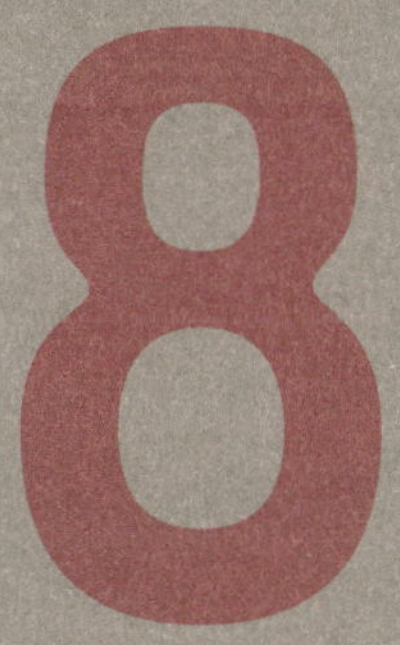

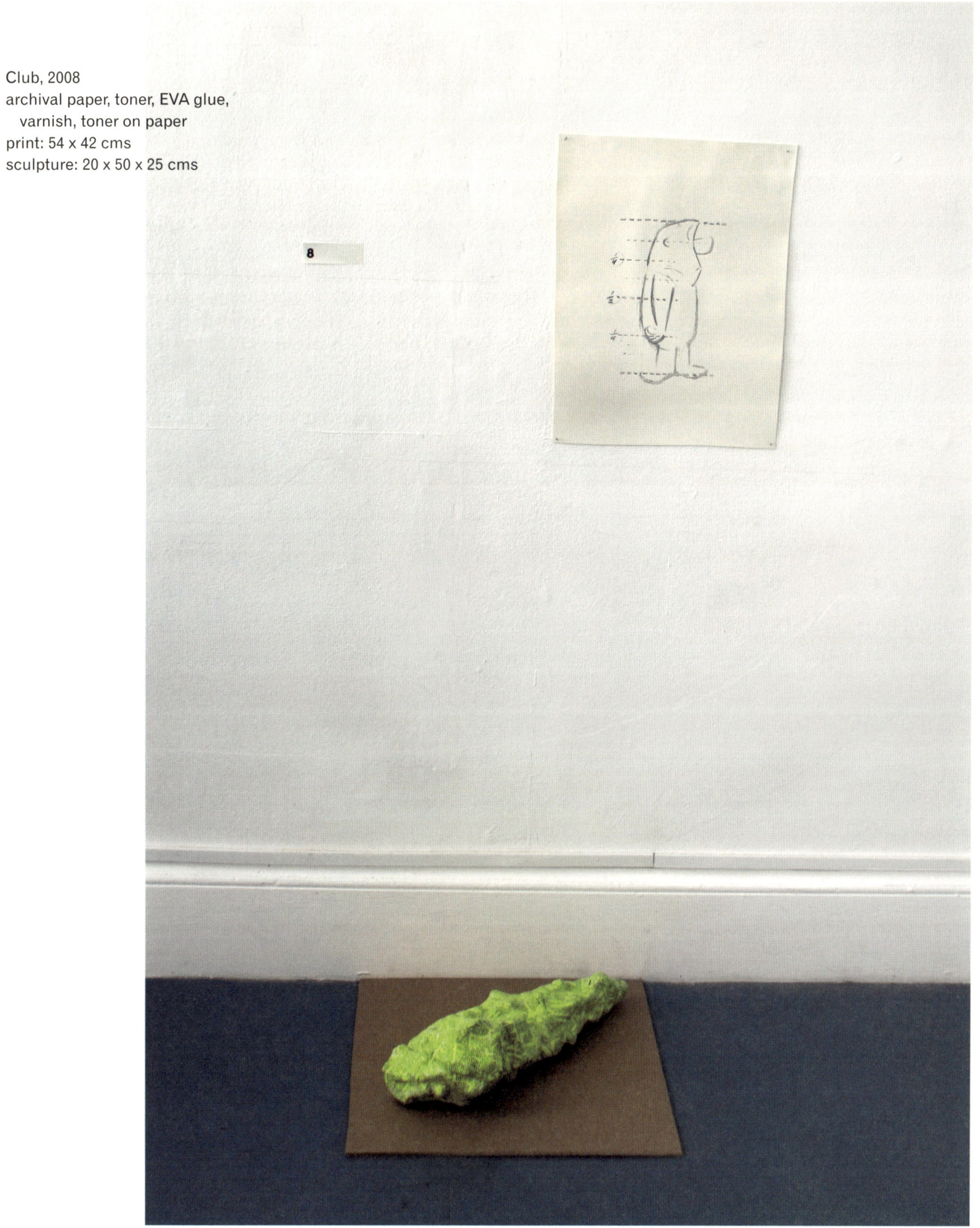


Club, 2008
archival paper, toner, EVA glue,
varnish, toner on paper
print: 54 x 42 cms
sculpture: 20 x 50 x 25 cms

Clubbed Baby Seals (he is not aware how Jews really seem to him? this is not how things really seem to you), 2009
archival paper, toner, EVA glue
15 x 107 x 95 cms
(papier-mâché made from index pages from the Wall Street Journal)

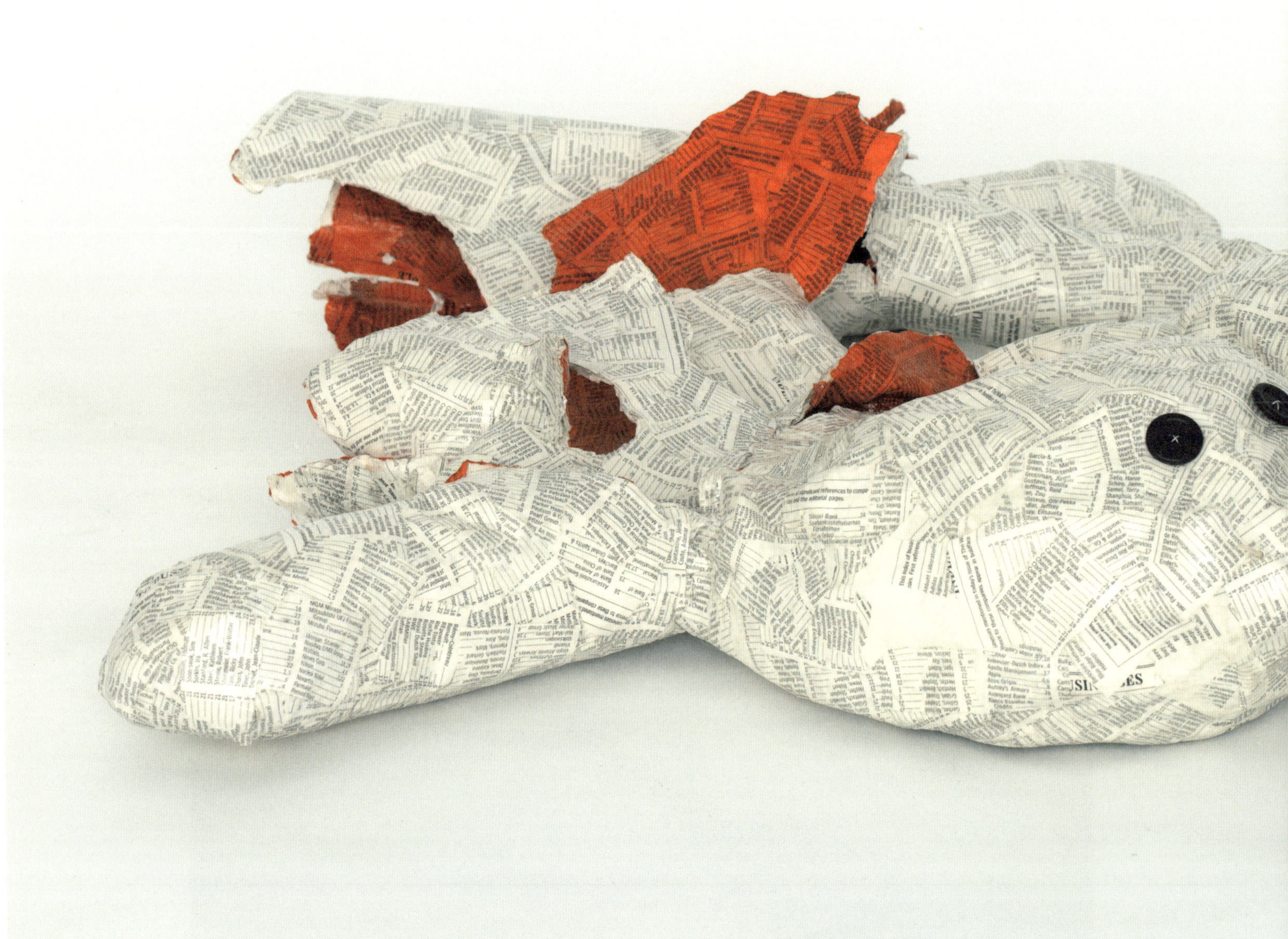

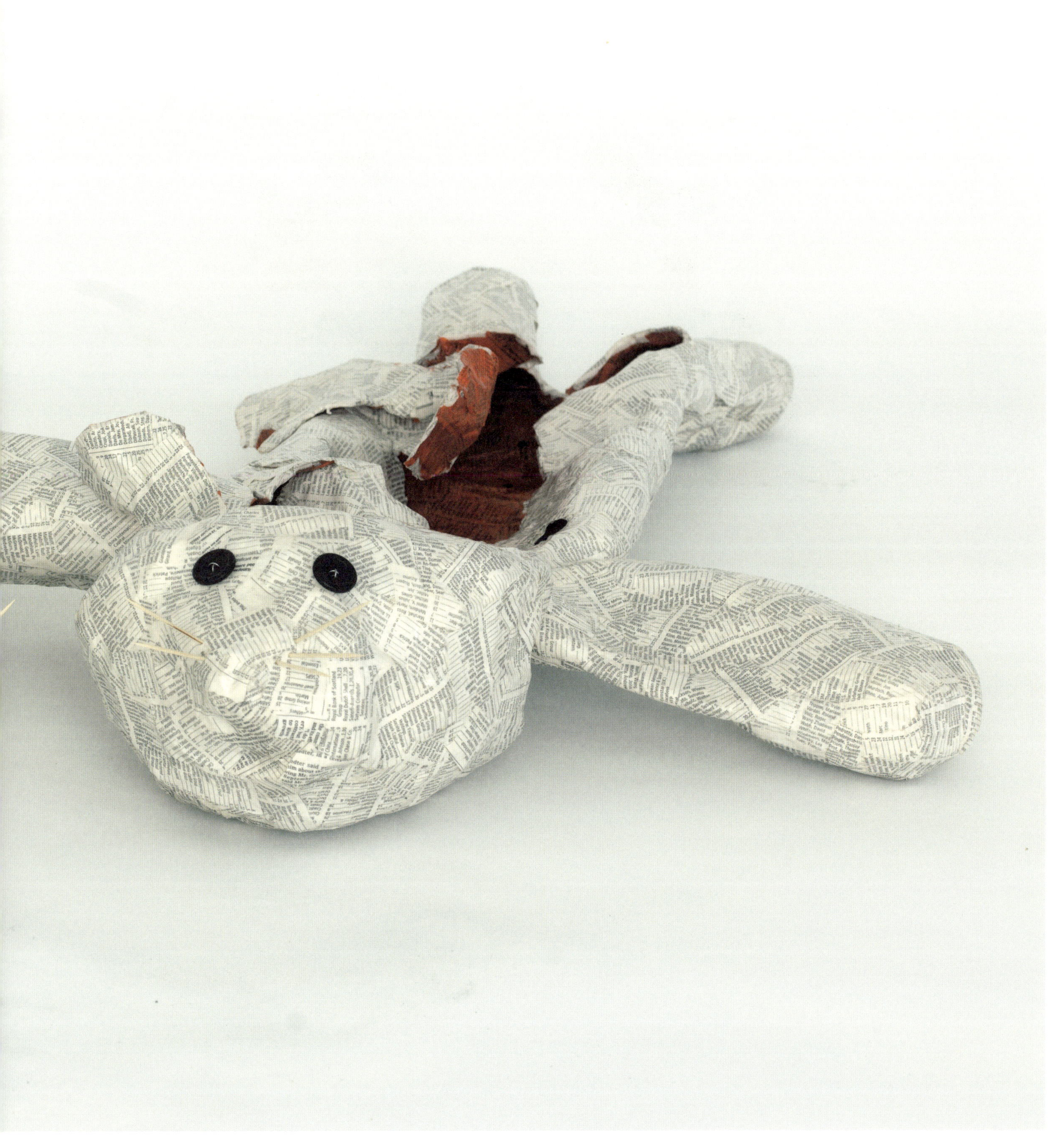

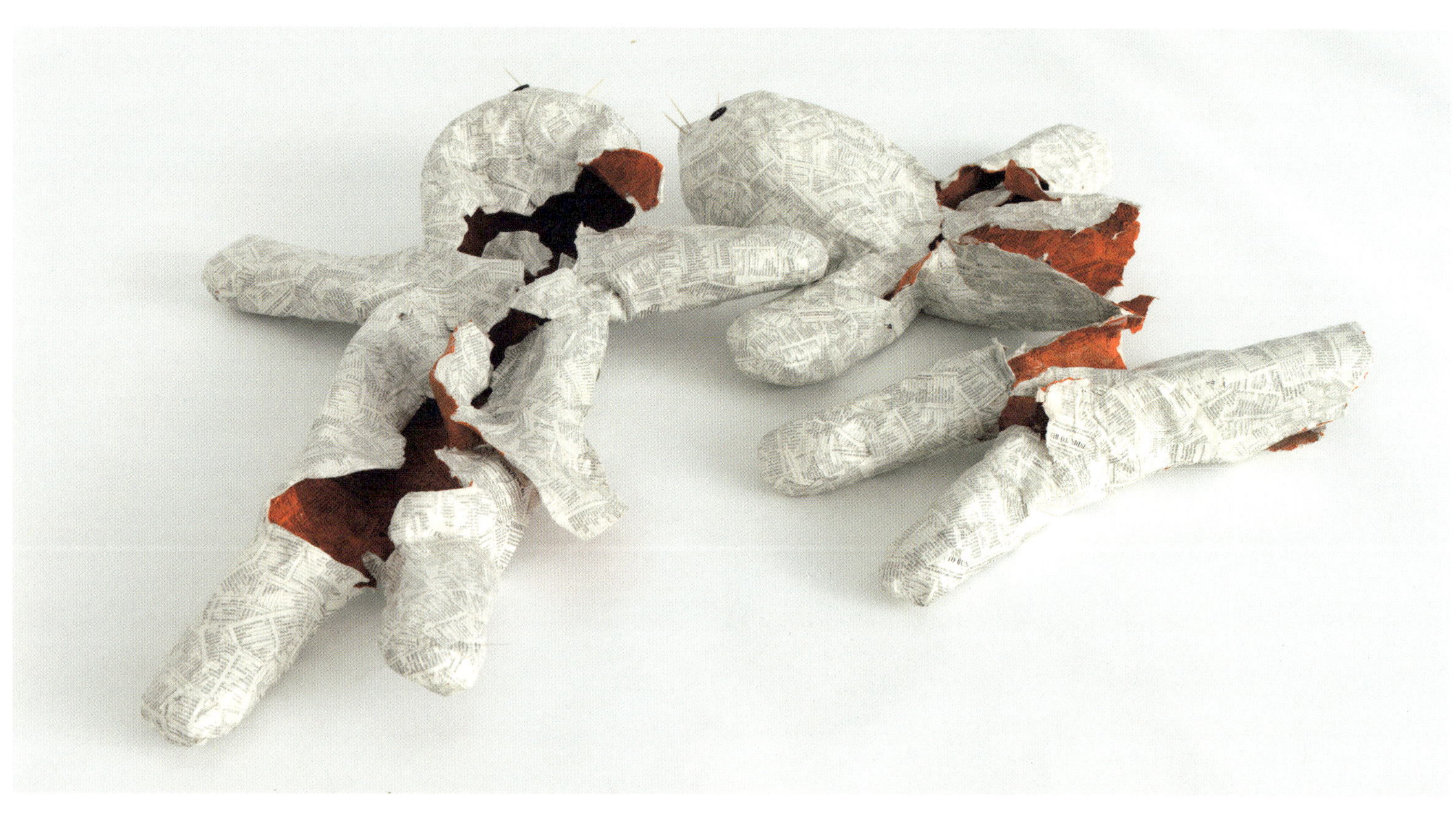

Clubbed Baby Seals (he is not aware how Jews really seem to him? this is not how things really seem to you), 2009
archival paper, toner, EVA glue
15 x 107 x 95 cms
(papier-mâché made from index pages from the Wall Street Journal)

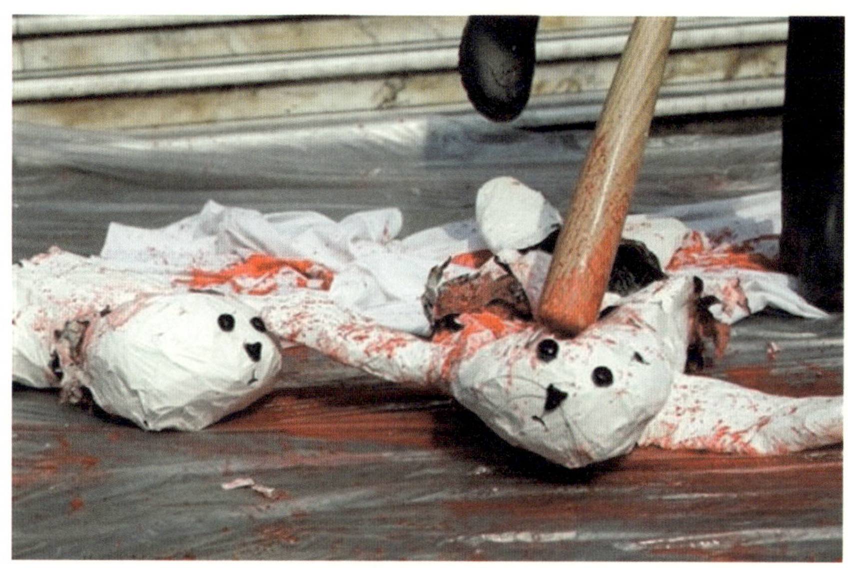

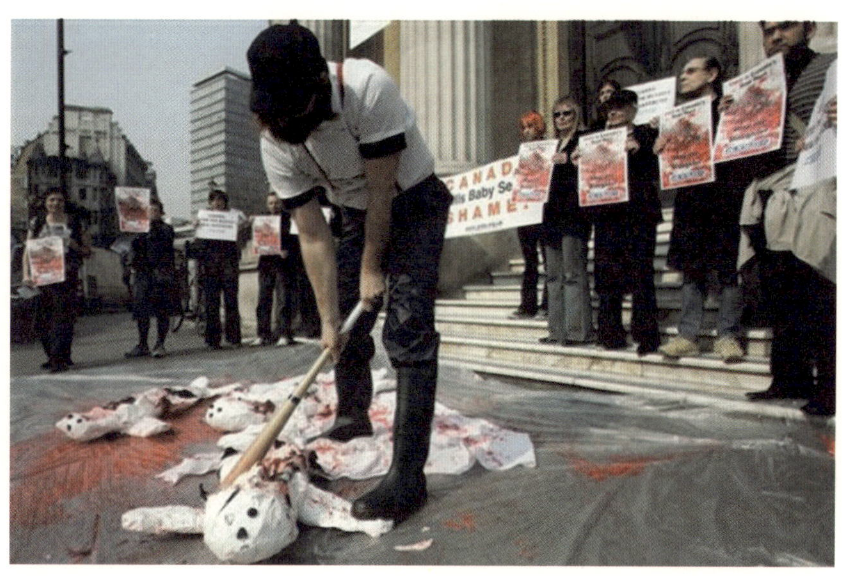

source images for Clubbed Baby Seals, 2009

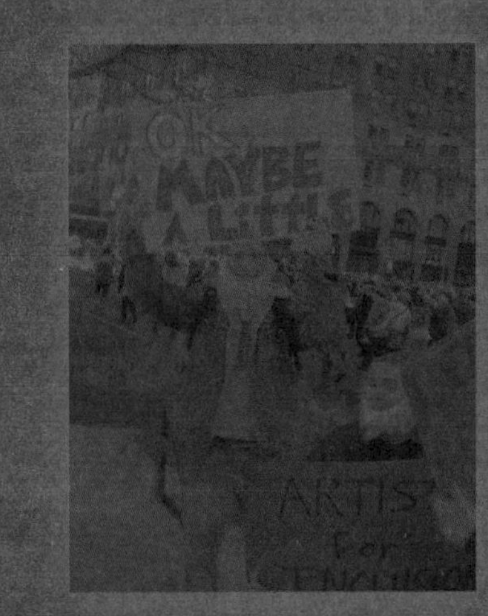
OK
MAYBE
For

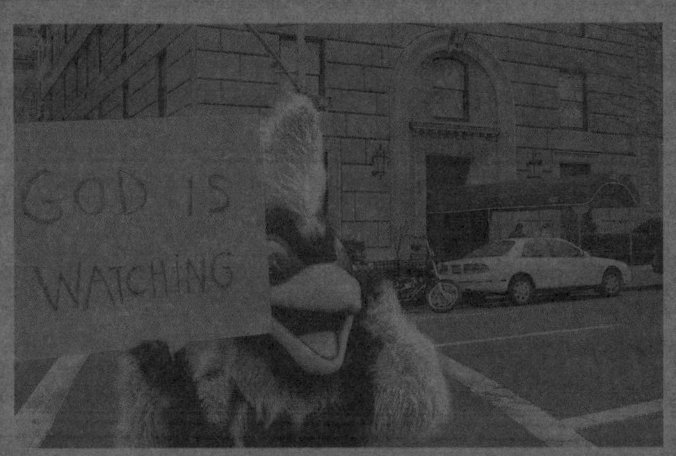
GOD IS
WATCHING

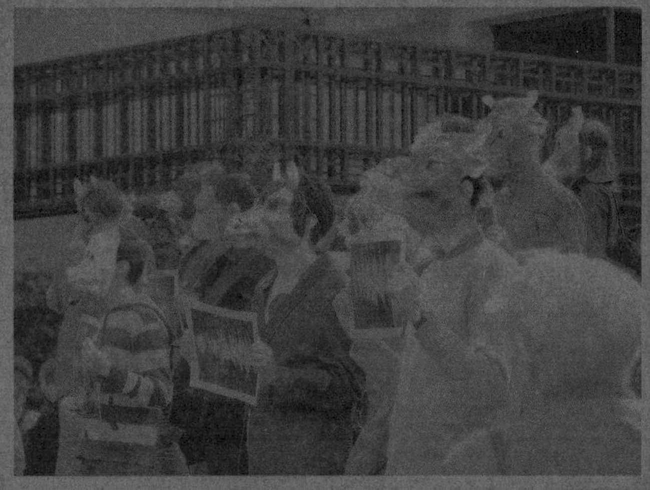

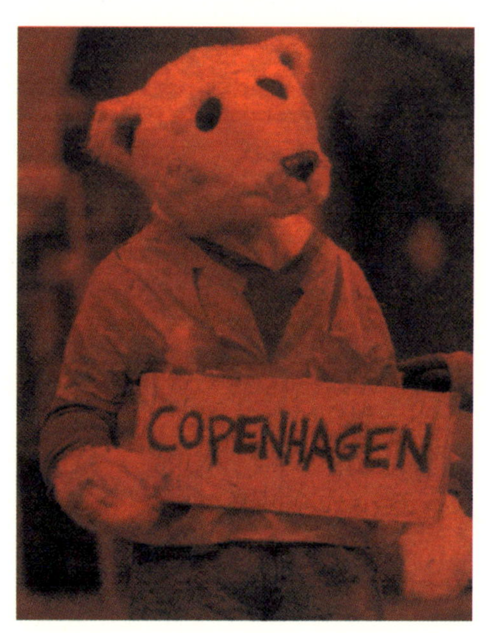
COPENHAGEN

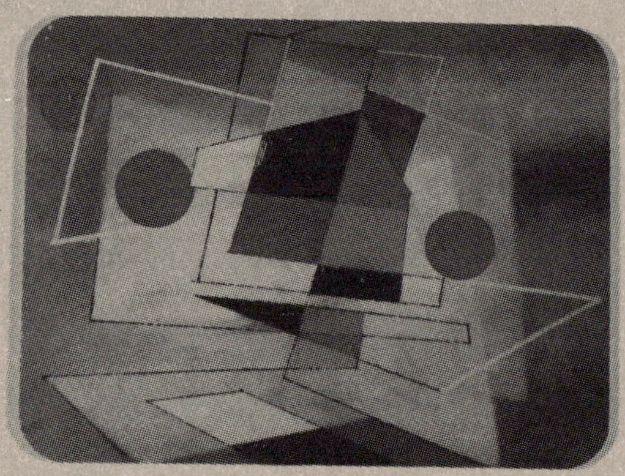

Hungarian Italian Abstraction, 2008
inkjet on mousemat
19 x 24.5 cms

9

act Ent-Scheidung Gap
because bosses do not wear them never was
beyond trauma not
excluded temporal eternal
temporal event eternity itself
repeat change (undo the effects of) eternity
itself not give up the ghost
give up their ghost confession Moses and
Monotheism confess betray
trauma agape agape
superegotize agape
eros within the confines of the Law
agape Blue agape
Vertigo Blue Vertigo Blue
freedom expansion agape
itself meaningless
identity the is appearance
this appearance appears
through hegemonic imaginary
qua appearance How do
stand with regard to – in the eyes of – Schelling? opposite
'What does mean in the eyes of God?

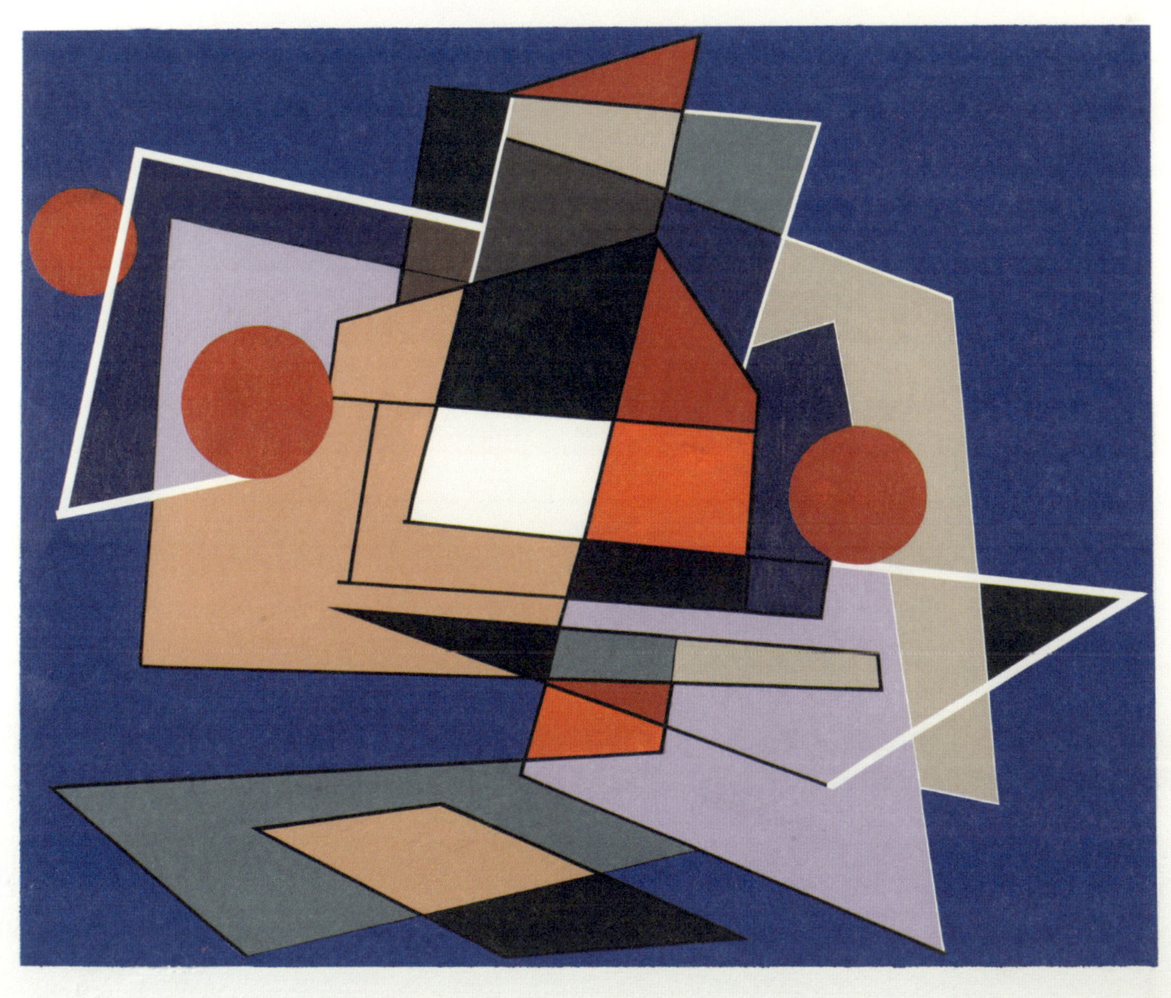

Hungarian Italian Abstraction (vertigo blue temporal event), 2009
acrylic paint and vinyl adhesive sticker on plasterboard
painting: 55 x 70 cms
plasterboard: 96 x 101 cms

Studio view of Hungarian Italian Abstraction (vertigo blue temporal event), 2009
acrylic paint and vinyl adhesive sticker on plasterboard
painting: 55 x 70 cms

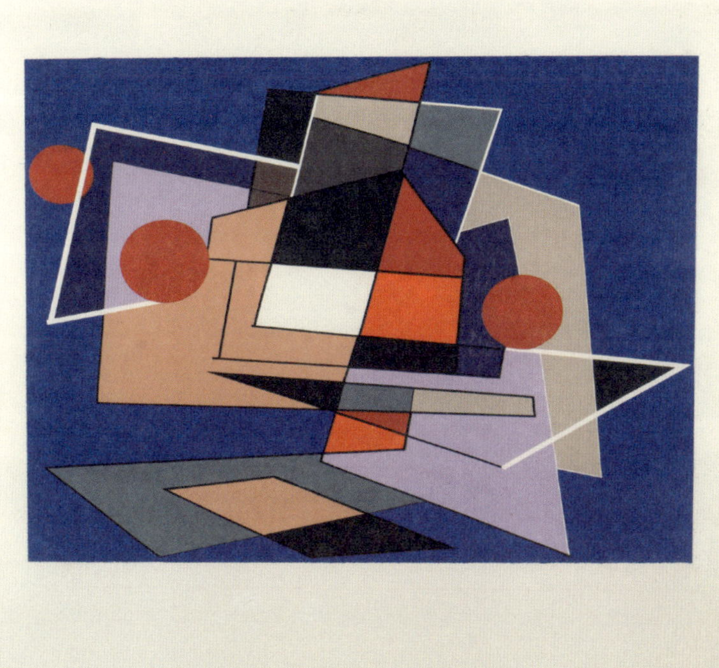

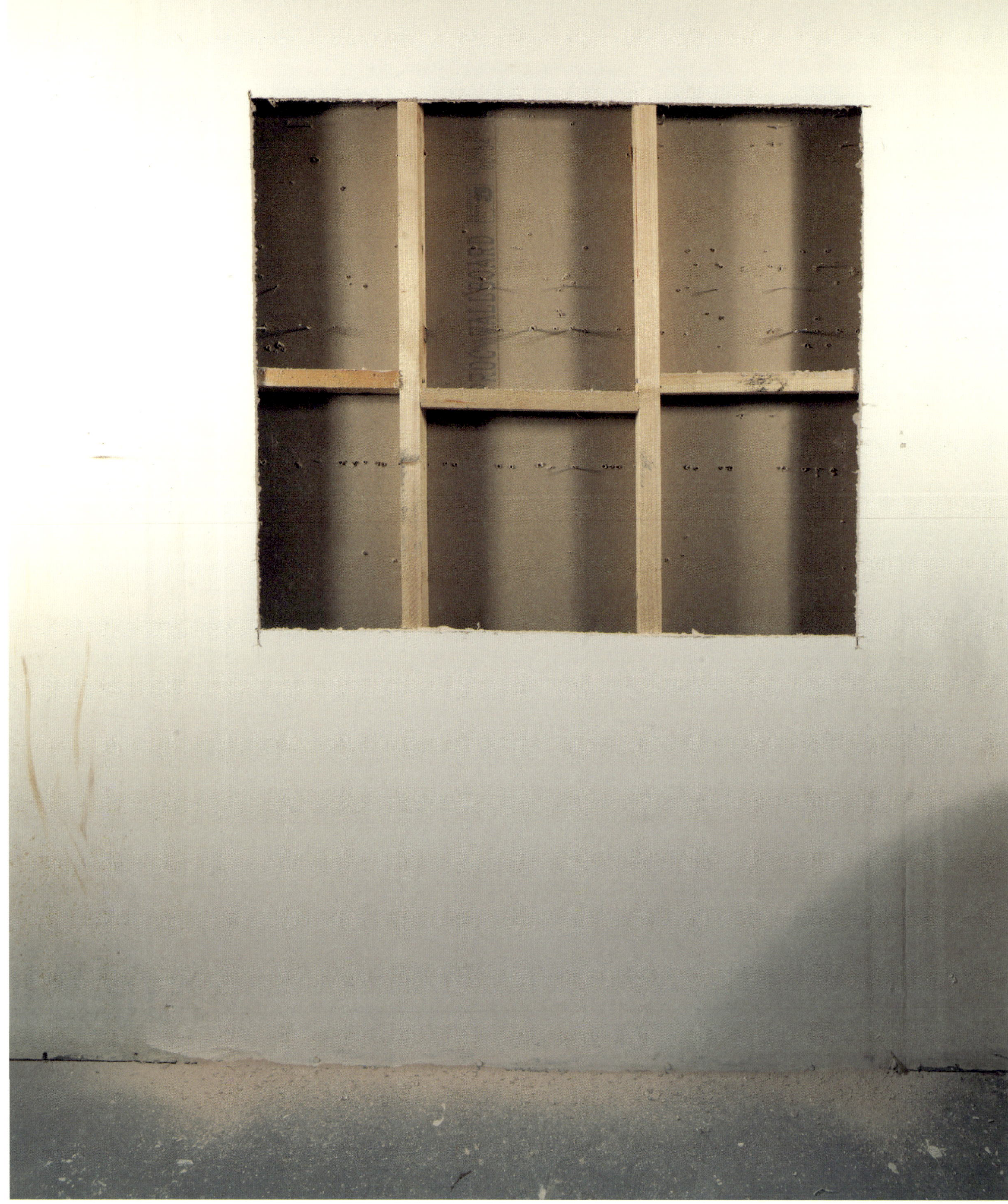

Studio view of Hungarian Italian Abstraction (vertigo blue temporal event), 2009 after removal
plasterboard hole: 96 x 101 cms

Bio Bits, 2006
Installation view composite,
The LAB, Dublin

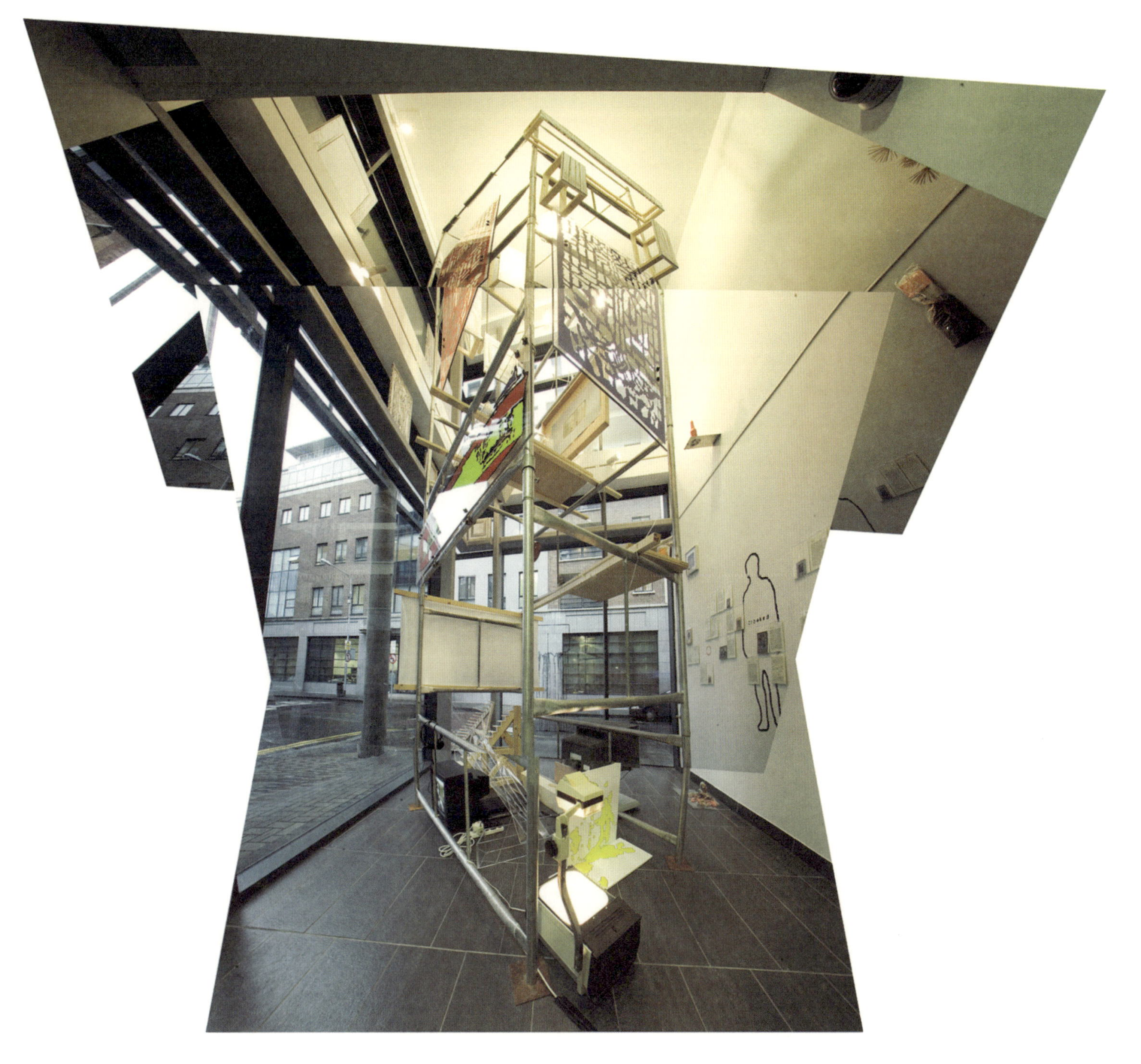

Hill of Shouts, 2004
photographic print on vinyl mesh
200 x 600 cms

# This Is Not How Things Really Seem To You

Seán Kissane

*"I know very well that the Other's culture is worthy of the same respect as my own:*
*nevertheless ... [I despise them passionately]."* [1]
—Slavoj Žižek, The Fragile Absolute

Fifteen Fragile Absolutes was the title of Alan Phelan's recent project at the Irish Museum of Modern Art during his period as artist-in-residence in 2008. The title refers to the work by the Slovenian sociologist, philosopher and cultural critic Slavoj Žižek, *The Fragile Absolute – or, why is the Christian legacy worth fighting for?* Phelan took the italicised words from that text and used them as random word associations towards 15 ideas for works. This assembly of words, while putting aside the content of the book, did manage to convey some of both Žižek and Phelan's mutual interests. Fragile Absolute #3, *World War I in Colour (the void itself)* (2009) is an example:

*it • it • it • more! • did • drink the Nothingness itself • objet petit • opposite •'culturalization' of the market economy itself • place • objet petit a • horror vacui • creating empty, unoccupied place • occupant without a place •correlative • only an element which is thoroughly 'out of place' • can sustain the void of an empty place • rien n'aura eu lieu que le lieu • suicide • imaginary • imagined • Real • passage à l 'acte • resists • cannot • resists • internal •passage à l 'acte • direct • directly • same • passage à l 'acte • passage à l'acte • symbolic • almost-nothing • opposite • this • L'objet du siècle • future anterior • rien n'aura eu lieu que le lieu • takes place • save • its own • à la •'objectively' ugly • 'represents' the function of ugliness • irrelevant •Verweisung • The Last Tycoon • But • behind • desublimation • directly depicting • had to be accomplished • the Void itself • trash itself • within •directly •*

Ferdinand de Saussure argued that in language, meaning emerges only in its use. That is, the meaning of sounds, words or images is only fixed when stabilised in a series with others. This points towards the fact that meaning is constructed only in the context in which elements appear to us .[2] Phelan's Fifteen Fragile Absolutes clearly disrupt the stability of language and meaning aligned by Žižek, but his dismembering of it provides a framework through which we can view his own work. As he reconfigures diverse elements they are lent a new voice – their context providing a means towards interpretation.

The exhibitions at the Irish Museum of Modern Art, Chapter Arts Centre, and Limerick City Gallery of Art form a synopsis and re-presentation of the Fifteen Fragile Absolutes project. The intention is to present one exhibition over three spaces, each exhibition project unique and defined by its context. From this we can extrapolate some of Phelan's strategies of display - works are constantly de-contextualised or re-contextualised through interdependencies which are interrogated by configuration and juxtaposition. Previous examples of this include Enthalpic Everything at the Limerick City Gallery of Art in 2000; and his recent Bio Bits exhibition at The Lab, Dublin in 2006 where, in a type of extreme parataxis, he erected a scaffold tower within the confined space of a window-box-gallery to which he attached various works from the previous ten years combining elements of many different projects in a dynamic new arrangement. While these reconfigurations have been a part of Phelan's work for the best part of a decade, it is interesting to note that it is a feature that he shares with Žižek. 'The practice of Žižek's work: the constant reworking of concepts, examples and even actual passages of prose testifies as much as anything to the repeated attempts to seize the Thing itself. As the Marxist cultural critic Fredric Jameson says ... the true Hegelian moment lies not in some mystical Absolute Knowledge, but in the practice that becomes substantial and worth doing in its own right, as an end in itself.'[3]

The central work commissioned for the formal gardens at IMMA, *Goran's Stealth Yugo* (2009) arose from Phelan's 2006 artists' residency in Belgrade, Serbia. While there his interest in modified car enthusiasts (commonly called Boy Racers) prompted a visit to the Zastava car production plant in Kragujevac, south of Belgrade. At the height of its production in 1989, just under 55,000 people were directly employed by Zastava and about 500,000 jobs were dependent on the company. Two years later in 1991 as war broke out, Yugoslavia splintered into separate states and the Yugo, the Zastava flagship car, "suddenly found itself named for a country that no longer exists; effectively, a car without a country, set to share the destiny of Yugoslavia"[4]. Through the 90s, monthly wages at Zastava dropped as low as $15 per month, and production stopped as many of Zastava's suppliers were located in Croatia. The international embargo on Serbia devastated its industries - as well as eliminating the country's industrial export markets, sanctions caused shortages of raw materials. In 1993, Serbia's industrial output and retail sales fell by 40% and 70% respectively. Approximately 60% of the industrial labour force in Serbia was laid off.[5]

The Kragujevac which Phelan visited in 2006 was a very different place to the thriving industrial hub of the 1980s. By then employment at the factory had fallen to a fifth of previous levels causing crippling unemployment throughout the area and the poverty and social problems associated with it. Talks with international car manufacturers such as FIAT were ongoing in the hope of securing foreign investment to revitalise the company. Unfortunately these talks were proving inconclusive with the result that that factory was operating in a strange kind of suspended animation. What Heiner Müller described as, 'the waiting room mentality' in Communist Eastern Europe:

There would be an announcement: The train will arrive at 18.15 and depart at 18.20 – and it never did arrive at 18.15. Then came the second announcement: The train will arrive at 20.10. And so on. You went on sitting there in the waiting room waiting, thinking, It's bound to come at 20.15. That was the situation. Basically a state of Messianic anticipation. There are constant announcements of the Messiah's impending arrival, and you know perfectly well that he won't be coming. And yet somehow, it's good to hear him announced all over again. [6]

Among the many specialists, engineers, mechanics and technicians still based at Zastava in 2006 was the car designer, Goran Krstić. He, among other projects, had been designing fantasy concept cars of the type beloved of modified car enthusiasts or Boy Racers. Phelan immediately saw the match with his practice and asked Krstić to design a CAD version of the Yugo, in the distinctive style of previous sculptures such as *Bennett Island* (2006), including 'blending in' pine twigs. The resulting drawing, a large format blueprint, was entitled *Goran's Stealth Yugo* (2006) and exhibited at Galerija SKC in Belgrade in 2006 at the end of his residency.

This work, and the relationship which had been built between the artist, Goran Krstić and Zastava, formed the genesis of a commission from IMMA to construct a sculpture to be erected in the formal gardens at the Royal Hospital Kilmainham alongside the 2009 exhibition. The sculpture, made from highly polished chromed steel, sits 4 meters above the fountain of the formal gardens. Its frame is covered with over 100 'pine twigs' made from extruded rubber of the type used to seal car windows which reference the 'Blending In' of some of Phelan's previous projects. The term 'blending-in' comes from a 'stealth' industry which seeks disguise or camouflage technology, for example disguising a mobile phone mast as a tree.

The context and references implicit in this work are numerous and complex. In a wider sense it forms a curious exercise to compare the foundation myths of Serbia and Ireland. Previous works of Phelan's including, *Eamon Often Spoke in Tongues* (2007), *Michael should have learned to blend-in better* (2006) and *Roger should have stayed in the jungle* (2006), each reference Irish revolutionary leaders. The personal and political histories of Éamon de Valera, Michael Collins and Roger Casement are in many ways, stories of sacrifice, betrayal and ambivalence. The site of the current exhibition at the Royal Hospital Kilmainham touches on these histories – the building itself was at the centre of the apparatus of the British Army, while the neighbouring jail was the site of the execution of the signatories of the proclamation of the Irish Republic. The partition of Ireland along religious divides and the 'Troubles' which resulted, have parallels to the split between the Croatian Roman-Catholics, the Serbian Orthodox Christians, and the Bosnian Muslims. But within that statement is contained the fault-line of time and modern warfare. What separates our recent histories is perhaps the modernist project itself - ostensibly, one of progress and historical improvement, it paradoxically led to means and methods of slaughter on an industrial scale.

James Campbell in his essay 'Interpreting the war' describes this evolution: "In many ways, the unprecedented mass slaughter of the first World War, inaugurates the twentieth century as a disruption of enlightenment. The products and techniques of industrial culture turn on their users: what had been tools for the efficient production of goods become weapons in the efficient production of death. Mass armies of draftees are marched to their mechanised destruction with all the organisation that industrial capitalism has learned from the factory and the abattoir. The machine has produced the machine gun, and the human individual, becomes merely one of the more vulnerable parts of that machine."[7]

Phelan's work *World War I in Colour (the void itself)* relies on 'objective' historical accounts such as those of James Campbell to frame his enquiry into historical events. The photographs presented are stills captured from an eponymous DVD offered free by The Irish Daily Mirror. Although less than a century has passed since the events represented took place, the Hussars with their busby hats, and the elaborately plumed Prussians literally look like something from another age, a sense conveyed through his manipulation of the printing process as by overlaying the images with vague striations, he creates a pseudo-painterly effect redolent of degraded hand-applied emulsion. The text on each still derives from the subtitles already present in the video frame from the narration of Kenneth Brannagh. The words of the protagonists remove them even further from our experience, 'Let's punish the Balkan monkeys, show 'em what the army of a great power is worth'. Of course, hindsight is a great thing and the arrogance of the 'great powers' was to be tested by this war, which initiated the Modern project but spelled the end of the Colonial one.

Ireland was one of the first states to attempt to profit from its colonial master's weakened state through the 1916 Rising. Therein is perhaps another dichotomy between her relative non-participation in two World Wars, and Serbia's 'blame' for the first through the assassination of Archduke Franz-Ferdinand in Sarajevo in 1914. There is a strange circularity or prescience between the events of 1914 and 1989 when 'Serb Unity the Only Survival' was declared by Slobodan Milošević, putting into motion a chain of events that would culminate in NATO's bombing of Serbia in 1999. While NATO's intervention in Kosovo and Serbia are well documented, in the context of Phelan's work it is worth noting that the Zastava factory was one of the 'high-value' targets of the NATO bombers. Zastava was possibly a legitimate target having, through its long history, made arms, rifles, tanks and the other paraphernalia of war. During the NATO bombing, the car factory, truck factory, power plant, machine and tool foundries all suffered to varying degrees. The factory was bombed twice and 140 Zastava employees were injured during the first raid, 30 seriously; while another 36 were injured in the second. Many of the workers formed a human shield around the factory in an attempt to protect their livelihood and in an open letter to NATO declared, "We, the Zastava workers and citizens of Kragujevac, are afraid of the future ahead. Now we wonder whether we have any future at all. Our children are hungry, and their eyes are filled with horror. We have no more answers to their questions."[8] While this bombing was certainly a human tragedy, it is ironic that one of the areas of the factory most badly damaged was its paint shop – its most modern wing fully equipped with robots. Ironically the NATO 'surgical' bombers missed the arms factory entirely! A factory spokesman at the time stated, "If we include all the other factories throughout Serbia that are part of the Zastava Group, it is estimated that the living conditions of about 200,000 people are in jeopardy and many a Western observer suggests that Zastava's ability to manufacture cars is entirely eliminated."[9] Collateral damage in Kragujevac included the destruction of the power plant which leaked toxic materials into the water supply - NATO immediately intervened to put right this damage.[10]

Žižek describes NATO's strategy as "perverse in the precise Freudian sense of the term: it was itself (co-)responsible for the calamity against which it offered itself as a remedy (like the mad governess ... who sets the family house on fire in order to be able to prove her devotion... by bravely saving the children from the raging flames)." He goes on to say, "The crucial point is thus to recognize clearly in this ideology of global victimisation, in this identification of the (human) subject itself as 'something that can be hurt', the mode of ideology that fits today's global capitalism. This ideology of victimisation is the very mode in which – most of the time invisible to the public eye, and for that reason all the more ineluctable – the Real of Capital exerts its rule."[11]

Phelan's project incorporates some of these notions of Capital through the economic and social relationships implicit in its exchange. While the collaboration with Krstić is informed by a

Relational standpoint, it is useful to differentiate Phelan's practice from the Gillick/Gordon/Parreno paradigm in which inter-relationality is confined to a specific social group. Phelan appropriates the methods of exchange posited by Relational Aesthetics but fractures those exchanges through the placing of economic (socio-political) subalterns within them. In doing so, Phelan implicates capital exchange within the art-market, particularly how it relates to global capital. The project also reverses, what was in 2006, the prevailing flow of labour between Ireland and Eastern Europe. A second work included in the exhibition *The Other Hand of Victory (Heibei version) (ontological madness)* (2009) more directly quotes exchanges of global capital. Based on Phelan's chance encounter with the 'hand of victory' at the Musée du Louvre – it is the right-hand of the *Winged Victory of Samothrace* (c. 220-190 BCE). The Winged Victory, one of the most iconic works of Hellenistic art, has been extensively quoted throughout art-history and popular culture.
A direct connection to *Goran's Stealth Yugo* might be Marinetti's 'Futurist Manifesto' of 1909 in which he states: "A race-automobile adorned with great pipes like serpents with exploding breath ... which seems to rush over exploding powder is more beautiful than the Victory of Samothrace."[12] This speed, so beloved by the Futurists, is referenced in the work *Blurred Chicken (you can because you must!)* (2009), the implication being that the chicken is 'blurred' because it has been seen from the window of a passing vehicle like a Futurist work of art. Phelan further adopts some of Marinetti's iconoclasm in his rendering of the 'other' hand of Victory. He purchased a wooden modelling hand from German mega-retailer, Lidl, and reconfigured an approximation of the Louvre hand. This model was then sent to Hebei in China where local craftsmen scaled it up in white marble.

Parallels between *Goran's Stealth Yugo* and *The Other Hand of Victory* can be drawn to the conceptual works made by the Italian artist Alighiero Boetti the late 1960s. Boetti hired groups of Afghan women in Kabul to make his tapestries, with the intention of removing as much decision making as possible from the artist. A result of these collaborations was an exposure of the constructs around the making of an artwork, the market and cycles of capital within that system. The women who crafted these works were disenfranchised individuals, unable to read the text which they were embroidering, and paid almost nothing for their work. Boetti demonstrated that once an object entered the art market, it was subject to systems of capital outside the space of its conception. The artist had little control over the fate of his object once he relinquished it to the forces of capital. It also exposed the osmotic transfer of value through economic systems along political lines of alignment from Non-Aligned (Third World) and Socialist states (Second World); through to consumerist Western economies.

Phelan's collaborations may be coloured by Boetti's Arte Povera, but his work seems to take a more cynical position in respect to global transfers of capital, a position possibly informed by US foreign policy, post 9/11. Naomi Klein in her recent book The Shock Doctrine (2007), coined the term 'Disaster Capitalism' for a new, pervasive and pernicious type of profiteering. Klein contends that 9/11 offered US multi-national corporations an opportunity to privatise the systems around the 'War on Terror' ensuring that war is now an entirely 'for-profit' venture. She cites a number of statistics to illustrate her point. In 2003 the US Government handed out 3,512 contracts to companies to perform security functions. By August 2005, the Department of Homeland Security had issued 115,000 such contracts transforming the "homeland security" industry into a $200 billion industry.[13]

Returning to Žižek, perhaps this is what he describes as Id-Evil, a violence grounded in no utilitarian or ideological cause. Phelan's 'Fragile Absolute #1', *Phantom Blanket (there is no Christ outside of Saint Paul)* (2008) obliquely references Id-Evil. The Phantom Blanket is an orange wool blanket into which Phelan cut out the outline of the face of Darth Maul, the apprentice to Darth Vader from George Lucas's Star Wars movies. Aside from its resemblance to the Shroud of Turin, this work could appear glib or humorous, referencing as it does, popular culture in a direct way and through the somewhat idiosyncratic medium of a found orange blanket.[14] However, Phelan's juxtaposition of the Phantom Blanket with chapter 1 of the Fragile Absolute, Giving up the Balkan Ghost, demands further enquiry. In this chapter, Žižek describes the Balkans as 'this vortex of (self-) destructive passions, the exact opposite, almost a kind of photographic negative, of the tolerant co-existence of ethnic communities, a kind of multiculturalist dream turned into a nightmare.'[15] He describes a type of 'reflexive racism' and takes an example from popular culture The Phantom Menace (1999), the first prequel to the Star Wars trilogy.[16]

"The usual leftist critical point that the multitude of exotic alien (extra-human) species in Star Wars represents, in code, inter-human ethnic differences, reducing them to the level of common racist stereotypes (the evil merchants of the greedy Trade Federation are a clear caricature of ant-like Chinese merchants), somehow misses the point: these references to ethnic clichés are not a cipher to be penetrated through an arduous theoretical analysis; they are directly alluded to, their identification is, as it were, part of the game...All the talk about foreigners stealing work from us, or about the threat they represent to our Western values, should not deceive us: on closer examination it soon becomes clear that this talk provides a rather superficial secondary rationalisation. The answer we ultimately receive from a skinhead is that it makes him feel good to beat up foreigners; that their presence disturbs him ..."[17]

Strangely Phelan does not portray the chief-villain, rather than Darth Vader he gives us Darth Maul, his lowly apprentice. This is a subversive, almost proto-political act, (think of *Michael should have learned to blend-in better*). Phelan manages to preserve the quality of Darth Vader's 'Beautiful Soul' by giving us instead, the dark, profoundly ambiguous figure of Darth Maul who does the 'dirty jobs' for his master. Žižek elaborates on this ambiguity in the context of the Nazi hierarchy: "Hitler knew very well how to play this double game apropos of the Holocaust, using Himmler ... In his speech to the SS leaders ... Himmler spoke quite openly about the mass killings of the Jews as 'a glorious page in our history, and one that has never been written and never can be written', explicitly including the killing of women and children."[18]

Repeatedly what we see in Phelan's work is a type of distancing himself from his subject. Very often there is a built-in dis-recognition inherent in the work as in the case of *Trees Don't Talk* (2006) which obliquely references Milošević's regime; *Roger should have stayed in the jungle*, the title of which implies that there could have been an easier option than losing one's reputation and life; and most explicitly, each of those works including *Goran's Stealth Yugo*, which through the use of pine twigs, 'blend-in' attempting to avoid identification or even detection. In a fictive 'historical' time line, the works in this exhibition begin in 1914 with the first World War, and end with the chilling Srebrenica Massacre of 1995.[19] In psychoanalytic terms, the artist has no choice but to obfuscate as, "images of utter catastrophe, far from giving us access to the Real, can function as a protective shield against the Real."[20] Žižek posits that this dis-representation is the very difference between modernism and post-modernism. Since classical times, playwrights had put the terrifying event outside of the scene, and only placed its effects and reflections on stage. The post-modern way (via Proust and Hitchcock) is not to even show the reflections of the scene, but rather to show the perfectly ordinariness of evil. "One shows an object or an activity which is presented as an everyday, even common thing, but suddenly through the reactions of this object's milieu being reflected back on the object itself, we realise that one is confronting a terrifying object, the source of an inexplicable terror ... What we perceived only a moment ago as being a totally common thing is revealed as Evil incarnate."[21]

Phelan's Fragile Absolute #11, *Bad Glue* (2006), originally took the form of a page from the Belgrade newspaper 'Novosti' (News) with the memoriam page from 16 March 2006. It showed notices taken by mourning supporters of Milošević, who died while in custody in The Hague during his trial for war crimes. The notices include text such as "Your ideas, your genius mind, energy in fighting for the truth, justice and comfort for your people, have been and will always be a source of utter inspiration for us". In an ever-evolving state of parataxis, Fragile Absolute #11 has now morphed into a portrait-head of the Canadian novelist Douglas Coupland in the work *Douglas (lacked the dimension of radical Evil)* (2009). Like many of Phelan's recent sculptures including *Bent (striking at himself)* (2009) and *Woman who stole from farmer (it is only truth that matters)* (2009), the work is constructed from papier-mâché. The paper used is derived from various periodicals; in the case of Bent the source is a column by the fictional writer Ross O'Carroll-Kelly from The Irish Times referencing the recent global financial crisis, while Douglas is composed of pages from

Coupland's 2006 novel jPod where a sinister yet minor character called Douglas Coupland appears, oddly and overtly self-reflexively affecting the main characters of the narrative. In these works we can see Phelan humorously undermining the content of his own work by making somewhat inappropriate or even tasteless relations between his subjects. Coupland is probably best-known for his 1991 novel Generation X, which coined terms such as 'McJob' to describe the malaise of the post Cold-War generation. Milošević is probably best-known for trying to wipe out a generation of Bosnians...

In order to work towards a conclusion, it seems apposite to return to Žižek, but this approach is problematic as, like Phelan, his very practice refuses easy categorisation or completion:

> 'We may thus observe the following paradox in Žižek ... throughout his work as a whole, one can find him reversing his position many times. He writes ... prolifically and seemingly with little concern for consistency. It is as though the activity of writing itself is Žižek's chief motivation, the reason why he writes at all. This is reflected in the very form of his texts, where there is inevitably an unnecessary final chapter, consisting of faits divers or 'related matters' added on, after the main theoretical work of the book has been completed. In fact, strangely enough, what Žižek actually wants us to see is this very nothingness, this 'nothing-to-say' or 'empty speech' that underlies his texts. Let us call it his theoretical drive, or in more technical language a kind of enunciation without enunciated.'[22]

In effect, it could be that Phelan has played with us by offering a seemingly infallible key to interpretation. It would be wise to consider Virgil's words *timeo Danaos et dona ferentis*[23] for he has presented us with little more than a Trojan Horse. He describes the structures which he created from The Fragile Absolute as a 'fictive boundary ... a self-imposed limit which conversely frees up the flow of creativity.' Of the italicised words from Žižek, he compares them to 'meta tags in HTML head section coding' - keywords hidden in the code that provide the instructions for the display of a web page. Phelan makes parallels to this system to the provision of information around an artwork, he adds 'Google, as far back as 2002, stated that meta tags could not be trusted as the information was being manipulated by coders. By repeating the same meta keyword several times or using certain combinations of words, many sites believed they could increase their ranking (keyword stuffing and spamdexing). It is more likely that a search engine will ignore the meta keyword element completely.'[24] This splintering of experience or erasure of meaning in some ways can be explained by the Lacanian concept of 'the Real' and Žižek's 'empty place'. "The 'empty place' precedes and makes possible the object that fills it: objects are, for sure, out of place – but in order for them to be out of place, the (empty) place must already be there, and this place is rendered by 'minimalist' art, starting with Kasimir Malevich."[25] The implication here is that the absence of 'meaning' or 'interpretation' is an absolute prerequisite for both. In fact Žižek suggests that we, the post-modern audience, should have assumed a void, 'one is tempted to propose one of the possible definitions of 'realism': a naïve belief that, behind the curtain of representations, there actually exists some full, substantial reality. 'Post-realism' begins when a doubt emerges as to the existence of this reality, that is, when the foreboding arises that the very gesture of concealment creates what it pretends to conceal.'[26]

> *'What, hear I the light?'*
> —Richard Wagner, Tristan und Isolde

> *'He lies like an eye-witness!'*
> —Stalinist Soviet proverb[27]

— Notes —

1 Slavoj Žižek, The Fragile Absolute – or why is the Christian legacy worth fighting for? (London: Verso, 2000), p. 6.
2 Ferdinand de Saussure, Course in general linguistics, trans R. Harris. (Open Court Publishing, 1986), p. 118.
3 Slavoj Žižek, Interrogating the Real. R. Butler and S. Stephens (eds). (London, Continuum, 2005) p. 6.
4 Zastava Official website: http://www.zastavanacionale.com/Default.aspx?lng=en-us&mode=heritage&id=2007
5 Ibid.
6 Heiner Müller quoted in: Slavoj Žižek, The Fragile Absolute, pp 41,42.
7 James Campbell, Interpreting the war. The Cambridge companion to the literature of the First World War. Ed. Vincent B. Sherry. (Cambridge, Cambridge University Press, 2005) p. 261.
8 Zastava Official website.
9 Ibid.
10 Sriram Gopal and Nicole Deller. Precision Bombing, Widespread Harm Two Case Studies of the Bombings of Industrial Facilities at Pancevo and Kragujevac During Operation Allied Force, Yugoslavia 1999. Institute for Energy and Environmental Research, 2002.
11 Slavoj Žižek, The Fragile Absolute, pp 59,60
12 Nick Mansfield (ed), Subjectivity: Theories of the Self from Freud to Haraway. (New York, NYU Press, 2000). P. 150.
13 Naomi Klein, The Shock Doctrine.(New York, Penguin, 2007). p 12.
14 Coincidentally, this blanket was removed from a bag on its way to a charity shop – disrupting both the flow of capital and charity, its supposed opposite (symbiotic co-dependent).
15 Slavoj Žižek, The Fragile Absolute, p 3
16 Ibid.
Žižek returns to the subject of Darth Vader in chapter 11. "The film endeavours to answer the question to the 'origin of Evil', how did Anakin Skywalker, this sweet boy, turn into the monstrous instrument of cosmic evil? Two hints are crucial here: first the 'Christological' features of the young Anakin, (his mother hints that she became pregnant with him in an immaculate conception; the race he wins clearly echoes the famous chariot race in Ben Hur, this 'tale of Christ'); second, the fact that he is identified as the one who has the potential to 'restore the balance of the Force'.
17 Slavoj Žižek, The Fragile Absolute, p 7
18 Slavoj Žižek, Interrogating the Real, Why is Wagner worth saving? p.293. "I did not regard myself as justified in exterminating the men – that is to say, to kill them or to have them killed – and to allow the avengers in the shape of children to grow up for our sons and grandchildren. The difficult decision had to be taken to have this people disappear from the earth."
19 Both events precipitated by Serbian aggression.
20 Slavoj Žižek, The Fragile Absolute, p. 78.
21 Slavoj Žižek, Interrogating the Real, pp. 133, 134.
22 Ibid., p 2.
23 "Beware of Greeks bearing gifts" Virgil, The Aeneid, Book II
24 Pers. con. March 2009
25 Slavoj Žižek, Interrogating the Real, p. 362.
26 Ibid., p. 150.
27 Ibid., p. 294.

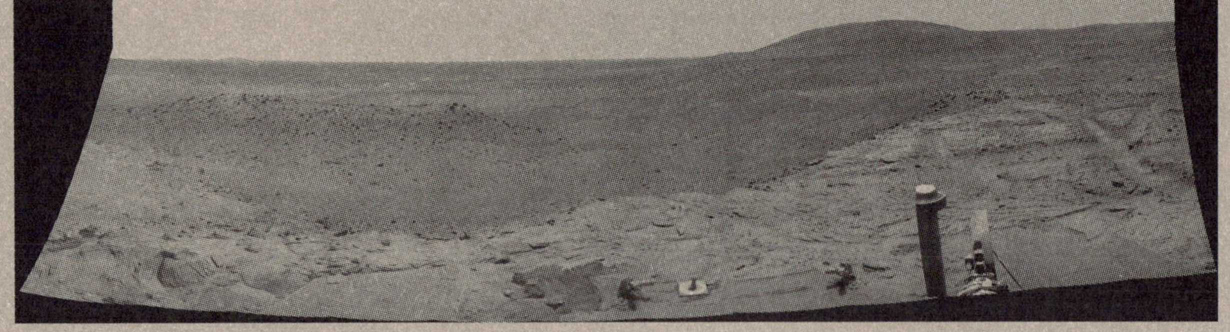

Source image for Mars Piece, 2008

p.175

Men are from Mars, Women are from Venus
coitus a tergo externally imposed, contingent and traumatic
semblable qua hystericizes
jouissance anti-narrativist
Rights to violate the Ten Commandments lie
kill directly not beyond
semblant inhuman Dead Man
Walking qua and Yes!
defences qua generated
before my countenance

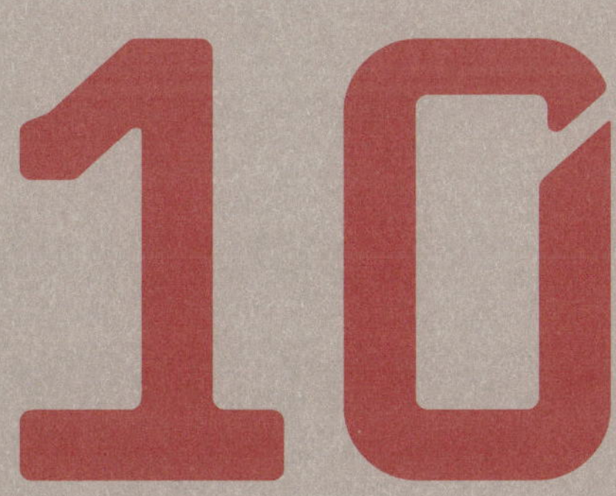

p.176

Mars Piece, 2008
ink-jet print
136 x 1900 cms

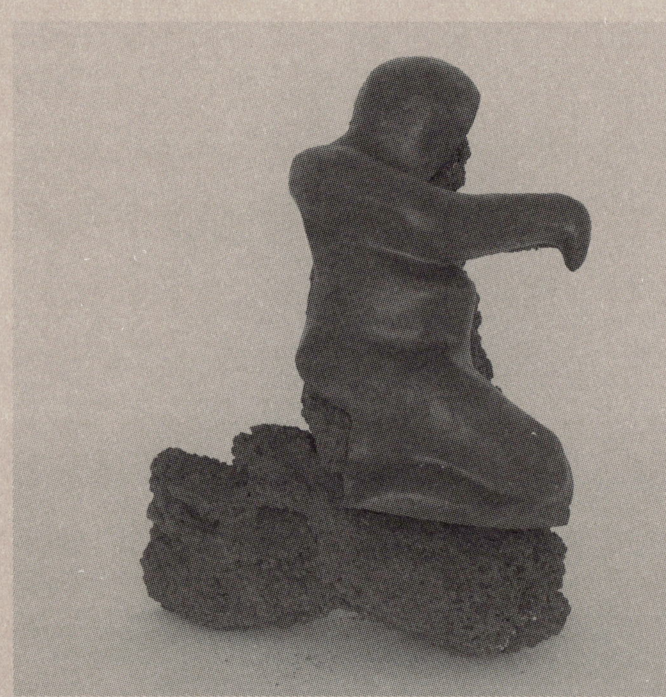

Lady from Mars (coitus a tergo), 2009
spaghetti rock, fibreglass, EVA glue, spray paint
74 x 63 x 45 cms

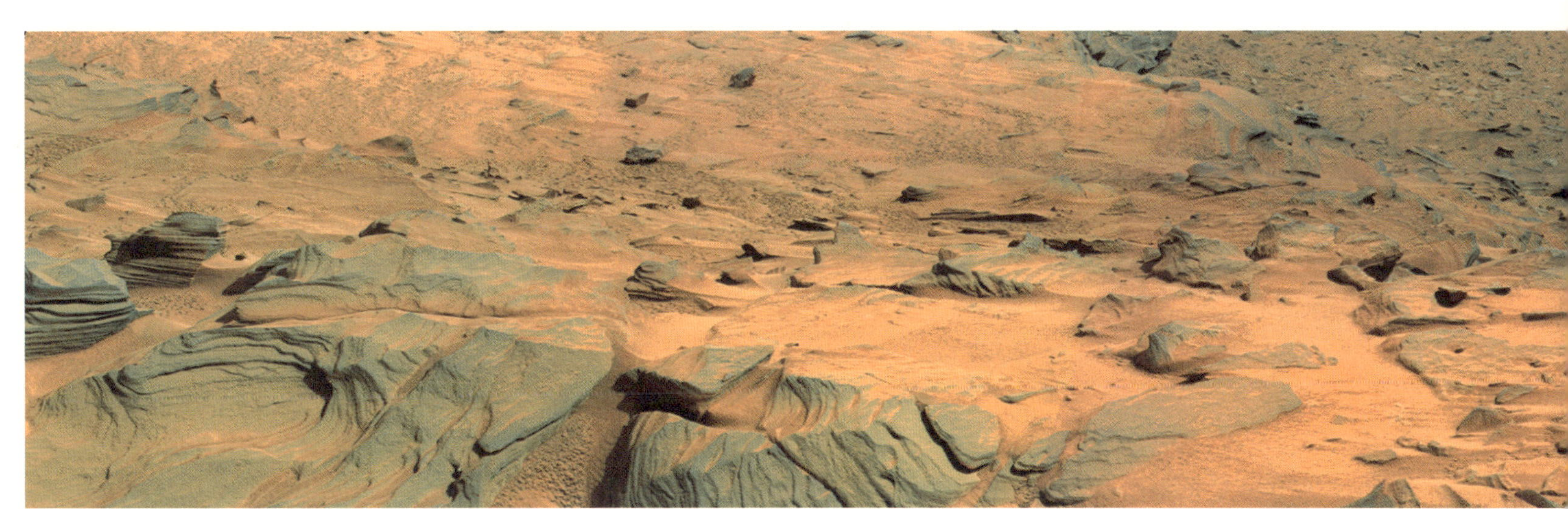

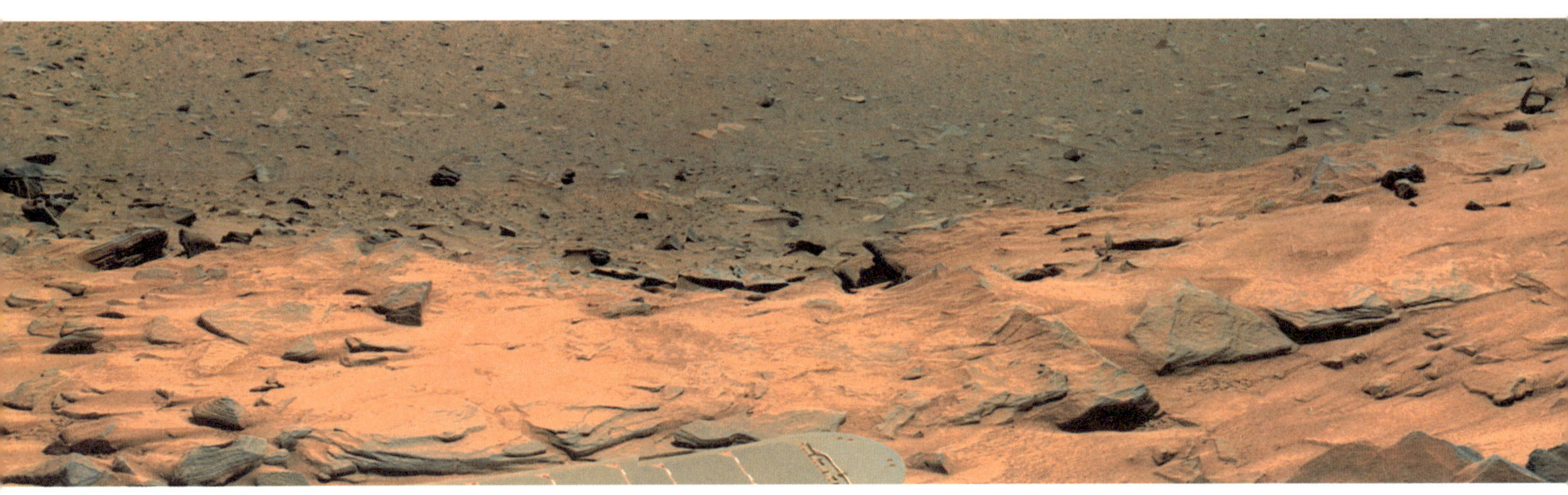

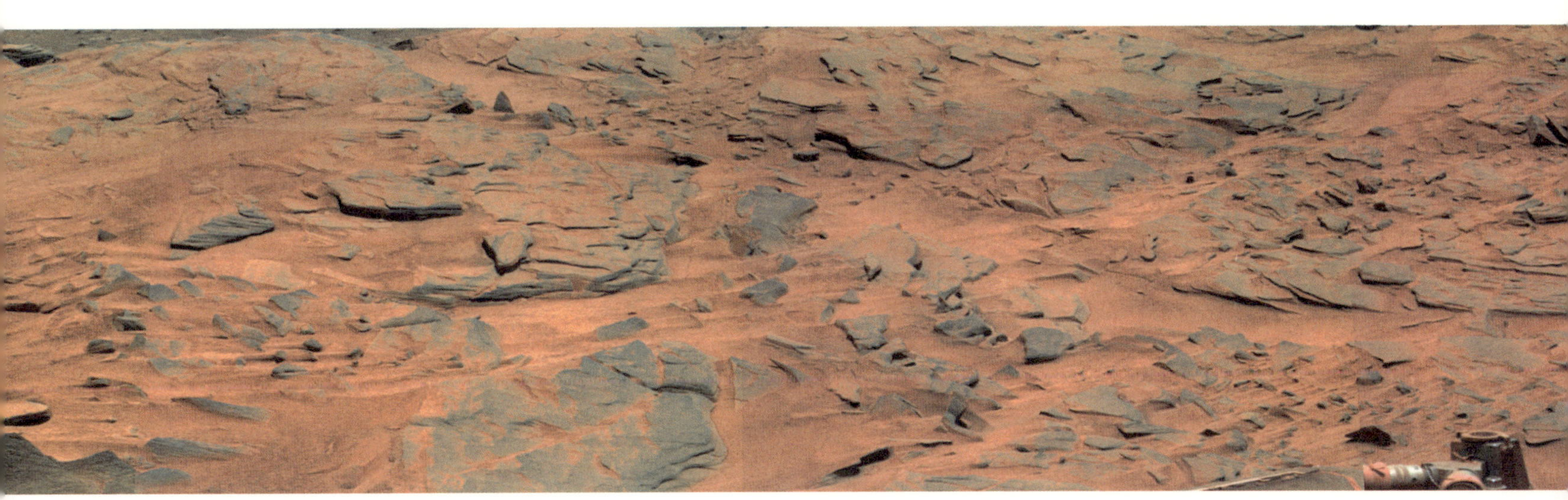

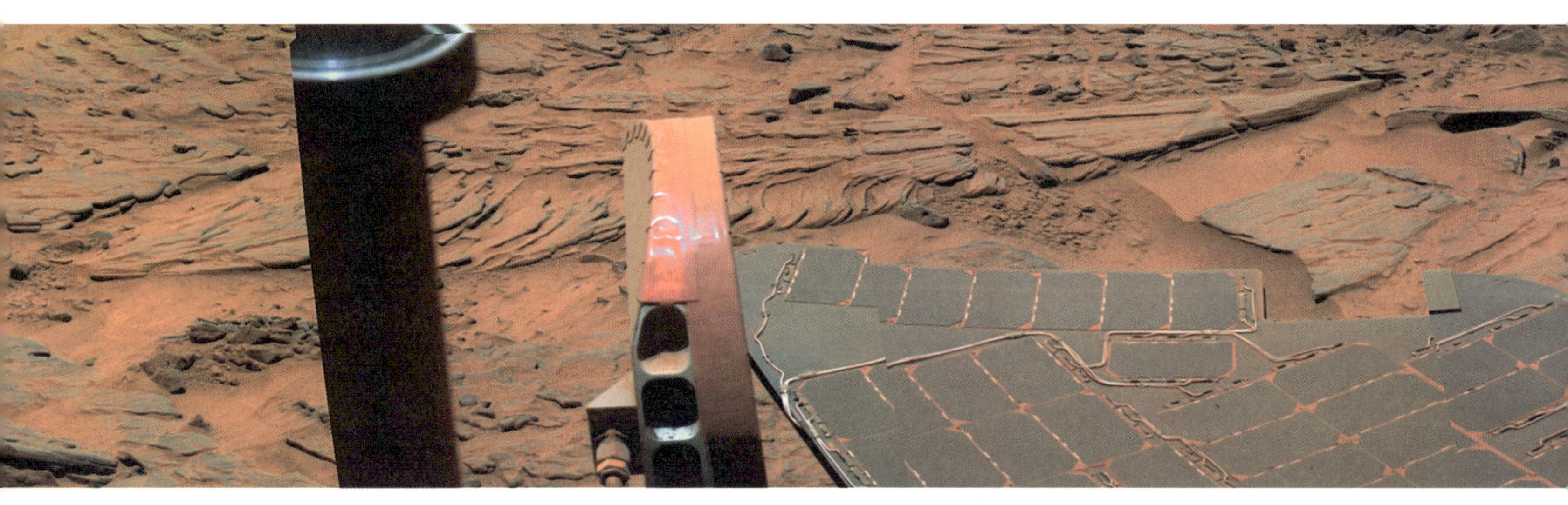

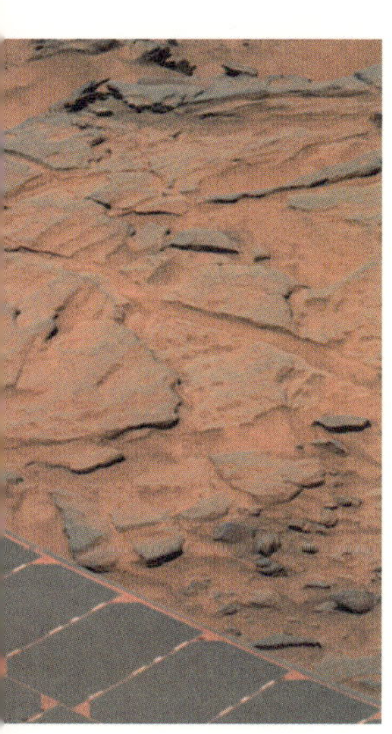

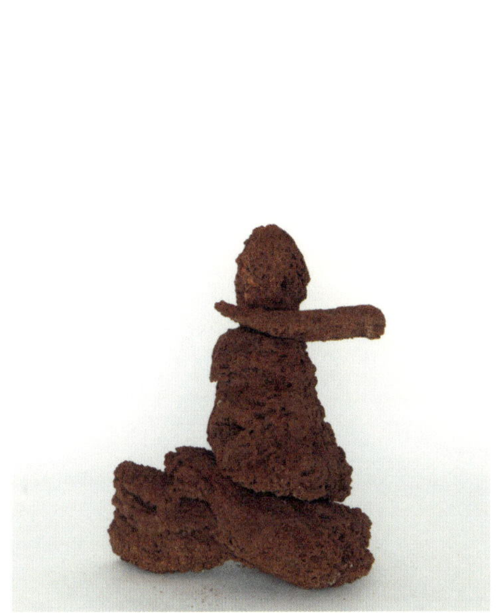
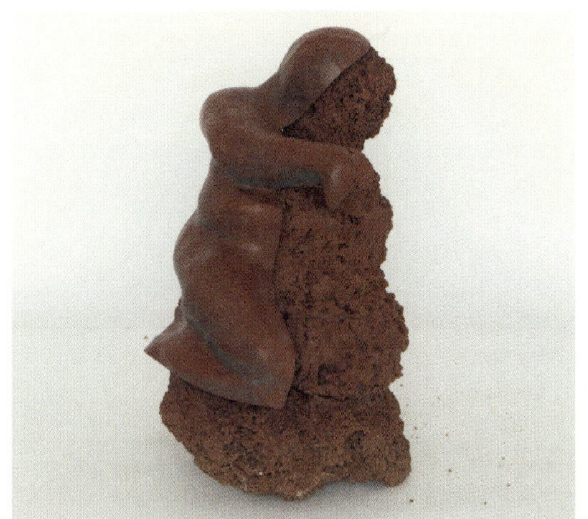
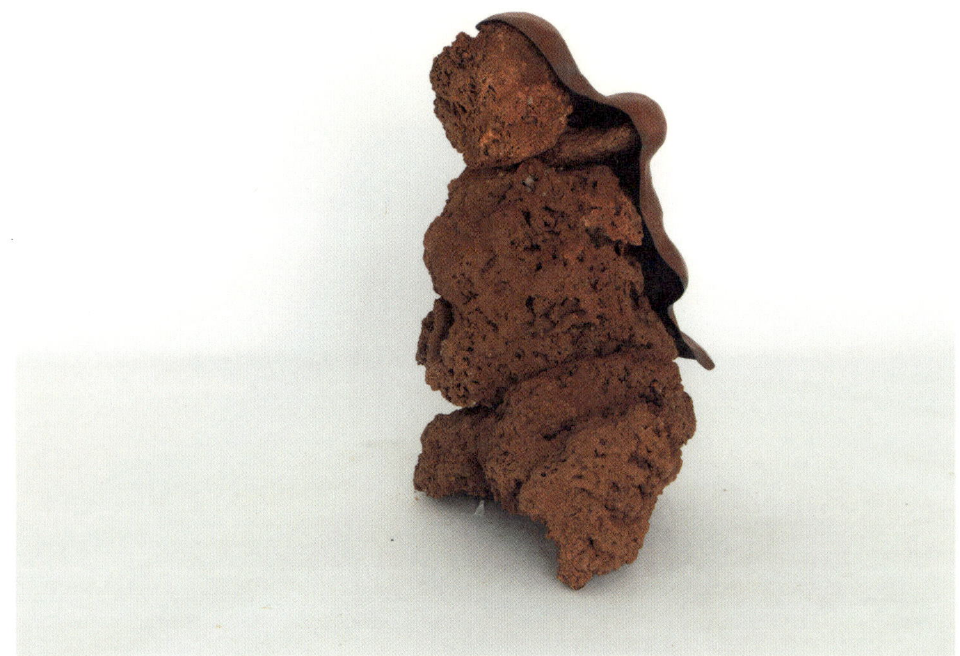

Lady from Mars (coitus a tergo), 2009
spaghetti rock, fibreglass, EVA glue, spray paint
74 x 63 x 45 cms

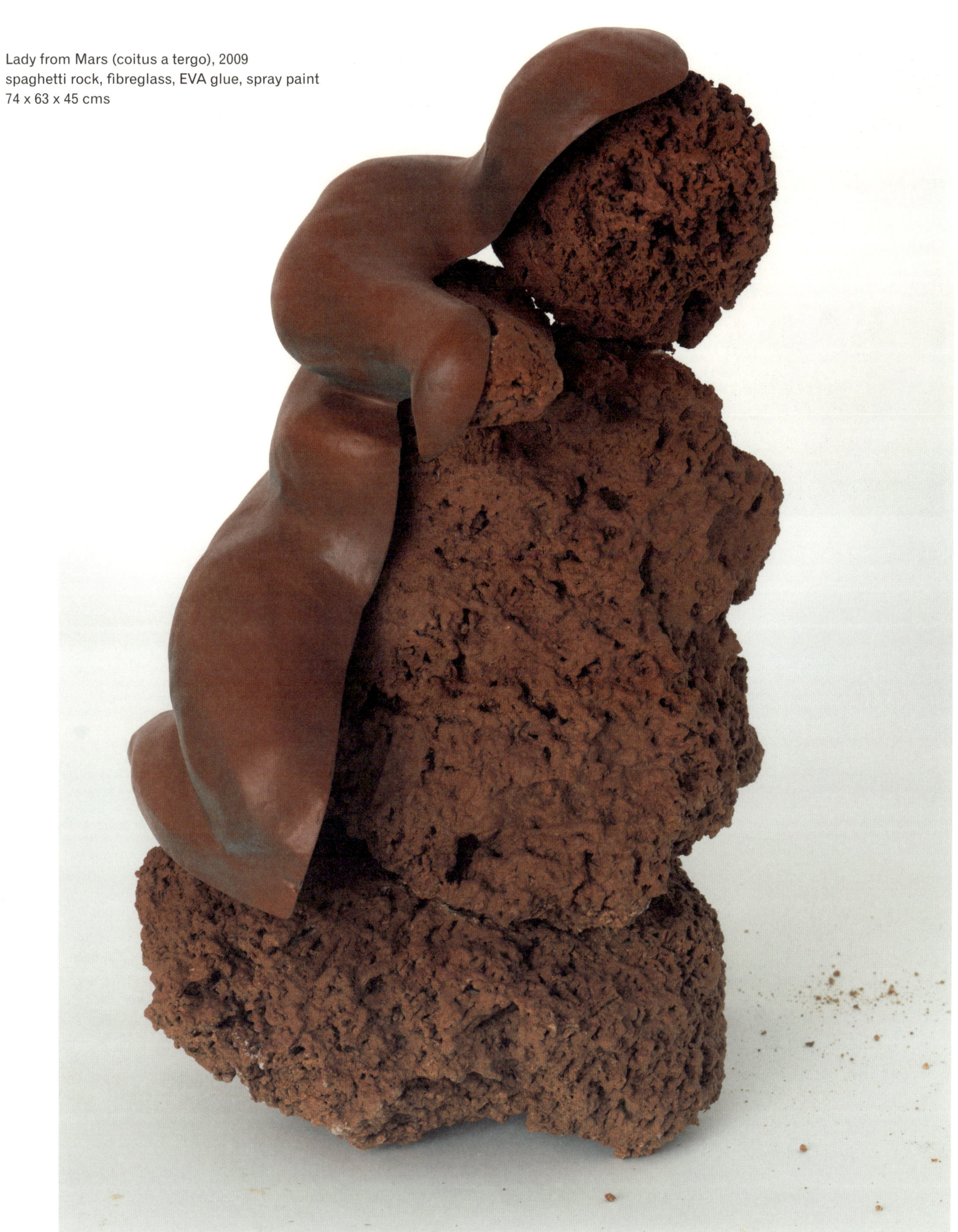

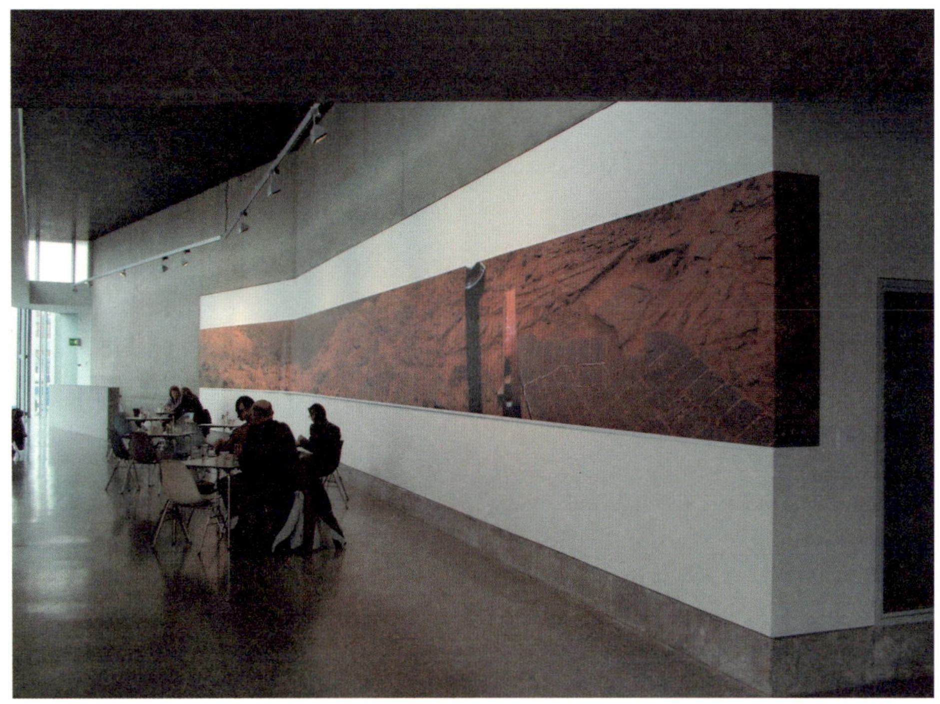

Mars Piece, 2008
ink-jet print
136 x 1900 cms
installed at Solstice Arts Centre,
Navan

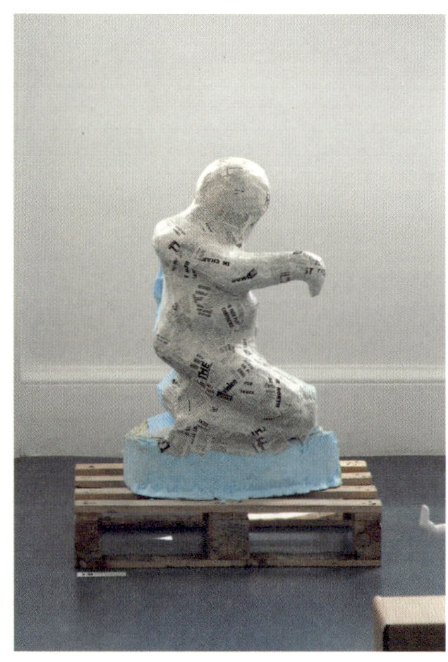

p.185

Lady from Mars, 2008
high density insulation foam, hole filling foam, clay, archival paper, toner, EVA glue, wood pallet
85 x 55 x 40 cms

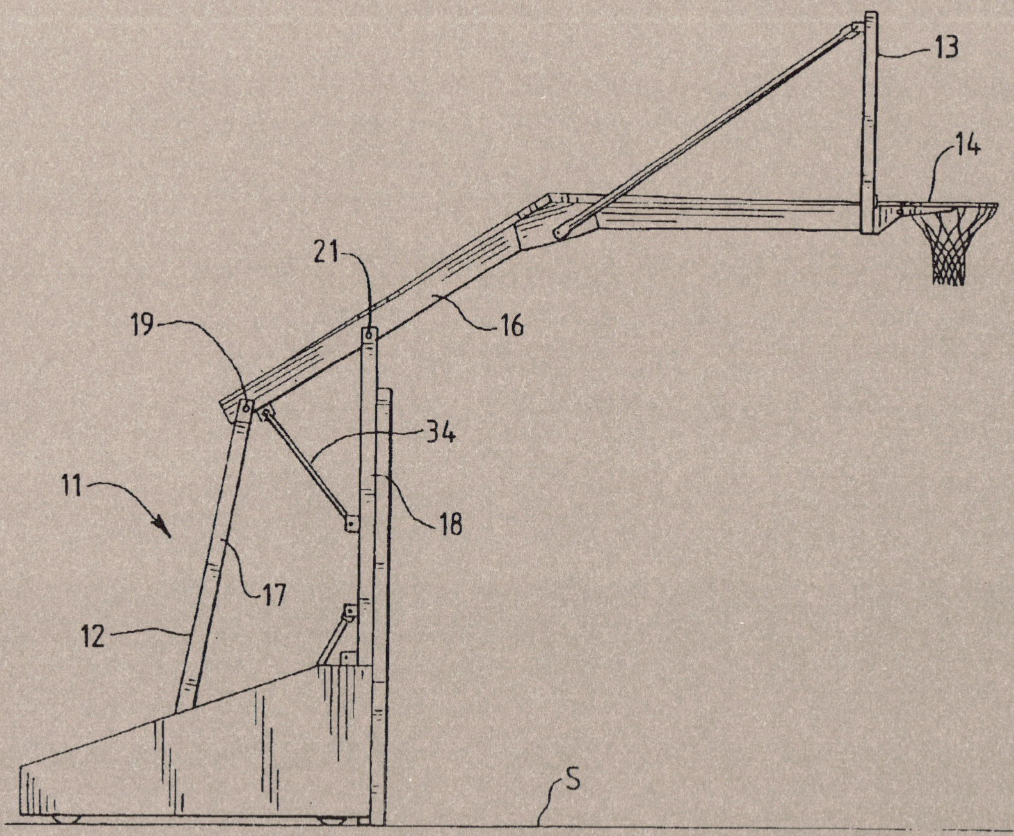
13
14
21
16
19
34
11
18
17
12
S

agape Inquiries into Truth and Interpretation
fake cosa nostra ignorance
break Seminar XX: Encore directly coincide
exceptions no only
Seminar XX jouissance
jouissance 'sinthome' Vertigo
sinthome sinthome charity
Seminar XX qua a contrario
Parsifal backwards not
rupture Parsifal
global universal immediate
directly irrelevant agape
maya separation throws the
balanced circuit of the universe off the rails Star Wars I:
The Phantom Menace how did Darth Vader become Darth
Vader Ben Hur Star Wars
correct it lacked the dimension of radical Evil
in favour of the Good? did
Weltalter Ent-Scheidung

11

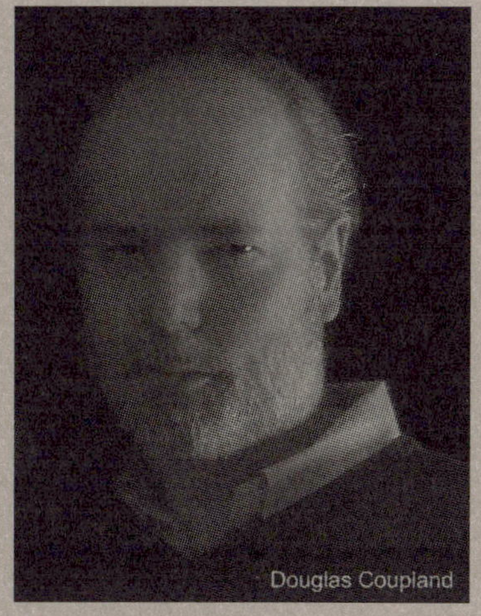

**p.188**

Bad Glue, 2006
newsprint, PVA, card
41.5 x 30 cms

Уснуо је у Господу

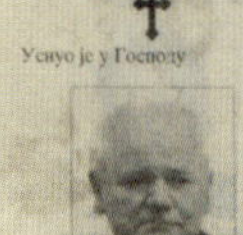

Живот људски је трен, он је трава пролетња! Живот је сјен и сан. Ми смо само путници у овој долини плача, у овом привременом живљу. У осами хашког сужањства- сам, без икога свога, без ријечи утјехе и потпоре, прођи слике свог живота од рођења, припремајући се да му крај буде хришћански, без бола, миран и непостидан и да добар одговор да на страшном суду Христовом! Вјечнаја памјат помјани, Господе, слугу свога Слободана. Господа просимо да ти састави твоју намучену душу у рајским обитељима, гдје душе праведника обитавају!

**Александар В. Јовићевић, Подгорица**

---

"Нек се овај вијек гордљи, над свијема вјековима, он ће ера бити страшна, људскијема кољенима, у њ се девет близанаца у један мах изњихаше из колевке Белоније и на земљи показаше: Наполеон, Карло, Блихер, кнез Велингтон и Суворов ..." Бесмртноме

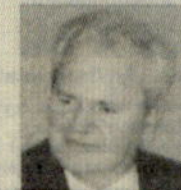

**Слободану Милошевићу**

**Драгољуб Буровић, Сретња, Петар Камберовић, Живко Цвијовић, Слободан Стојадиновић и Душица Бојовић**

---

Највећем хероју за слободу и правду

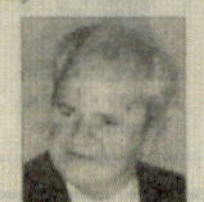

**Слободану Милошевићу**

Почивај у миру, Див јуначе, Српски мучениче, људска величино. Имао си се рашта и родити.

**Стеван Баљњар, Владо Царичић, Момир Недељковић и Боро Вуксановић**

---

Председниче, у историји која долази, живећете и остаћете легенда

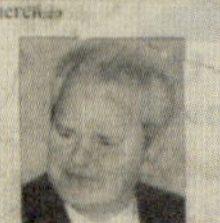

**Слободан Милошевић**

Пред очима целог света остали сте победник, у очима свога народа и своје земље, јер ништа вам нису могли учинити ни неоснованим и мрачним оптужбама.

**Сава Веселиновић, Београд**

---

Наш председник

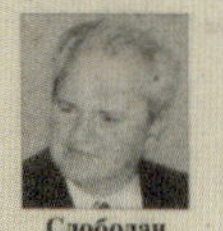

**Слободан Милошевић**

Борио си се за мир, почивај у миру.

Твоји: **Веља, Деса, Биса, Пера, Анка, Вујица, Жика, Влада и Снежа из Новог Београда**

---

Последњи поздрав

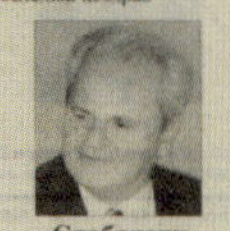

**Слободану Милошевићу**

од породице **Бановић**

---

Последњи поздрав великом борцу, вољеном лику неизмерне харизме за Србију, истину, правду

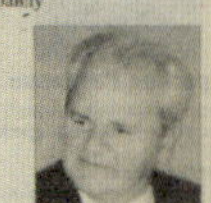

Уз Вас до краја. **"ММГ"**

---

Последњи поздрав драгом председнику, великом српском сину, браниоцу српства и отаџбине, хероју и легенди.

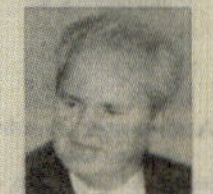

Нека ти је вјечна слава и хвала.

**Перо Спасојевић с породицом из Пљеваља**

---

Последњи поздрав председнику СПС

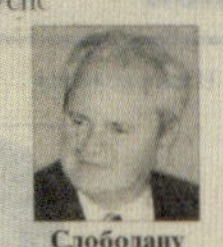

**Слободану Милошевићу**

Поносни смо што си нас достојанствено водио и што смо били Твоји следбеници. Вечна ти слава и хвала.

**Општински одбор СПС Мали Зворник**

---

Последњи поздрав највећем српском сину

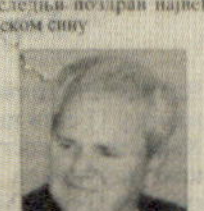

**Слободану Милошевићу**

од четири сестре са Косова: **Анђе, Разуменке, Станиславе и Слободанке**

---

Поштовани

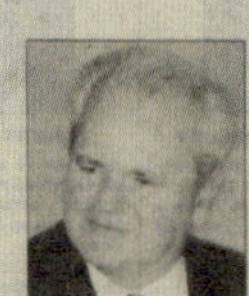

**Председниче**

твоје идеје, твој генијални ум и неисцрпна енергија у борби за истину, правду и интересе свога народа, били су и биће извор нашег надахнућа.

**Социјалисти Лесковца**

---

Друже

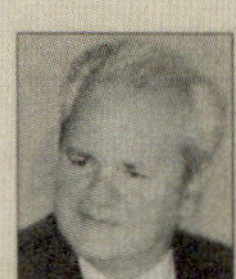

**Председниче**

храбро си се борио за истину, правду и слободу нашег народа, док те нису убили. Твоја борба неће бити узалудна.

**Саша Рудић** и **пријатељи**

---

Највећем борцу за Србију

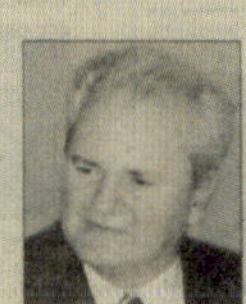

**Слободану Милошевићу**

Храбро си водио Србију у најтежем периоду. Твоја борба за истину и правду остаће наш путоказ у будућност. Поносни смо што си био на челу наше партије, државе и народа.

**Социјалисти Јагодине**

---

Поштовани

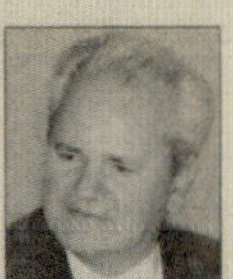

**Председниче**

хвала Вам за све што сте учинили за свој народ, своју државу и СПС.

Адвокат **Драган Богдановић** и **Општински одбор СПС-а** из **Велике Плане**

---

Последњи поздрав

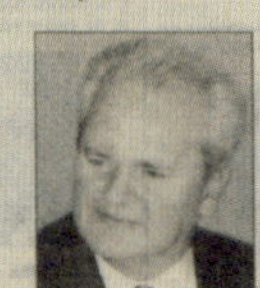

**Слободану Милошевићу**

Припадао си ретким изабраницима у историји Срба који су са толико енергије и храбрости опстајали на бранику своје земље и народа. Твој људски и национални понос и достојанство надахњиваће будуће генерације да скину вео срама у који су наш народ завили они од којих си нас храбро бранио. Слава ти.

**Јагош Бабић, Никола Сарић, Миго Самарџић** и **Петар Јакшић**

---

Борећи се неколико година достојанствено и храбро, истином против неистина, пред Хашким трибуналом, жртвовао си и живот за свој народ

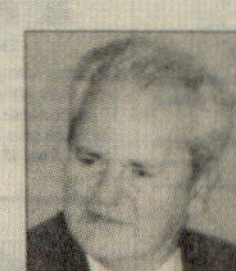

**Слободан Милошевић**

Посљедњи поздрав. Нека ти је вјечна слава и хвала.

**Борислав Микелић, бивши премијер владе РСК**

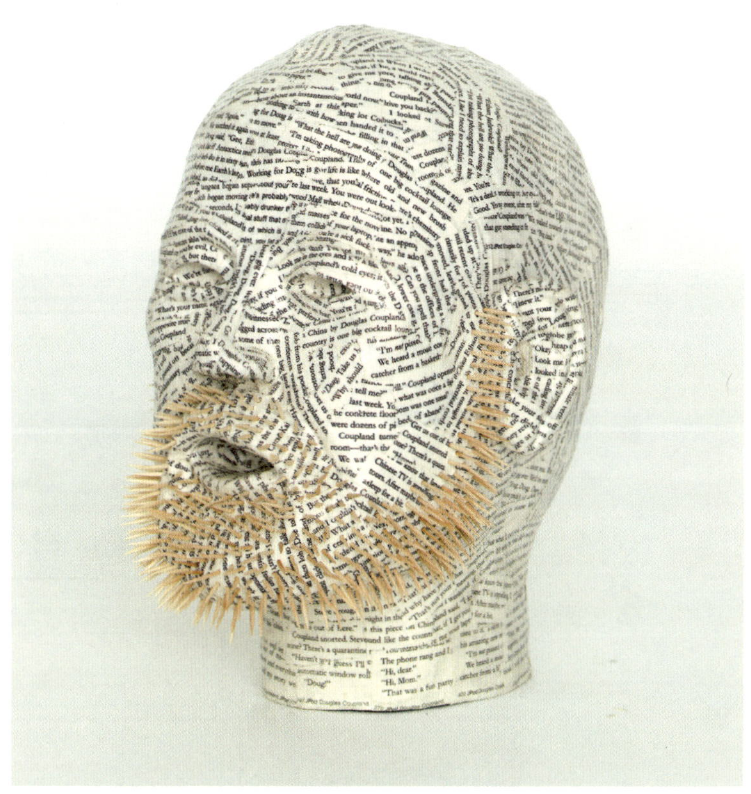

Douglas (lacked the dimension of radical Evil), 2009
archival paper, toner, EVA glue, cocktail sticks
34 x 21 x 28 cms
(papier-mâché made from pages in jPod 2006 novel where the character
Douglas Coupland appears in the story)

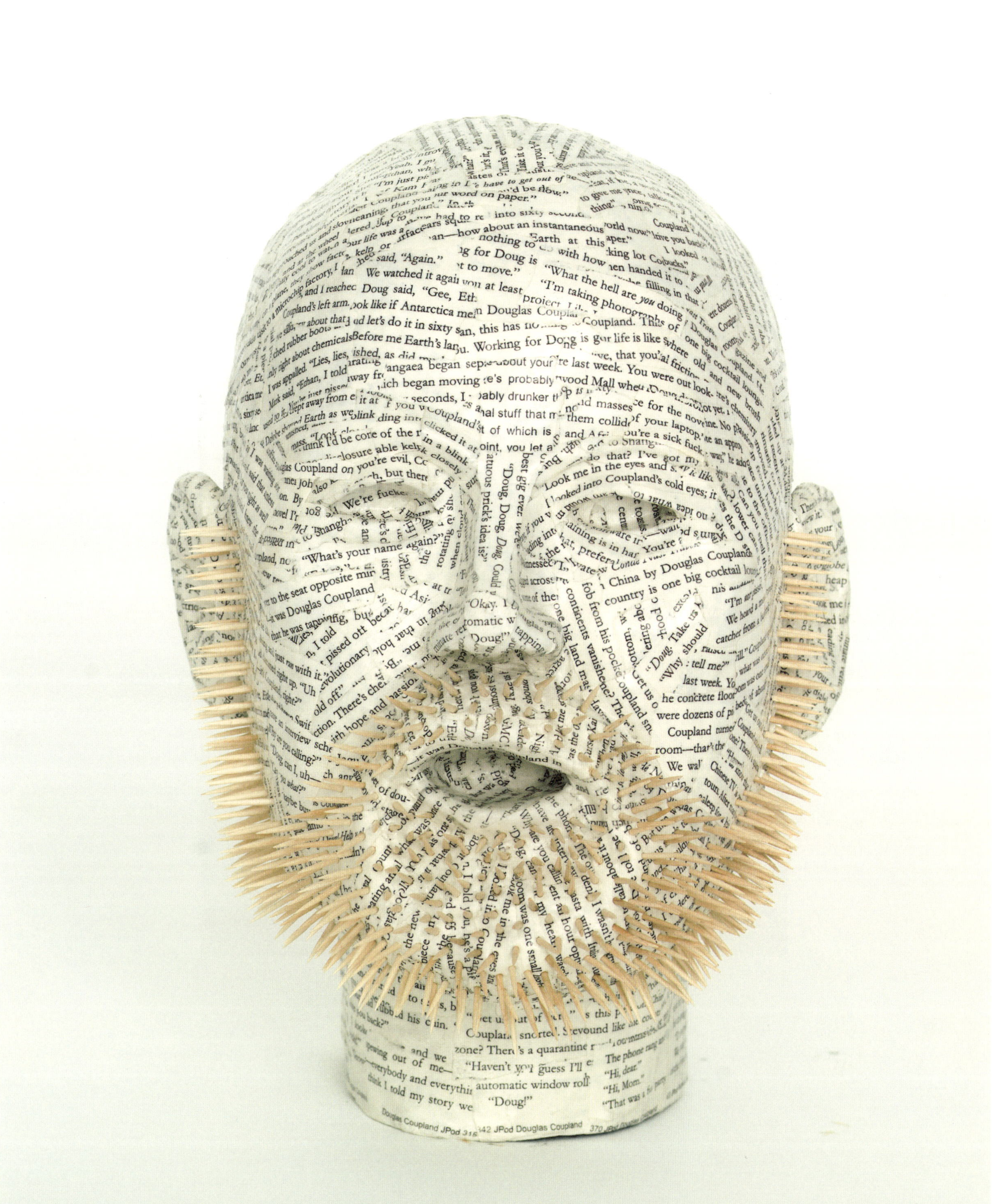

"What's your name again?"
to the seat opposite mi
was Douglas Coupland
Look me in the eyes and s
I looked into Coupland's cold eyes; it
China by Douglas Coupland
country is one big cocktail lo
"Haven't you guess I'll
automatic window roll
"Doug!"
"Hi, dear."
"Hi, Mom."
think I told my story we
Douglas Coupland JPod 316
342 JPod Douglas Coupland

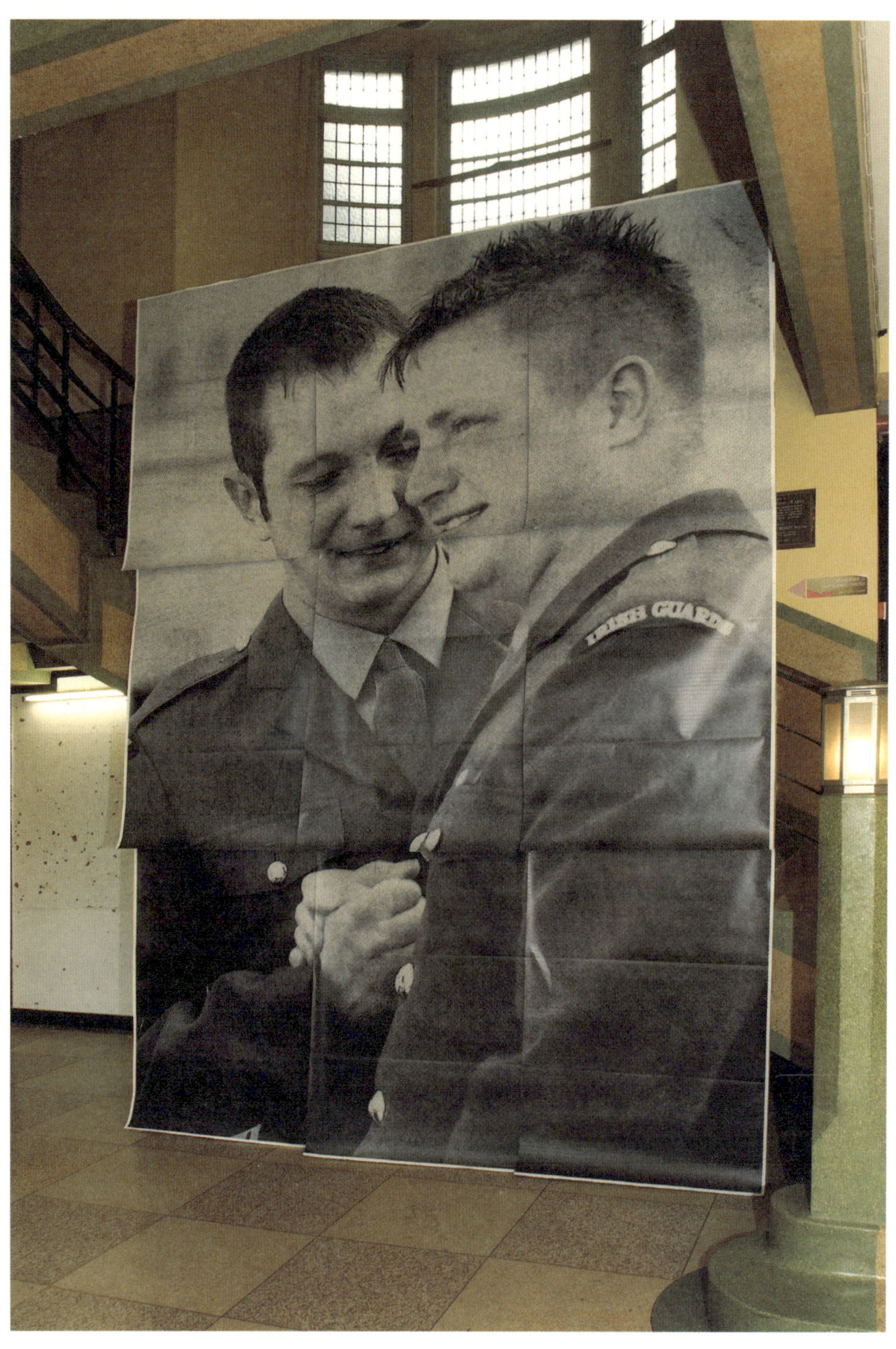

Irish Guards, 2006
inkjet billboard sheets
396 x 270 cms

Irish Guards, 2006
inkjet billboard sheets
dimensions variable

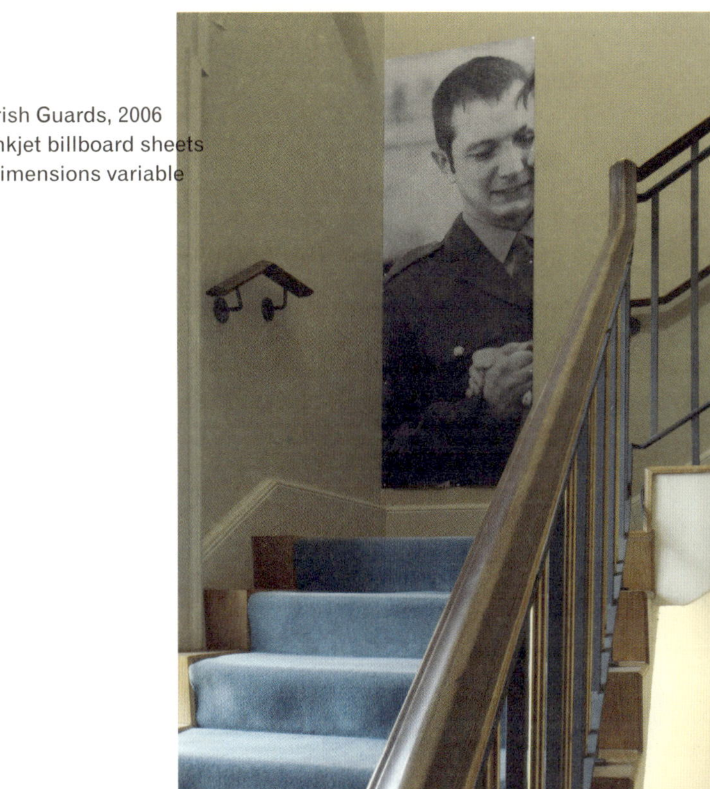

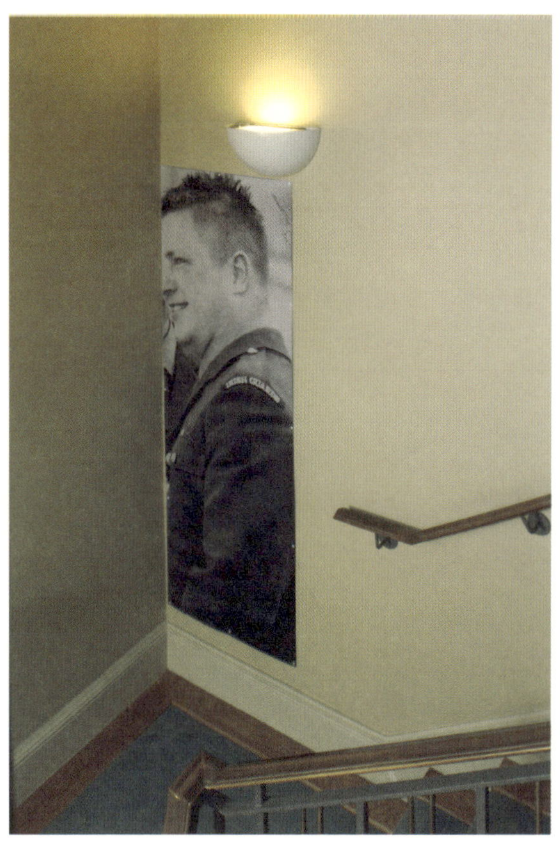

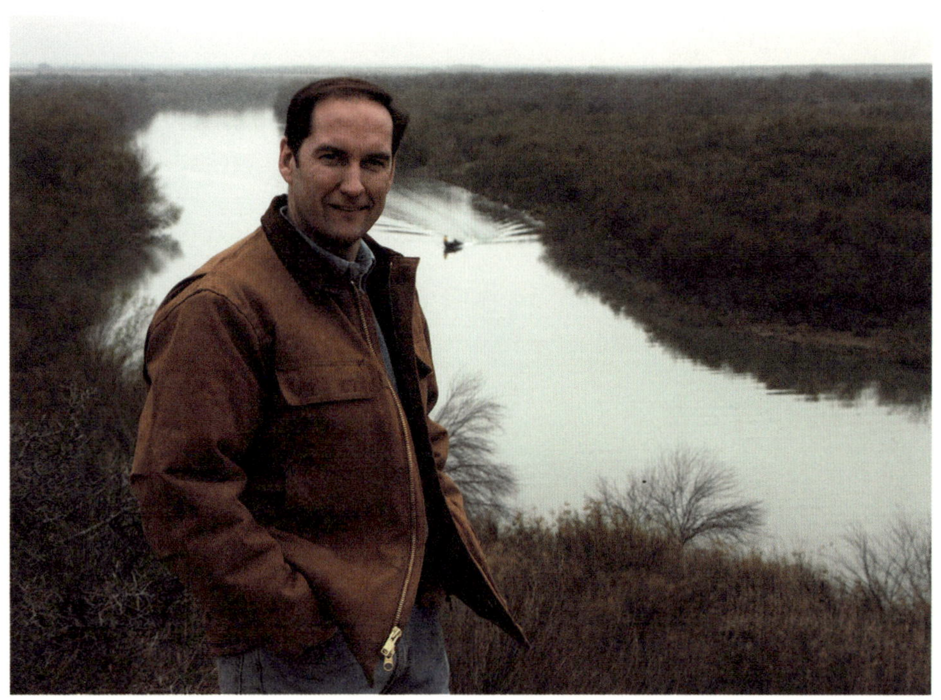

Brian Kennedy, 2006
c-print
25 x 36 cms

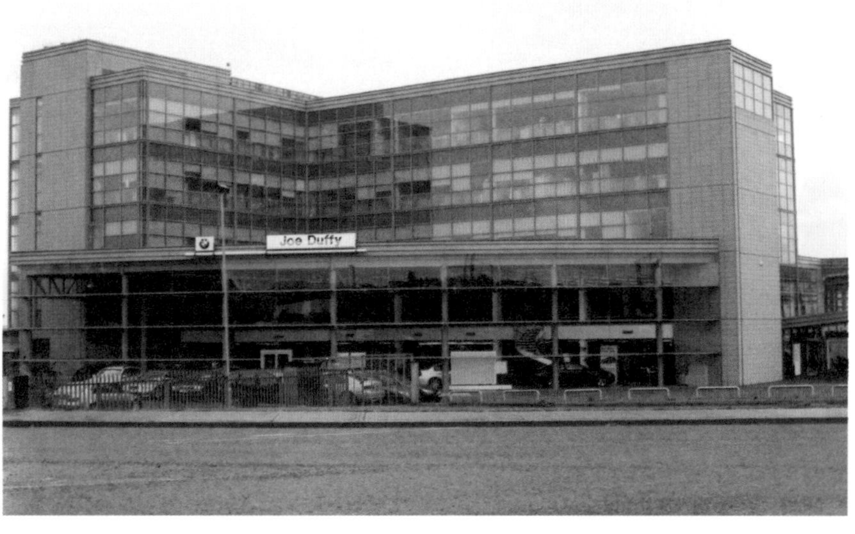


Joe Duffy Motors, 2006
c-print
25 x 36 cms

p.197

Crowd Psychology is qua
wo es war, soll ich werden interrupt the circular logic
of re-establishing balance because he is the lowest outcast
hate the beloved what dimension
agape singular point of
subjectivity sublimation violence
death drive 'love believes everything – and yet
is never to be deceived' les non-dupes errent
extremely fragile idealization sublimation
work this Bhaghavad-Gita
not work
alternative the proper Christian
uncoupling suspends not so much the explicit laws but, rather, their implicit
spectral obscene supplement

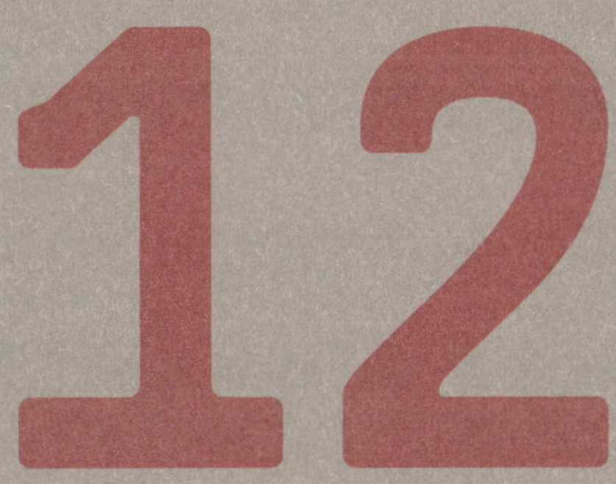

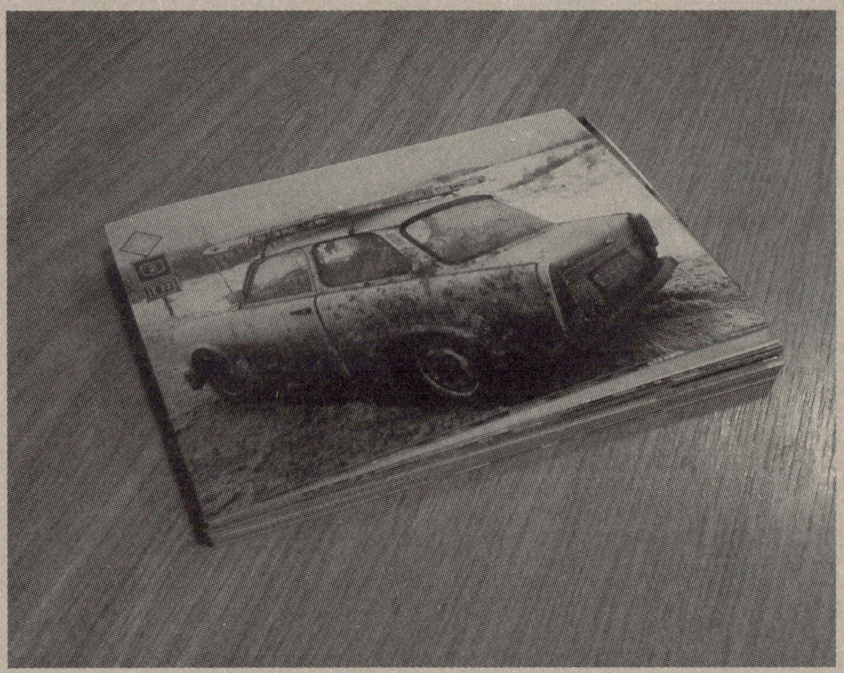

Dirt Car Stack, 2008
c-print
20 x 25 cms

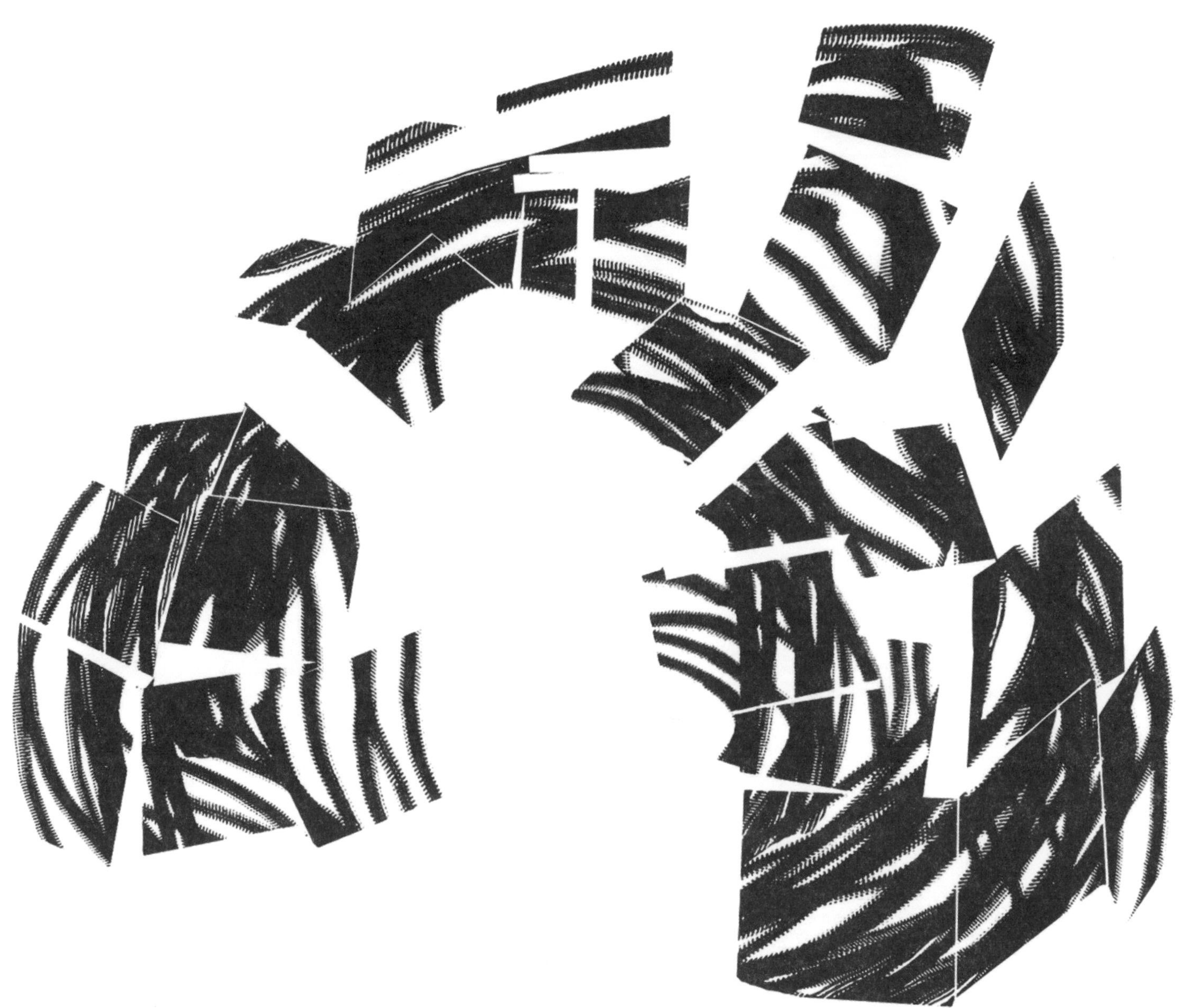

designs for Death Drive (interrupt the circular logic of re-establishing balance because he is the lowest outcast), 2009

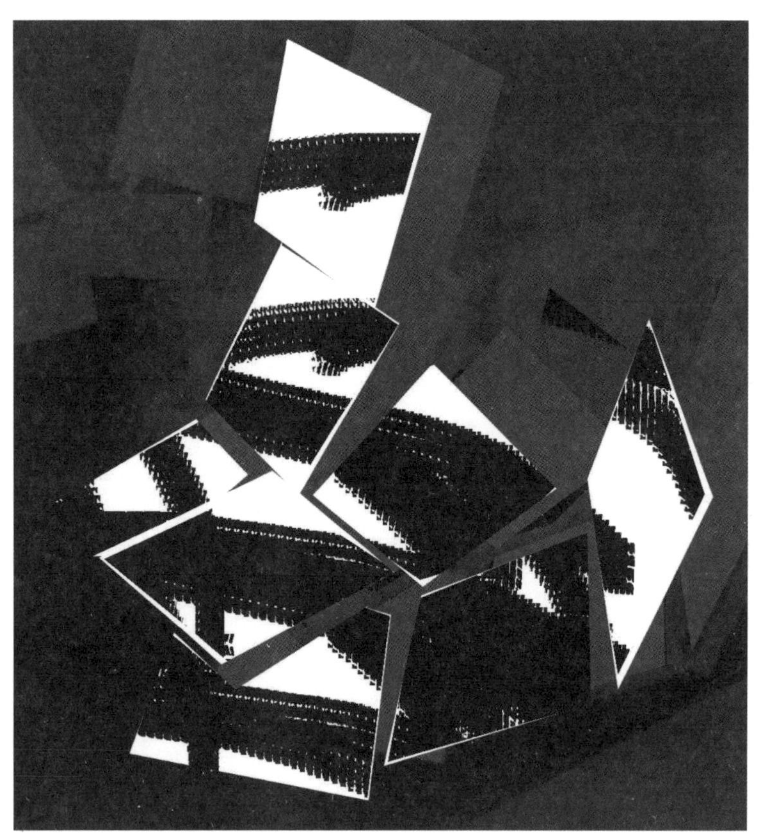

design for Death Drive (interrupt the circular logic of re-establishing balance because he is the lowest outcast), 2009

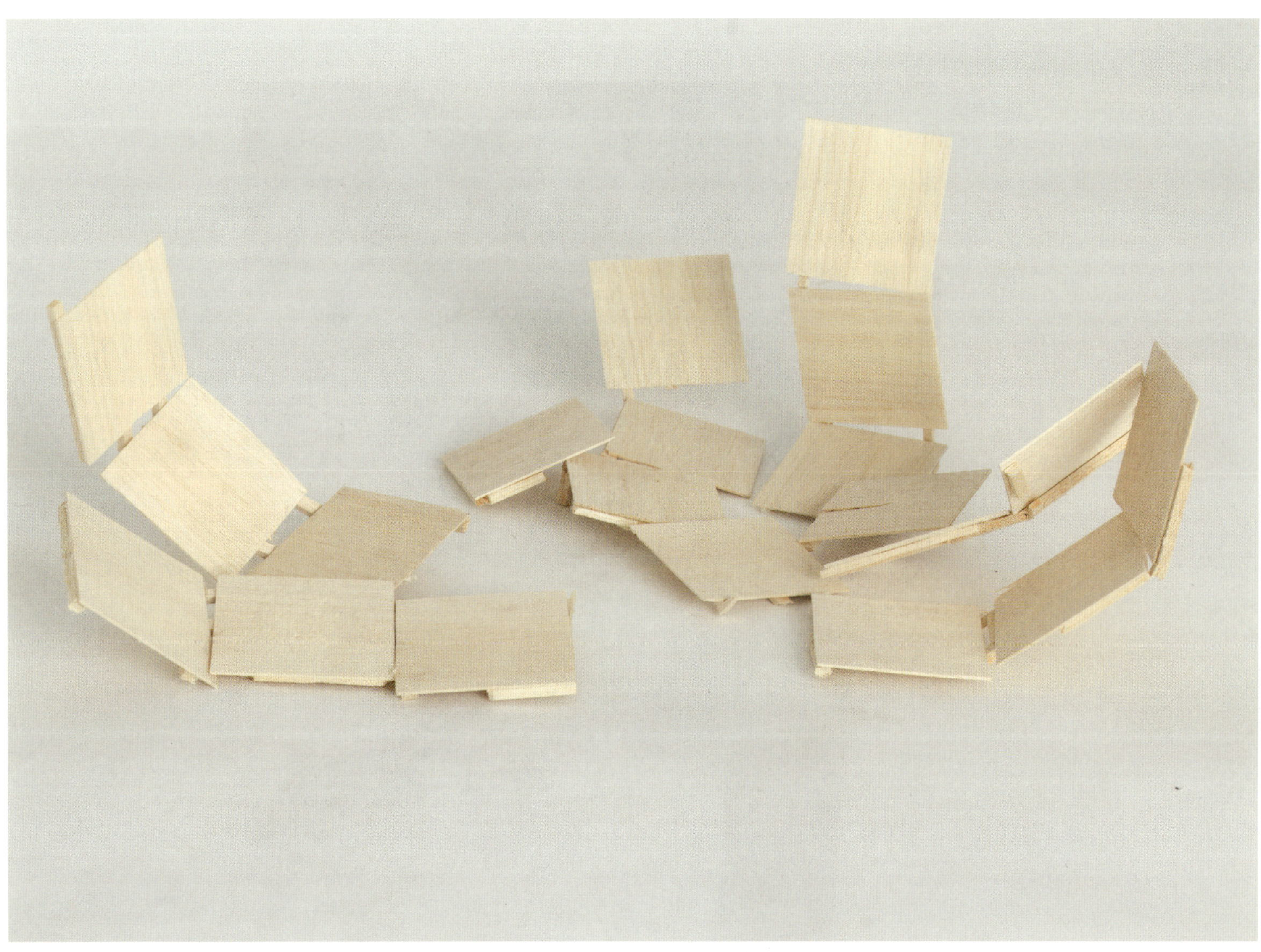

model for Death Drive (interrupt the circular logic of re-establishing balance because he is the lowest outcast), 2009

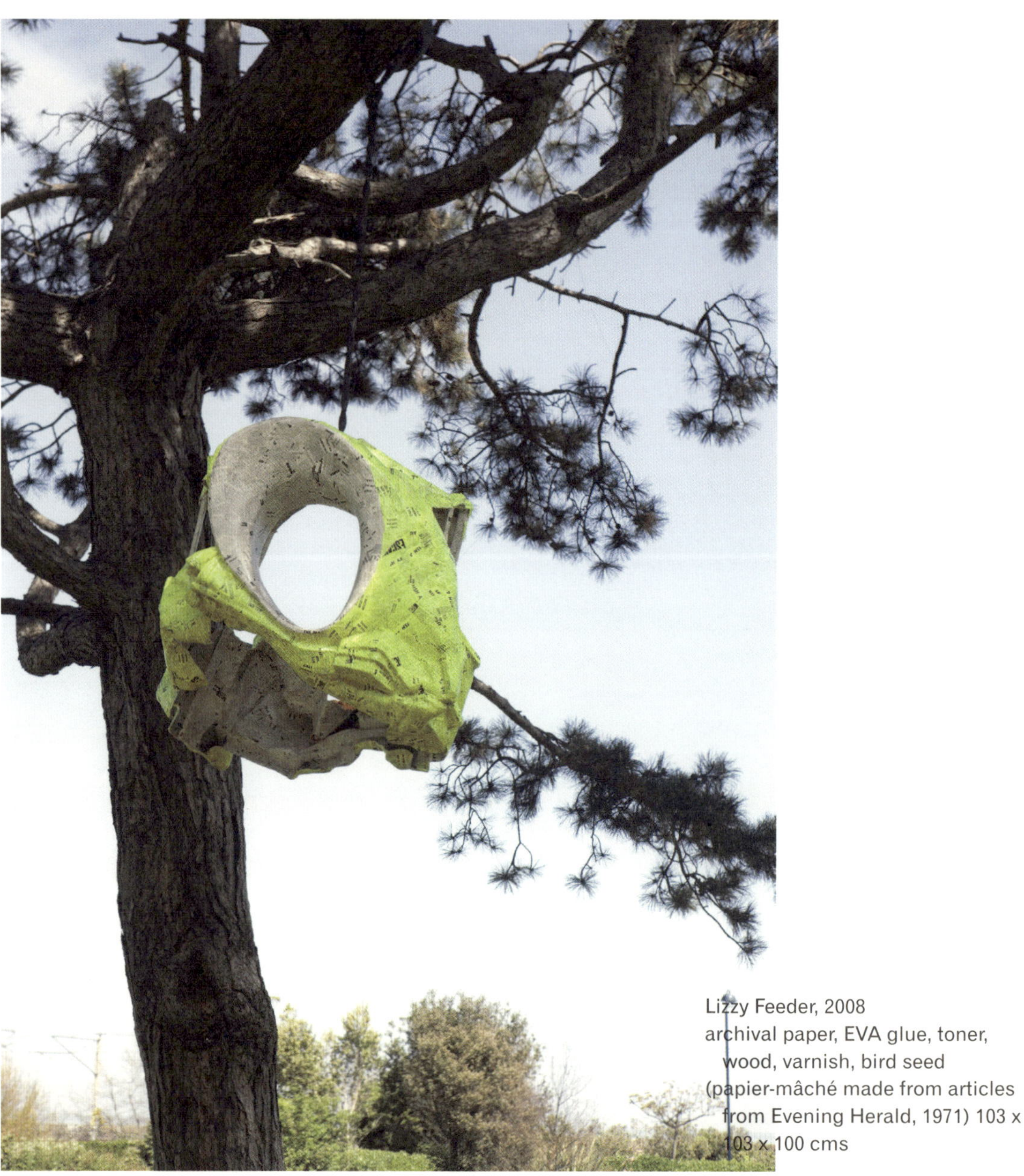

Lizzy Feeder, 2008
archival paper, EVA glue, toner, wood, varnish, bird seed (papier-mâché made from articles from Evening Herald, 1971) 103 x 103 x 100 cms

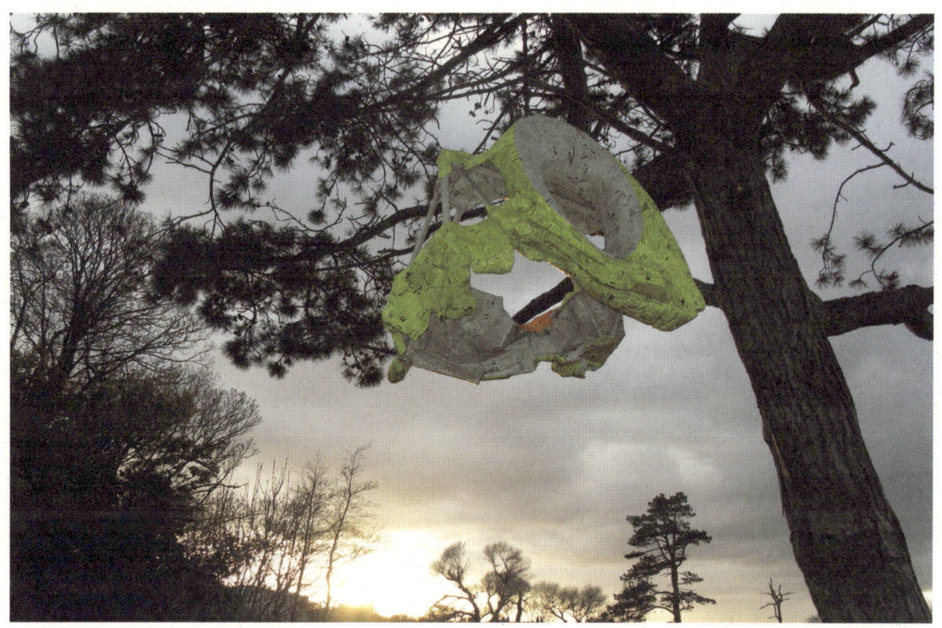

Lizzy Feeder, 2008
archival paper, EVA glue, toner, wood, varnish, bird seed
(papier-mâché made from articles from Evening Herald, 1971)
103 x 103 x 100 cms

source image for Lizzy Feeder, 2008

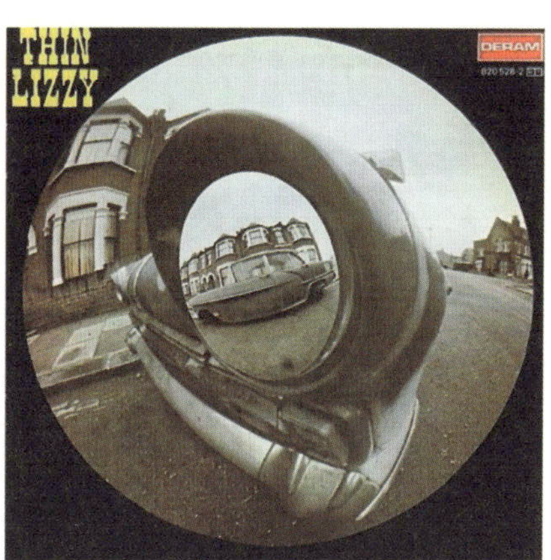

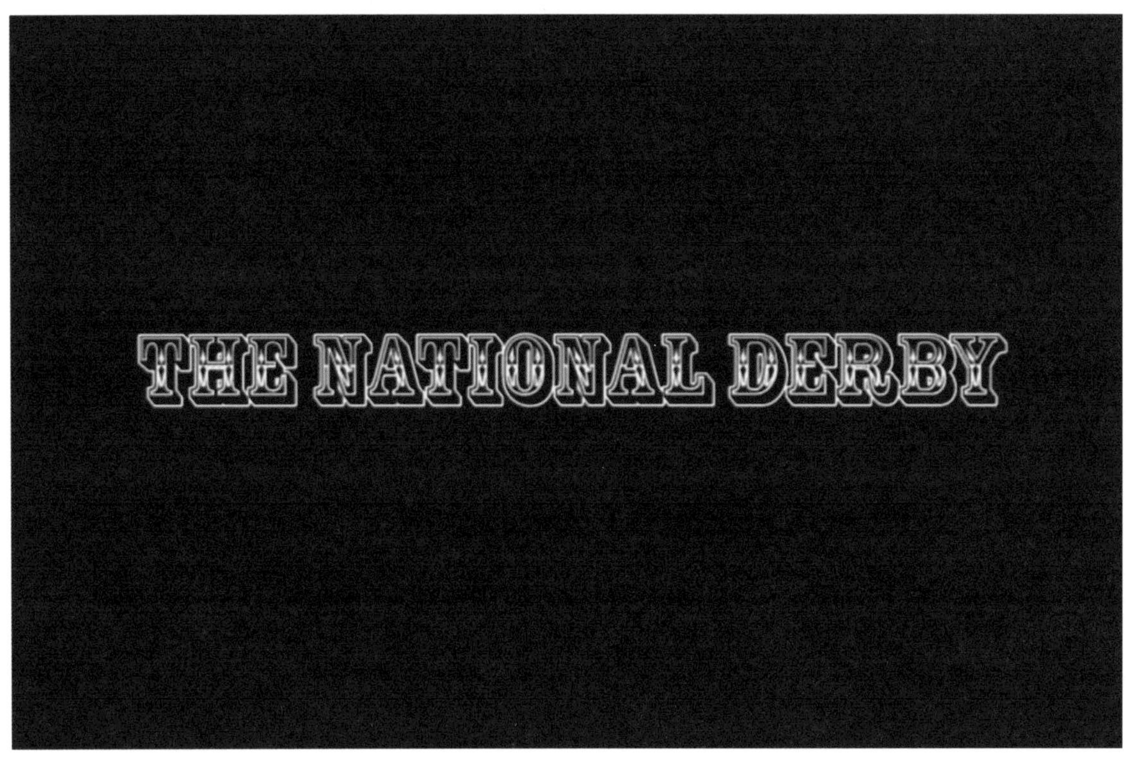


The National Derby, 2006
DVD video
duration: 2:54 mins
(images from bootleg copy of 1979 film by Goran Marković "Nacionalna Klasa" with subtitles from a text written by James Joyce in 1903 called "The Motor Derby")

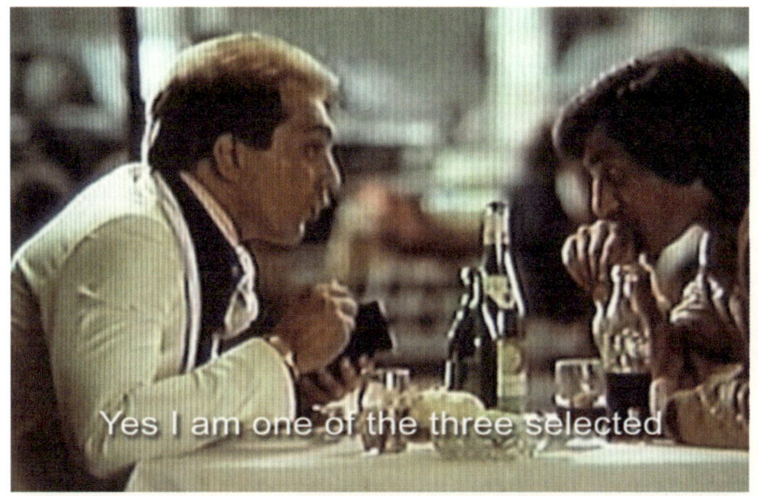
Yes I am one of the three selected

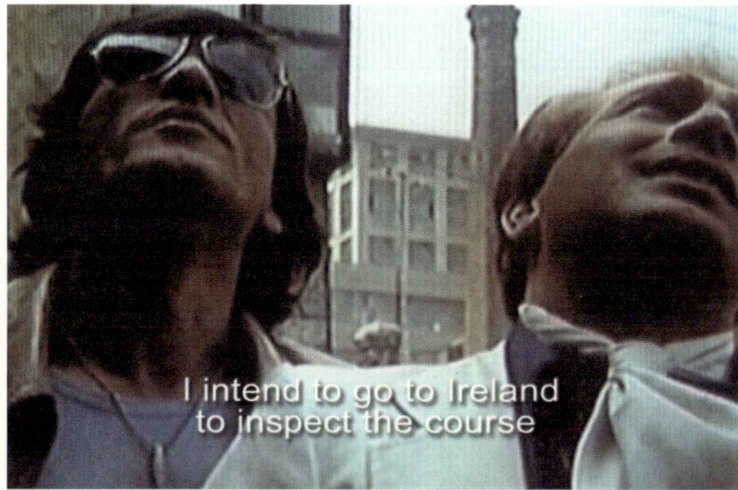
I intend to go to Ireland
to inspect the course

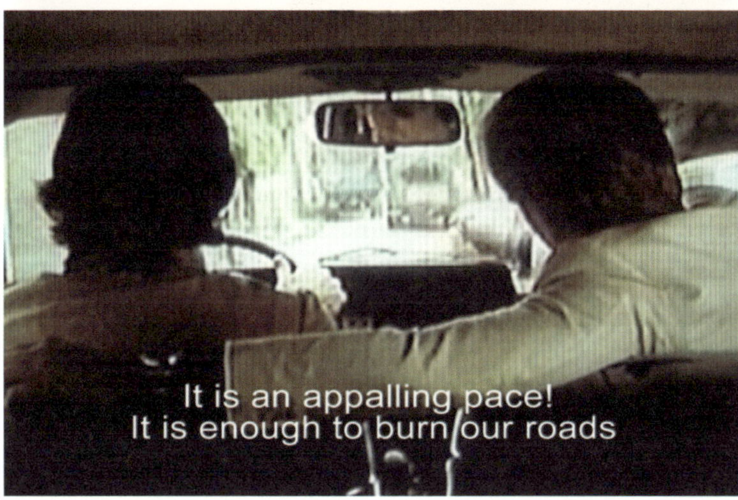
It is an appalling pace!
It is enough to burn our roads

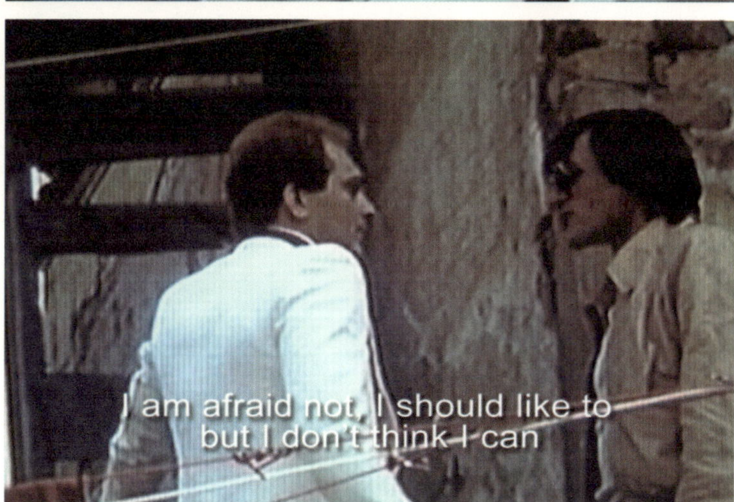
I am afraid not, I should like to
but I don't think I can

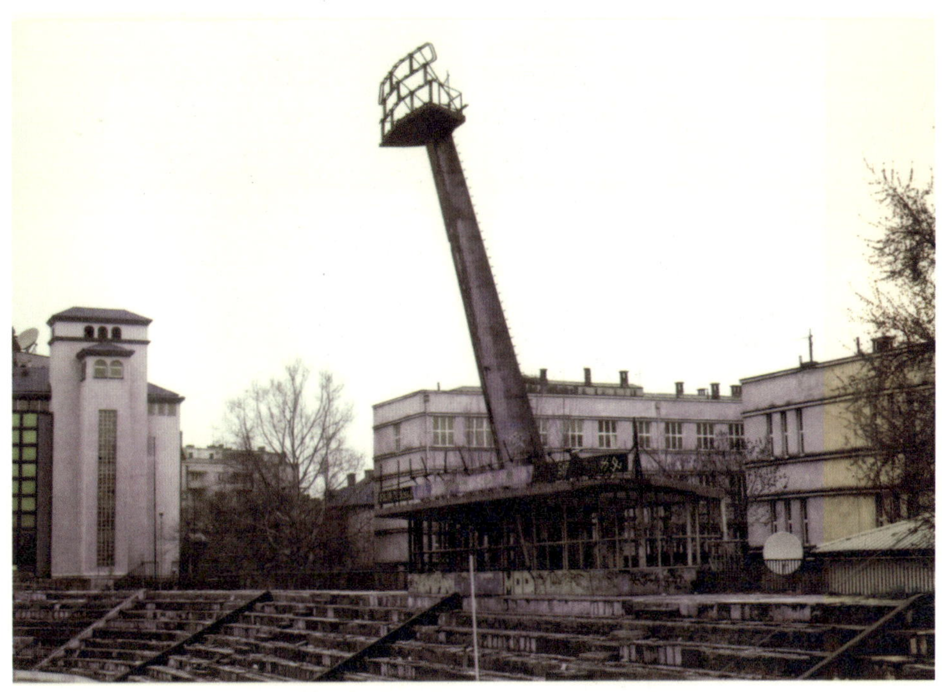

View of disused sports stadium,
Belgrade, Serbia, 2006

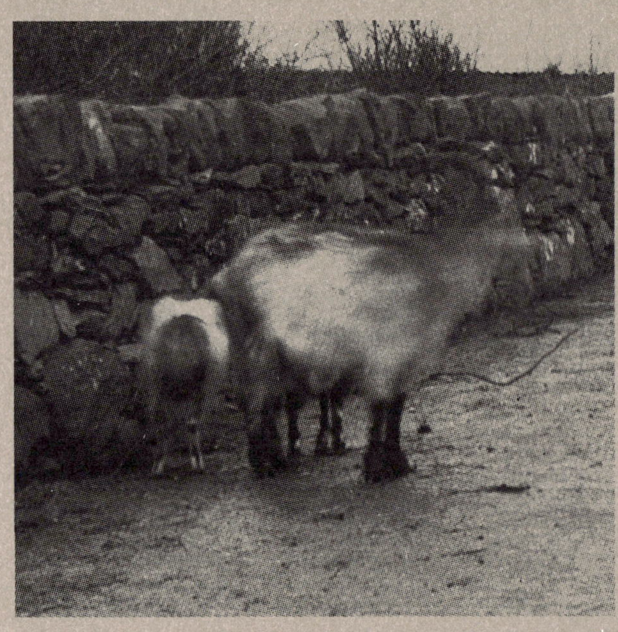

source images for Blurred Chicken
and Lumpy half-Goat, 2008

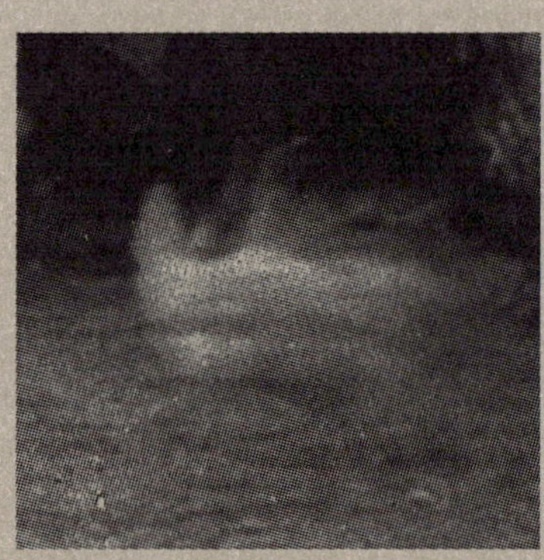

turns around defence superego
Das Ding das Ding
beyond jouissance You may!
Du kannst, denn du sollst! (You can [do your duty] because
you must [do it]! You can, because you must!
You should [you must], because you can authoritarian
totalitarian really want enjoy
doing your duty duty to enjoy yourself
act

# 13

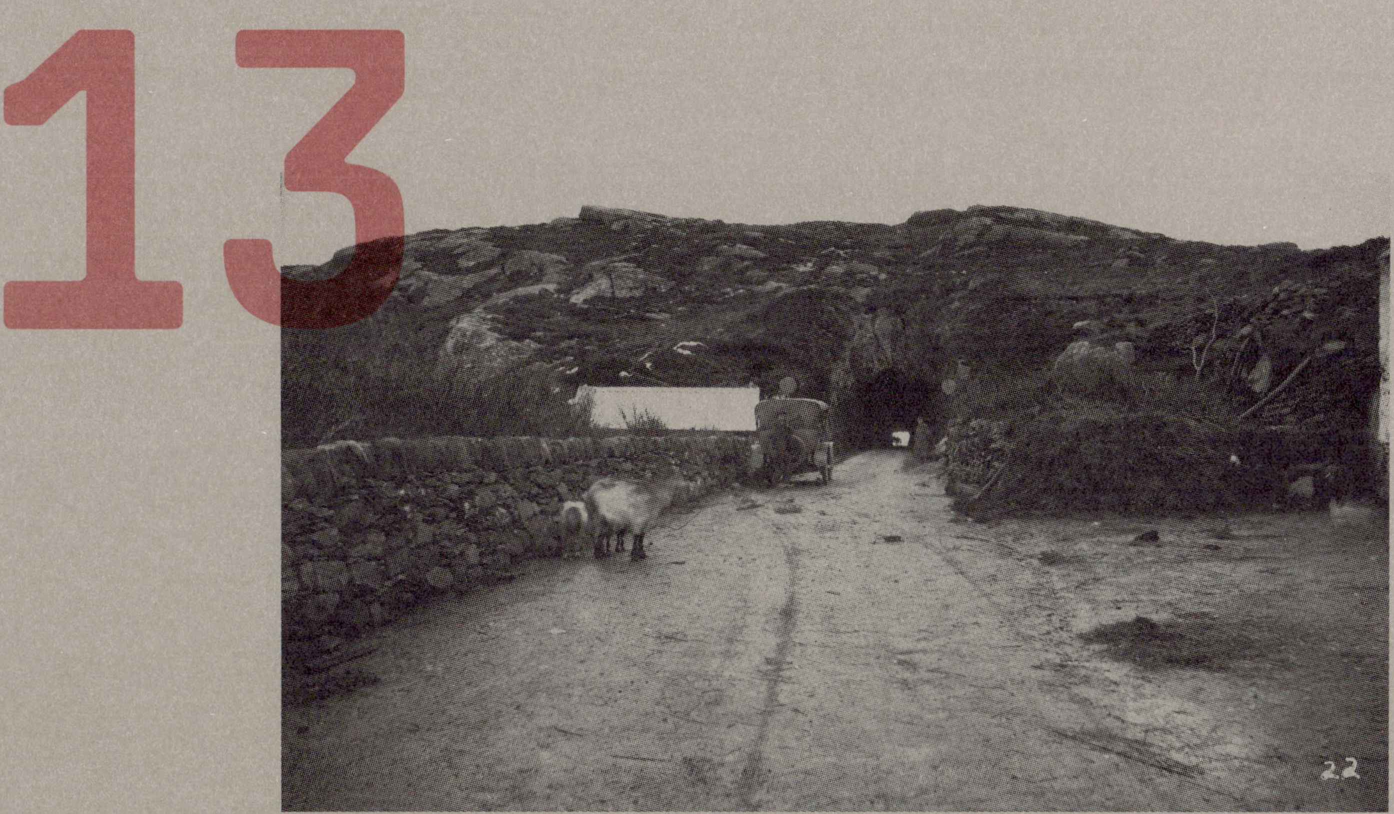


Ralph Gifford
Tunnel on a pass between counties Cork and Kerry, Ireland, 1910-1919
scan from nitrate negative

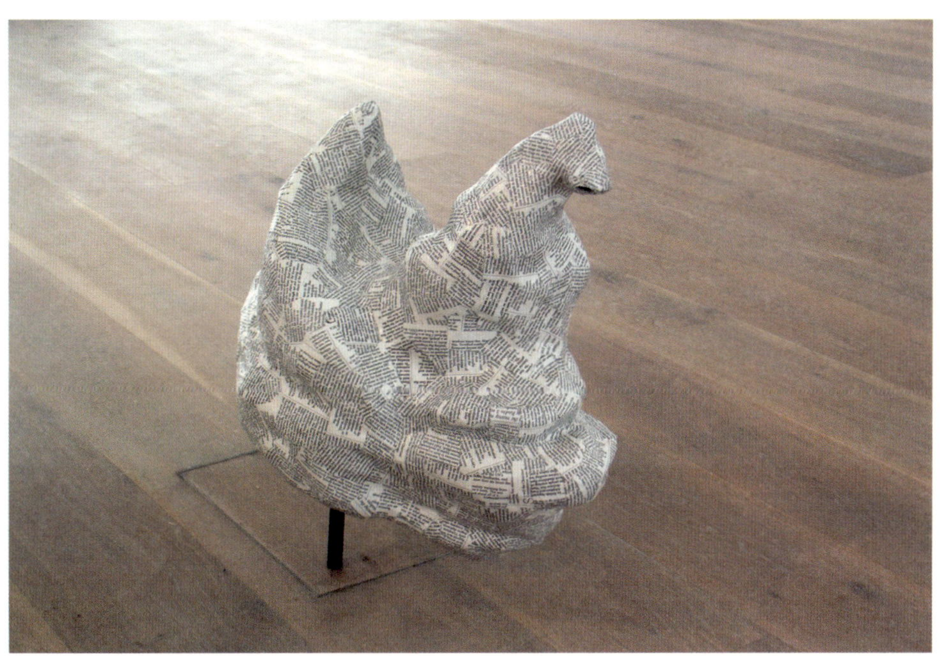

Blurred Chicken, 2008
archival paper, toner, EVA glue, metal, paint, polish
28 x 65 x 40 cms
(papier-mâché made from articles from the Daily Telegraph)

Blurred Chicken (you can, because you must!), 2009
archival paper, toner, metal, paint, polish, solar powered motor, wood half pallet
total: 66 x 54 x 45 cms; chicken 54 x 40 x 29 cms
(papier-mâché made from articles from the Daily Telegraph)

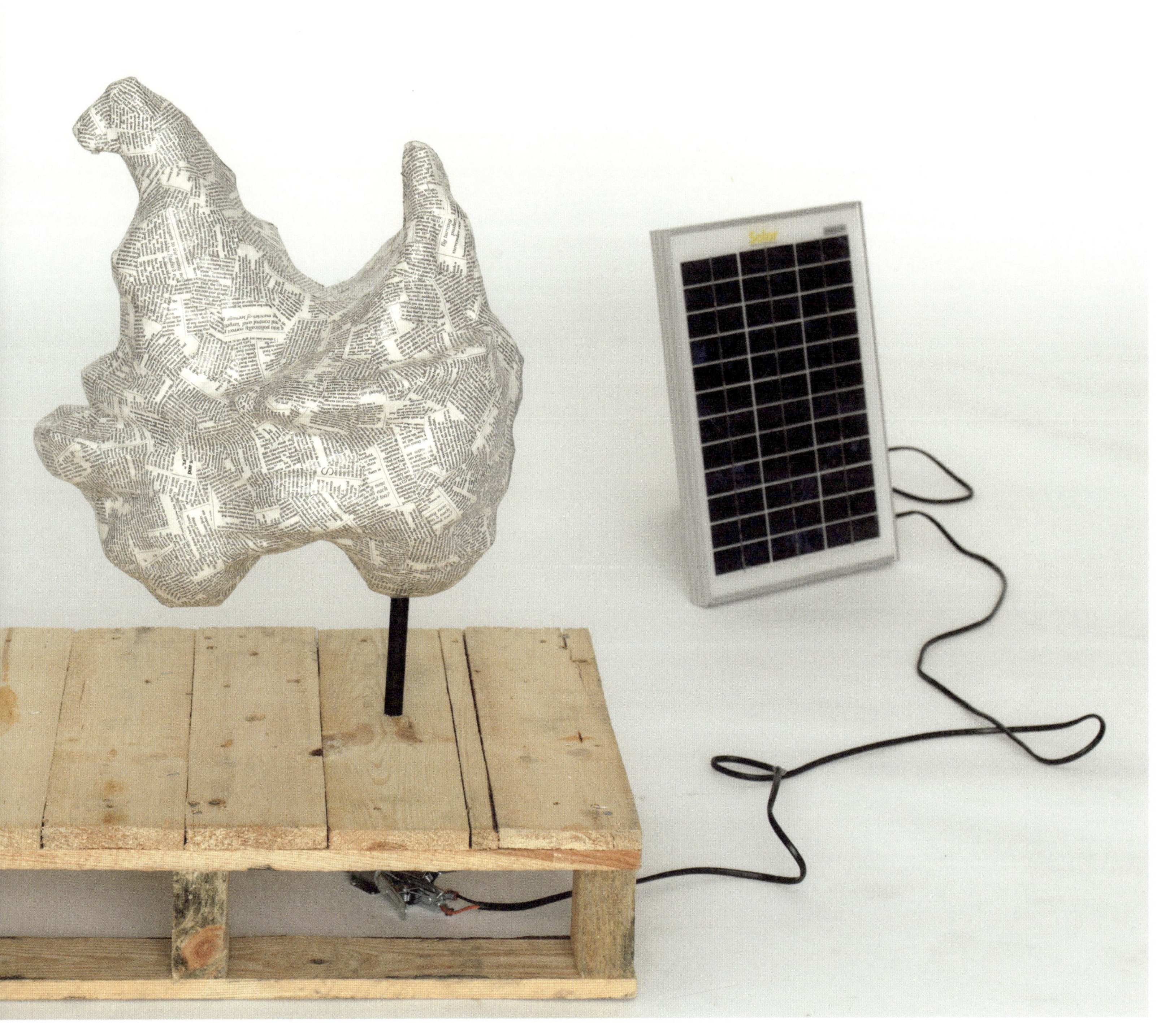

Lumpy half-Goat, 2008
archival paper, EVA glue, metal,
paint, polish
57 x 65 x 23 cms
(papier-mâché made from articles
from the Daily Telegraph)

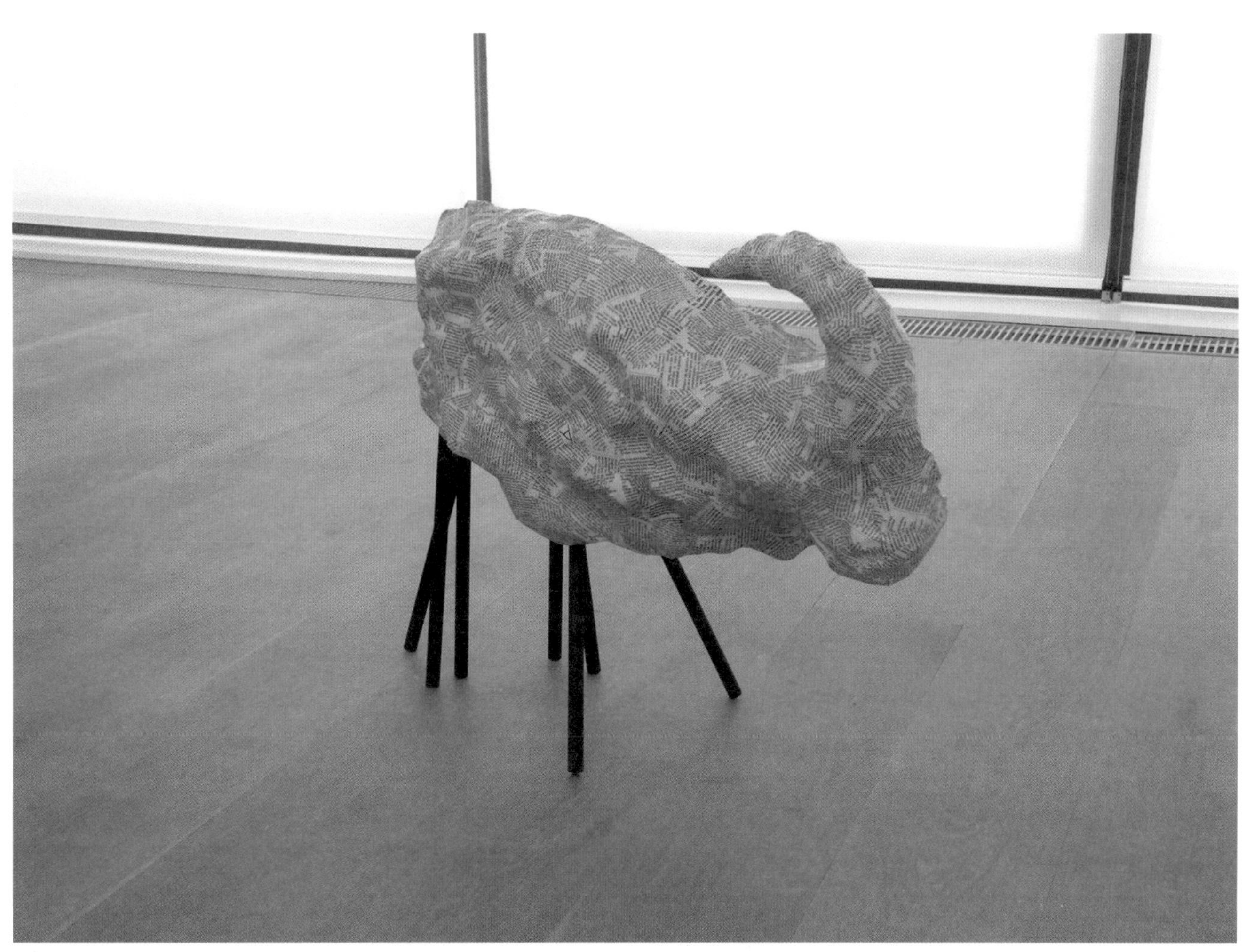

Ralph's Crawl Space, 2007
polyurethane foam, fibreglass, latex, ink
37 x 45 x 155 cms

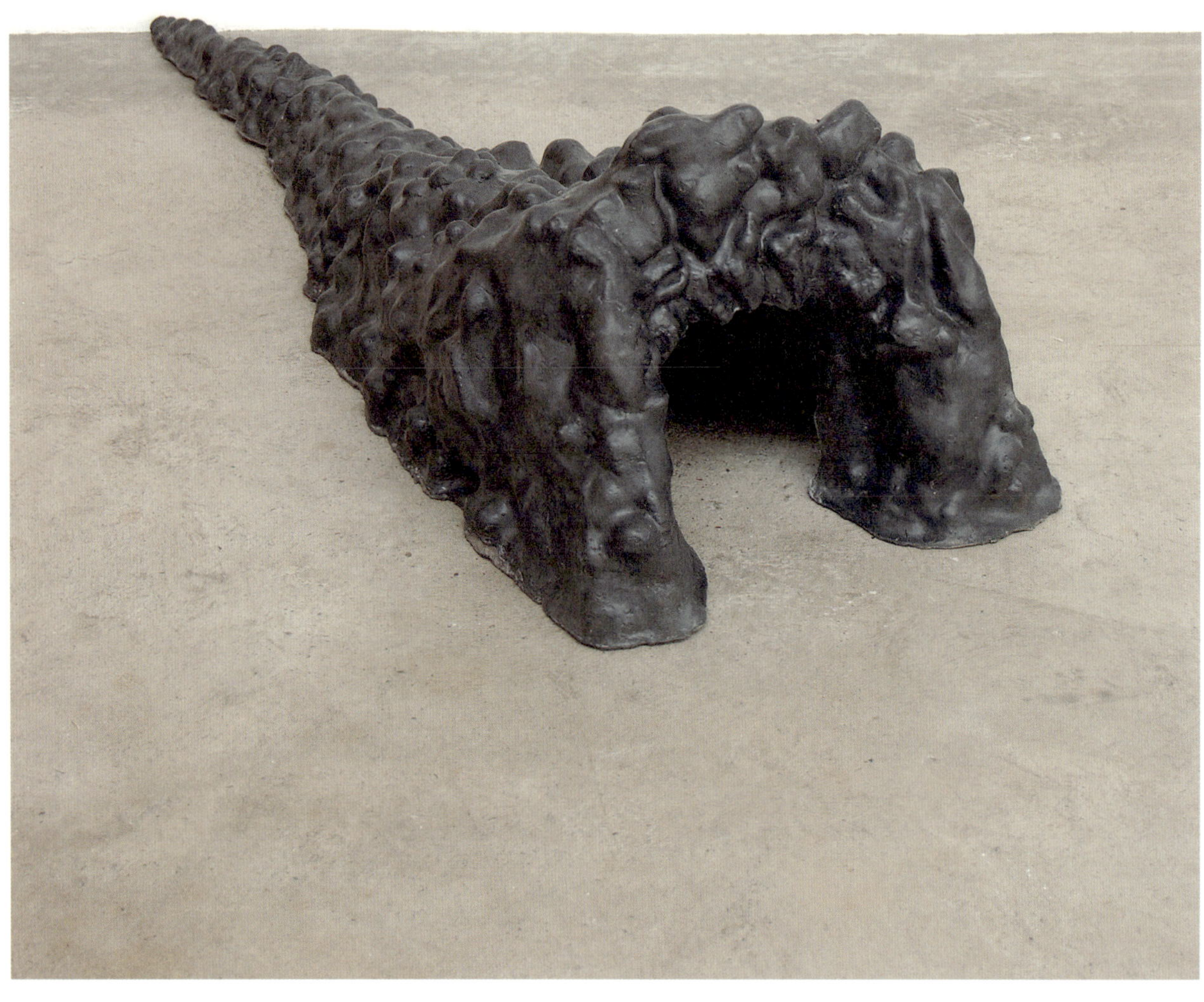

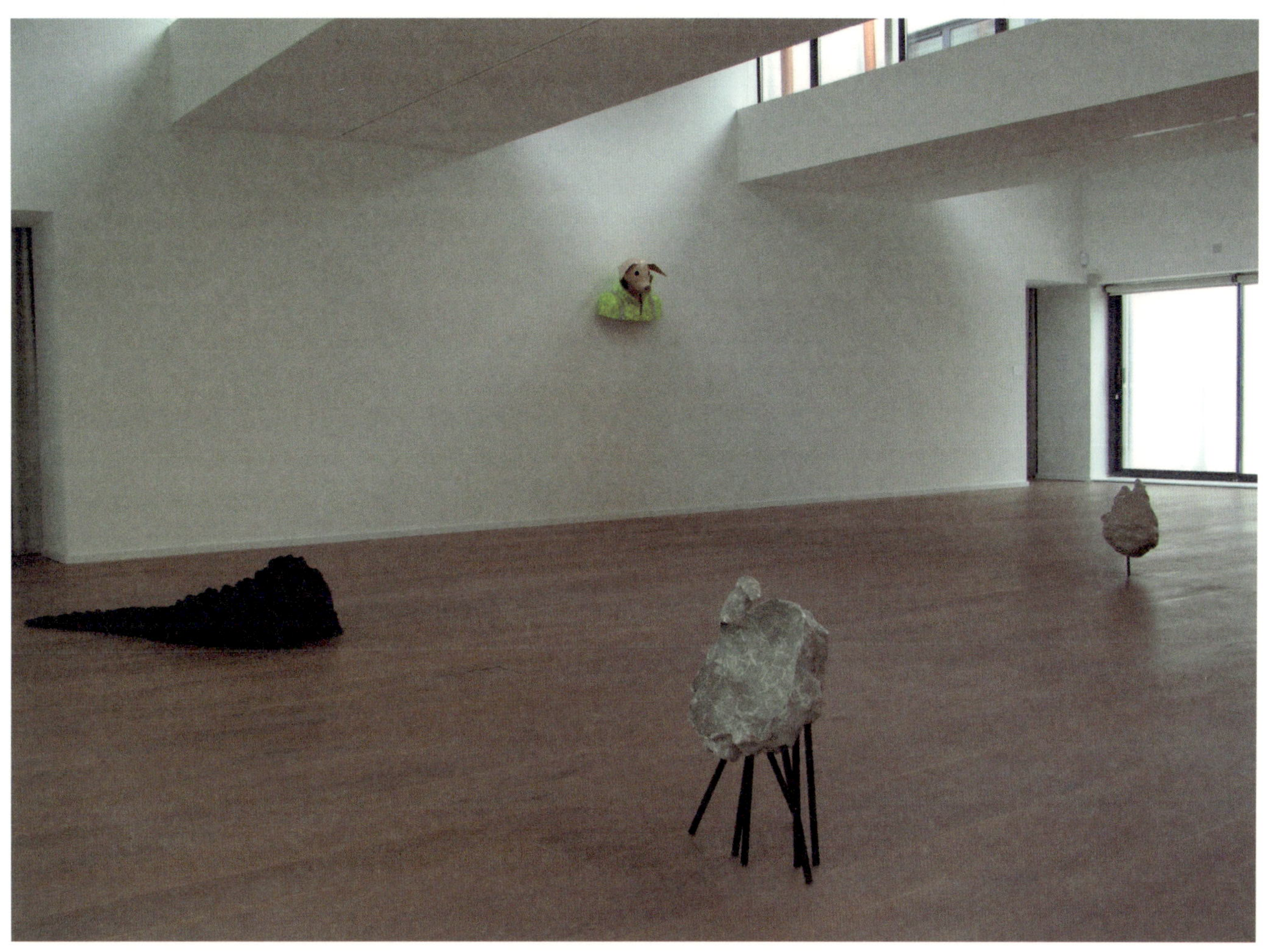

Exhibition view
Solstice Arts Centre, 2008

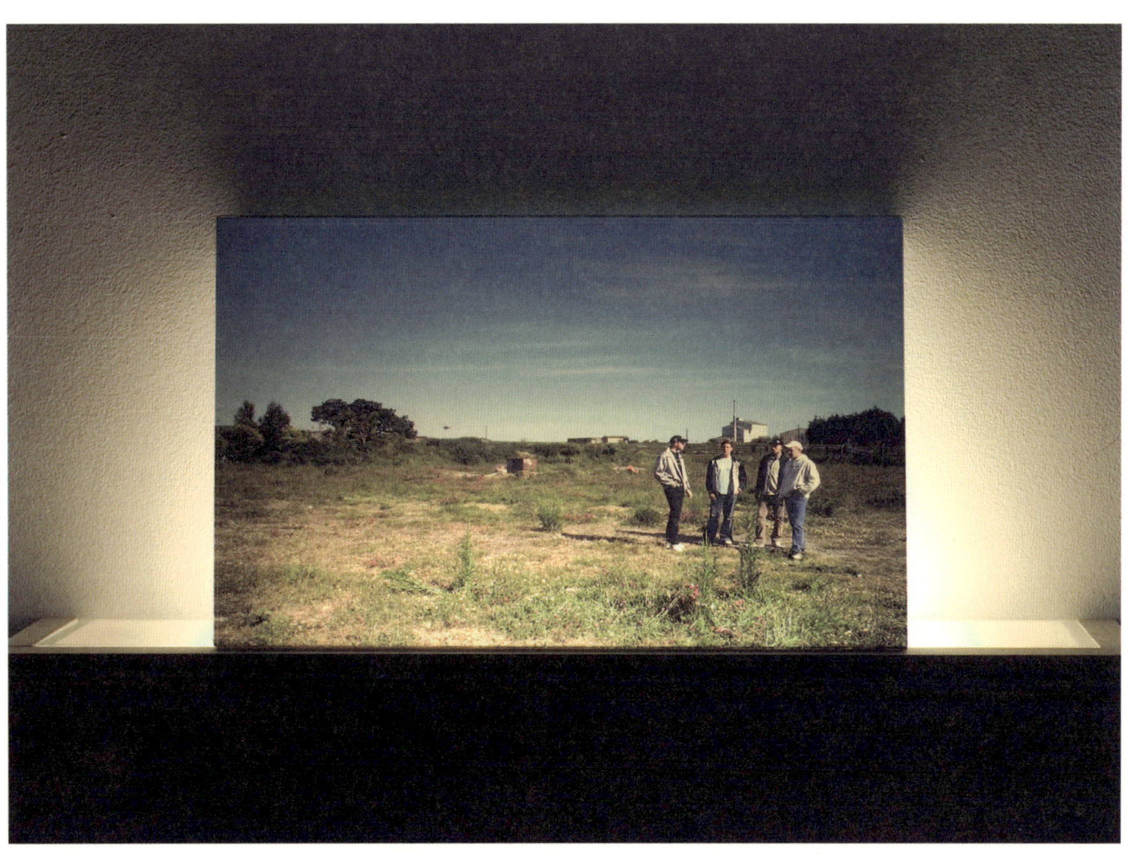

Arklow Racers, 2004
face mounted duratrans photograph,
light fixture, glass, wood
27 x 51 x 9 cms
image: 26 x 31 cms

# Speaking of drives... routes and meanderings

Medb Ruane

## PROLOGUE

Imaginary place, imaginary time. Footballer's girlfriend Charlene Hume-Berkeley encounters former Carmelite nun, Dame Judy Tutler, at a Show and Shine spectacle provoked by Alan Phelan.

Status and achievement fascinate Hume-Berkeley (25). She's obsessing about what men want, however, because of an ebbing sexual rapport with her partner. Determined to star in her own reality TV show, she recently discarded her research into later Lacan and the art of handbagging because it's bad for her image. Dame Judy (39) lives currently as a celibate. Sometimes, she dreams of driving in the *Leggenda e Passione* at Maranella, with her ideal lover by her side. A mechanic in her Carmelite years, Judy loves tinkering with various Scaglietti-designed, pontoon-fendered Ferrari 250 TRs. Her wish list number one is to inspect all 22 constructed between 1957 and 1958.
In another life, Arthur Griffith (1872-1922) might be Dame Judy's ideal. Editor, essayist and politician, his article 'The Resurrection of Hungary' (1904) questions how sovereignty evolves for smaller countries within larger entities, there the Austro-Hungarian Empire.

Coincidentally, the 15 years he spent (1895-1910) as an engaged man overlap with key moments in Sigmund Freud's articulation of psychoanalysis.
They meet in a rather clumsy attempt to tease out a few psychoanalytic strands in the project, without overt referencing or footnotes. Three short dialogues follow.

### Dialogue 1: Driving dialectics in the hyper-modern era

Dame Judy (DJ):
You all know something about motors? I want to talk about their carnal delights. At the level of the body, I'm like a Mongolian horsewoman readying her steed for competition when I'm shinin' my car. The rituals are the same whether you're groomin' a Fiat Punto or a Ferrari. I wash, rub, preen; polish 'til the skin glows. I enjoy the standing back then, walking round, raising my eyes up, and down, as I seek wholeness and completion – in vain, of course, because there is never an *oeillade*, never a unifying moment where I can see it all at once and experience, what may I say, ecstasy? Mmmm ... and the fragrances - sweaty engine oil boosting waxy sleekness, leather's unguenty whiff, the interior's taut, expectant aroma hovering, veiling ...
Arthur Griffith (AG):
You sound like Teresa of Avila, my dear! I'm more interested in the drives you inadvertently describe. I wish to explore them, if I may presume. Prof. Freud believed that they regulate sexuality and make us distinctively human in distinctively individual ways. It was a shock at the time, may I say. They've nothing to do with biology, he found. Not one connects to instinct. The tragedy is that the drives are unsatisfiable, relentlessly partial, condemned to spark off their discontinuous components of pressure, end, object and source.

Hume-Berkeley (HB):
With respect, Arthur, that's so old handbag. Your friend Freud changed his topography, you know, on top of opposing life drives and death drives. Yes, the opposition mirrored old literary binaries like Apollonian and Dionysian, or Eros and Thanatos, but Lacan sorted that. He's more useful here because, after all, we're considering something that's creative and destructive – the art of boy racing versus the crime of boy racing. What's different here? The drives are analogous to boy racers: they enjoy by pursuing a circuit, a closed circuit, quite repetitively. There's no final destination, it's the doing, the re-doing, and re-doing some more. It's about dicing with desire.
DJ: A moment please, Charlene. I admire your poeticism Arthur, I always have. Let me share my thoughts about the boy racers, remembering the Mongolian horsemen … and my darlin' Ewan McGregor filming there…
HB: Pardon me, Judy. I'm trying to articulate something here and your cuts aren't helpful. Every drive is a death drive for Lacan because it's excessive, repetitive – even destructive. It's no accident that we're playing with the sound-sense of the boy racers' "driving" and the "drives" as over a century of psychoanalysis has it. These are important signifiers. And, it's no accident that many people hate boy racers at a gut level. It's almost primordial, that disgust, so we have to ask why. Something else is going on …
AG: You may think me old fashioned, Miss Charlene. I hesitate to correct a young woman yet I'm duty bound to introduce the term *libido*, which your master Lacan transformed into *jouissance*. I must inquire where the drives as you know them feature in your subjective panorama and how they are relevant there.
HB walks out.

## Dialogue 2: Myth and symbol in the hyper-modern era

DJ: Something marvellous happens when a human climbs inside a car and becomes as one with it. Vroom, vroom! The highway beckons, the future sheds limits. Years of enforced silence often leave me struggling for words, but in my imaginings, the racers are twenty-first century centaurs. Where does man stop and beast begin? Why are ...
AG: Shall I assist, Judy? You're implying, if I may be so bold, that the racers are a trope, like centaurs are. You're saying that they function rhetorically as fantasy figures carrying the burden of people's fears and aspirations. Centaurs are extravagant inventions, as I saw with my own eyes when reviewing Slavic mythology in the early (20th. They're Dionysian hybrids, liminal beings born out of conflicting territories: our human world or the nether regions which may be benign, but represent as likely malign, even malignant forces. We don't know if they're friends or foe, therefore we fear. We're clutched by anxiety's suffocating embrace.
HB (groans): Nature/culture? Limens and margins? Way too easy Arthur, too romantic. Next you'll be dissertating on the archetypal implications *à la* Jung. What a loser.
AG: I'm mystified as to why I irritate you, Miss Charlene. Surely there's room to consider the centaurs, and by association the racers, as giving free rein to *id* representations and thus to uncontrollable inner wildnesses. They represent the unrepresentable. Dame Judy, let me introduce you to Freud's second topography. He set it out during the Anglo-Irish negotiations which preoccupied me, although he doesn't mention them. *Id-ego-superego*: the *id*, or *das Es* as Freud writes, doesn't organise itself coherently; rather it's the 'great reservoir of libido', 'a chaos' of unrelenting drives, here, life and death as I noted previously. He says the ego is like a rider trying

to control a wild horse, it being the id. Is this the centaur's domain, the boy racer's?
HB: You may not mean to be so patronising, Arthur, but puh-lease give Judy a break. Me too before I cliché my life away. Get real! Think about the real, the real Real, the rim round *Das Ding*, the void, chasm, the nothing at the core of being. Think about racers inscribing the deadly space we can't name, challenging it like matadors, toreadors, whatever, brandishing red banners before huge, blank eyes that could kill.
DR: You're losing me.
HB: The racing knots the three registers, don't you get it? Real, Symbolic, Imaginary. It's a dazzling, desperate display of *jouissance* punctuated/punctured by limits. The car is like a carcass, an envelope - and the thought of it, the fantasy, is the hinge that knots carcass and subject together! Beyond, the death drive! Within, the hole of being! Or the other way round...
DR: I'm lost.
[A pause. Conversation resumes]
DR: The Gordon Bennett myth intrigues me. I understand he lived in real time yet if he did not, we'd have had to invent him.
AG: What an unusual man. Rather like the primal father in Freud's *Totem and Taboo* who enjoyed without limits. The exception. He did whatever he wanted whenever he wanted and no one could stop him, until the sons cooperated and killed him! Then they had to invent laws and regulations so it wouldn't happen again. In Bennett's case, his vast wealth and media empire made everything possible.
HB: Sounds like another speech is coming. Anyway, Darwin mentioned the primal father first. He was probably psychotic.
DR: Darwin?

HB: No, Bennett. Or perverse, perhaps, because he acknowledged the Law without obeying it. He skirted around it, toyed with it. Here, though, the only way the racers can do what they do is to respect limits.
DJ: Phelan's intervention interests me. Am I using the right word, intervention? I'm into cars. You two are talking about God knows what. I read newspapers. I listen to Joe Duffy. People hate boy racers at a visceral level but of course the racers they hate aren't the centaurs I love or the car-lovers I admire. What's the difference?
HB: Phelan created a system of administration to regulate it. It's hyper-modernism via Foucault's 'new relational mode' with the artist intervening almost as an analyst does; using *witz*, joke, parody, skill...
DJ: What team does your boyfriend play for, Charlene?

DIALOGUE 3: ON WHETHER OR WHAT INTERVENTIONS MAY BE POSSIBLE.

AG: I don't want to upset you Charlene, especially with all your love difficulties. But, my dear, your research is, shall we say, unfinished and inconclusive. Phelan stages events and makes rather beautiful pieces for our edification and delight. I am especially impressed by the hand he commissioned from China. A hand of friendship, or a clutch of betrayal, such as Éamon de Valera offered me in tragic times. The vast Chinese empire making a gesture to us... it moves me, I do not hesitate to admit.
HB: Event? Call it spectacle, after Debord. How smart is he? I may have walked away from all that but I still have my notes. Let's see (rummages through phone)... events such as Woodstock and the Beatles' global broadcast of All You Need is Love... nothing there really. Let me check for Bourriaud – yes, here he is hypothesising

in 2001 that the artist is like a social worker intervening in social and communal relations. Relational aesthetics (rummages further), hold on, no, the new signifier is altermodern. That's another way of saying hypermodern, I reckon. Or not…

DJ: But Alan has intervened. He's taken random-enough activity, linked fantasy to signification and shaped it symbolically. Are we so sure that his intervention is akin to a social worker? It's not curative or therapeutic. I wonder if it's indeed more analogous to the analyst, making an interpretation to the patient or client on the couch. I've read some of the Freud you lent me, Arthur dear, and some of the Lacan and Bersani you gave me, little Charlene. I didn't find Freud's joke book humorous at all, by the way, yet I was struck by how the joke or *witz* irrupts from the unconscious. It's an equivocation your earlier Lacan called the umbilical cord of the *parole* and, as you know, his later *Television* connects this – is the link metaphoric or metonymic? I confuse them – to the psychoanalytic act, to the very desire of the analyst as he or she intervenes to stitch the signifiers of sound and silence. I'm not being clear.

AG: Shall I recapitulate what you are saying, Judy?

HB: Please don't, Mr. Griffith. Judy, what you're saying is quite confusing. Alan's project is there before our eyes. It's in the specular field. No, don't worry, I won't get into Seminar XI, the Four Fundamental Concepts, I need to tease this out. If what appears is provoking whatever we call it – the primordial, the holes in being Lacan represented as *objets a*, o-objects – which make us look and fear… well, they're non-specular, we can't see them and we deceive ourselves if we try to think about them that way. I can't get my brain around that cut between specular and non-specular. I can't even talk without making them a binary and they're not, I think.

DJ: Oh dear, I am not up to speed on o-objects either, they're so counter-intuitive, but Arthur was saying something interesting about the drives, weren't you? That they are always partial and unsatisfiable. You lose your o-objects, don't you dear? Losing them mobilises your desire so they're causal from the moment they're lost. O-objects are primordial provocatives!

## Epilogue

Dame Judy Tutler googled an on-line psychoanalytic site that night, after a quick search for Maranella (population 35) and a hit on royal-tarot.com. She phoned the o-object help line, where a recorded voice listed six: breast, faeces, urinary flow, imaginary phallus, voice, phoneme, nothing. Asleep, she dreamed of baby seals wrapped in voile, smiling from a large basket on the back of Ewan McGregor's Harley-Davidson as it soared, shimmering, over the Mongolian plains.

Arthur Griffith didn't dream.

Charlene Hume-Berkeley removed her make-up intently while listening to Giovanni Trappatoni sing Gigli. Her dreams worked her furiously, frantically, with wishes for a romantic lunch of smoked salmon and Sancerre, to be shared by AG and DJ. The fish undid her. None in the fridge! Less in the freezer! She ran to the organic outlet, bare-footed, only to find it closed. Hunched over Howth pier, she saw tiny caviar eggs bubbling under the wet sea and reached out to save them. She could not.

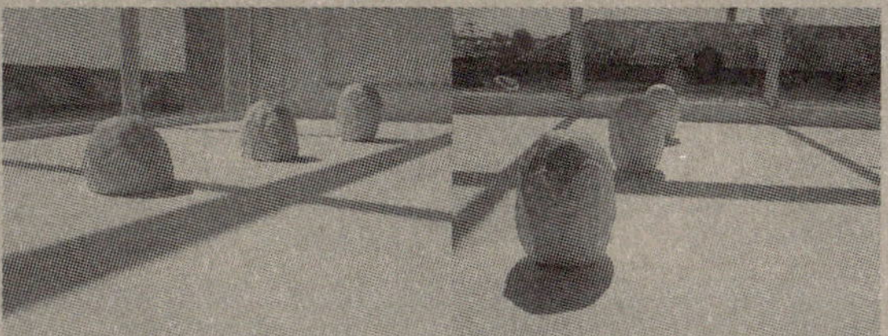

Buds, 2008
Various sizes, largest 7 x 5 x 5 cms
plaster, paint

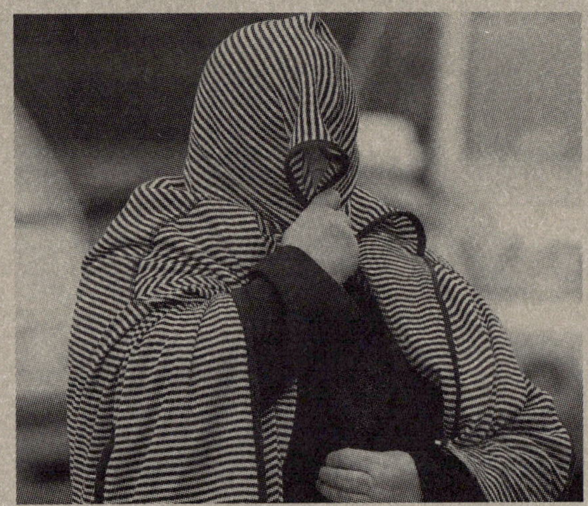

Source image for Woman who stole from farmer, 2009

Working model for Woman who stole from farmer, 2009
aluminum foil, plaster, clay, chicken wire, insulating foam, foam filler, paper, fabric, shellac
77 x 79 x 59 cms

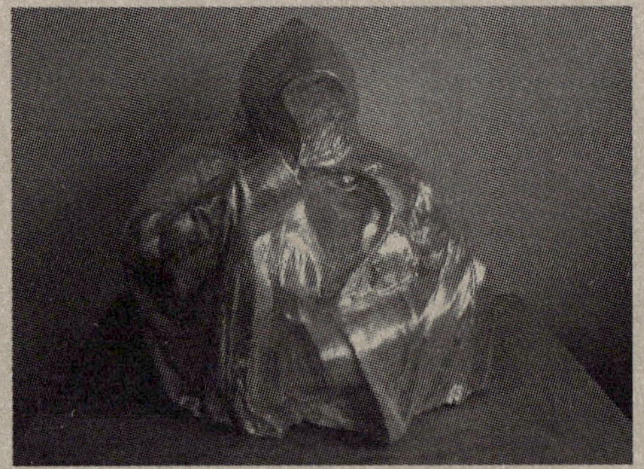

p.231

Darwin's Dangerous Idea The Subject – Encore against your will? false lie against your will? she knew perfectly well that if she answered 'No', the judge would order enforced transfusion statement enunciation true to herself without disregard does not deceive irrelevant The Institute for Judaism and Science literally indifference even if it helps you! pace against doing is do not feel any guilt it is only truth that matters always-already mediated by the (repression of the) desire to transgress the Law are is desire act Murder in the Cathedral this their not

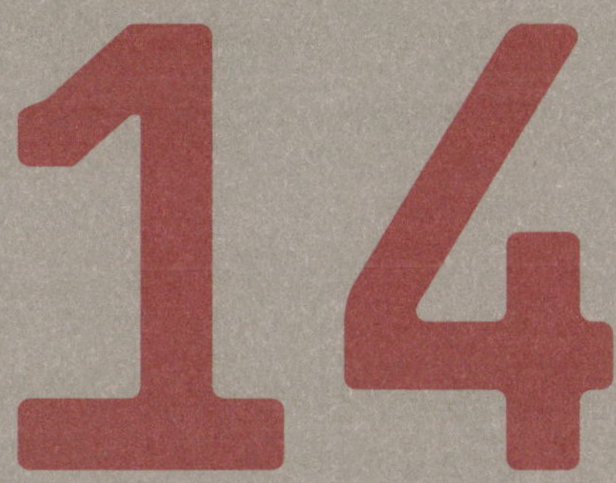

p.232

Woman who stole from farmer
(it is only truth that matters), 2009
archival paper, toner, EVA glue
77 x 79 x 59 cms

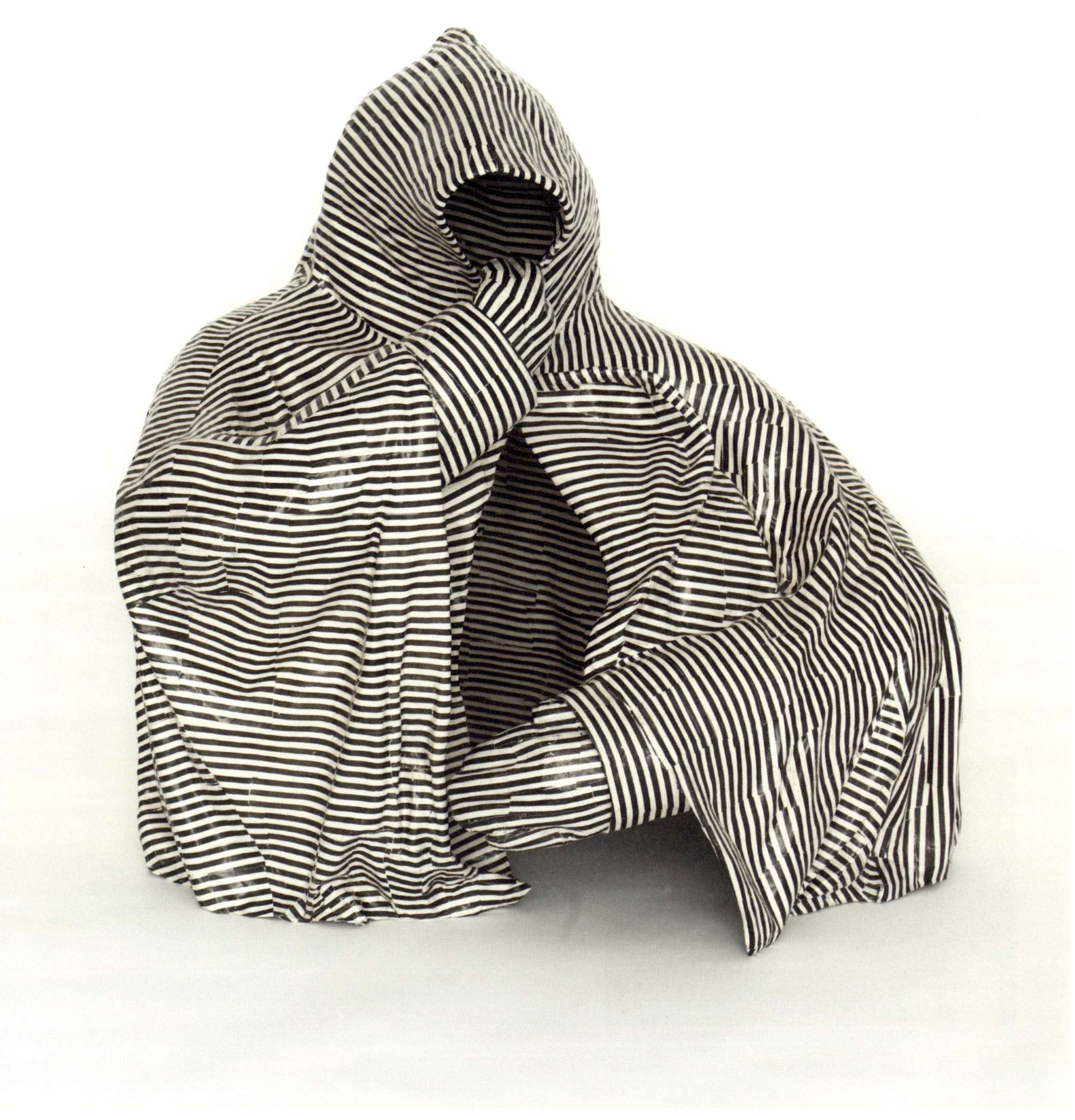

Journey to the Centre of the Blanchardstown Roundabout, 2003
duratrans photograph with solar powered turning mechanism, PVC, vinyl adhesive sticker, paint, video monitor, VHS video player
installation size: 225 x 125 cms, duration: 3 minutes

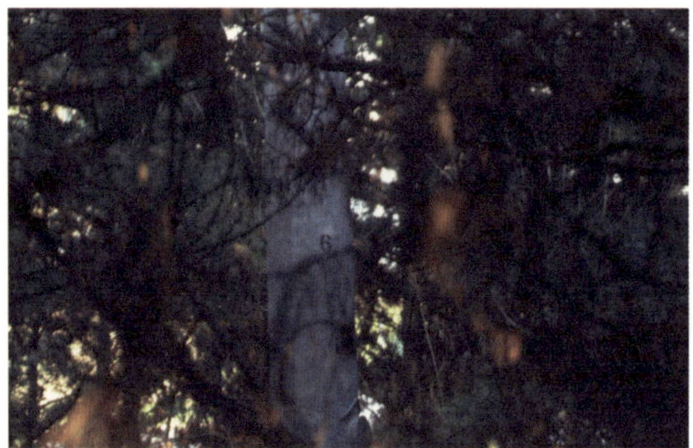

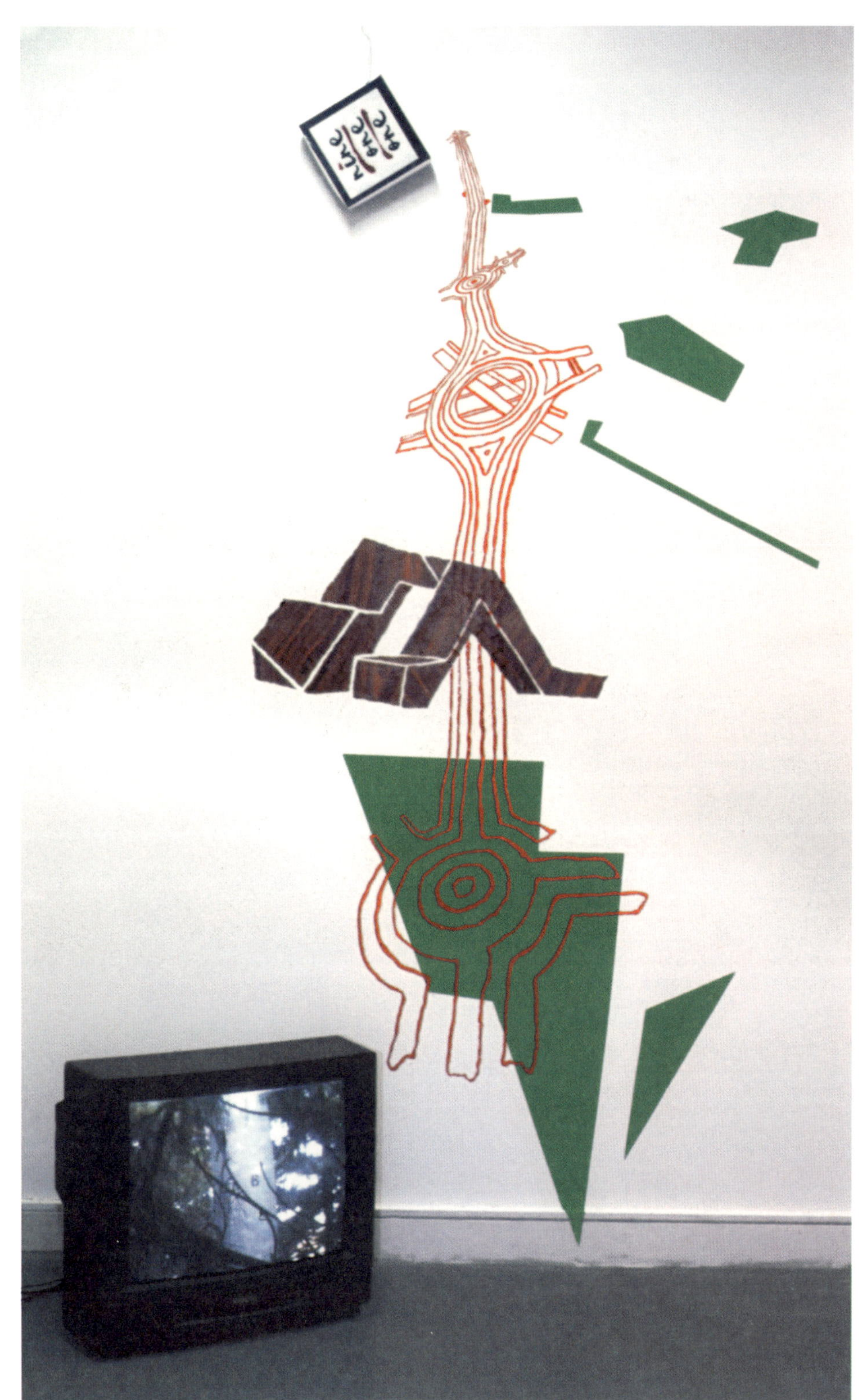

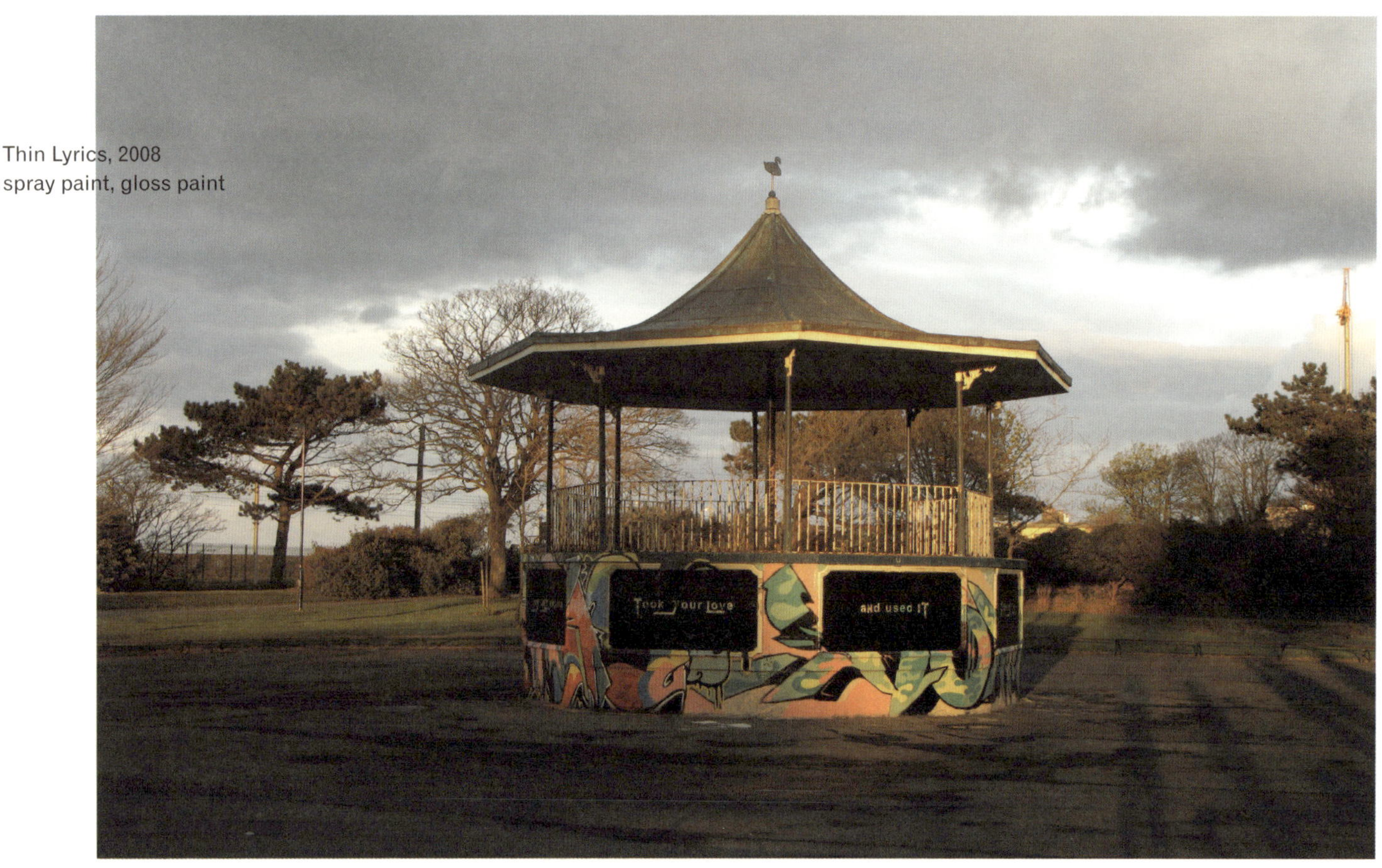


Thin Lyrics, 2008
spray paint, gloss paint

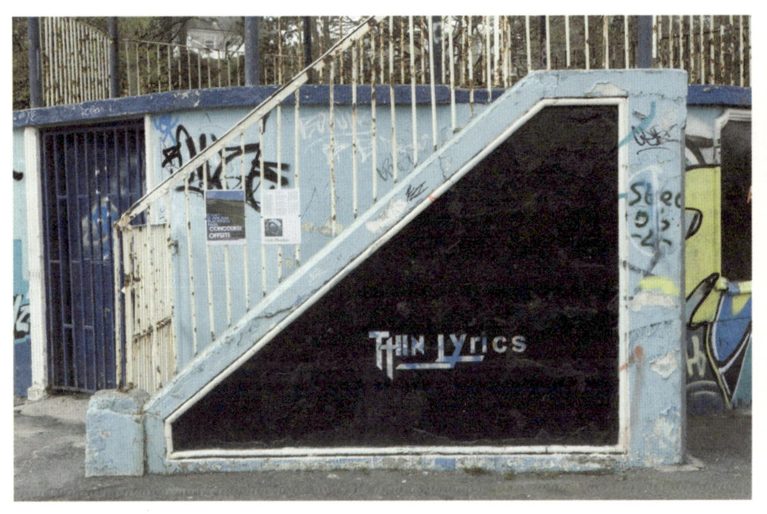
THIN LYrics

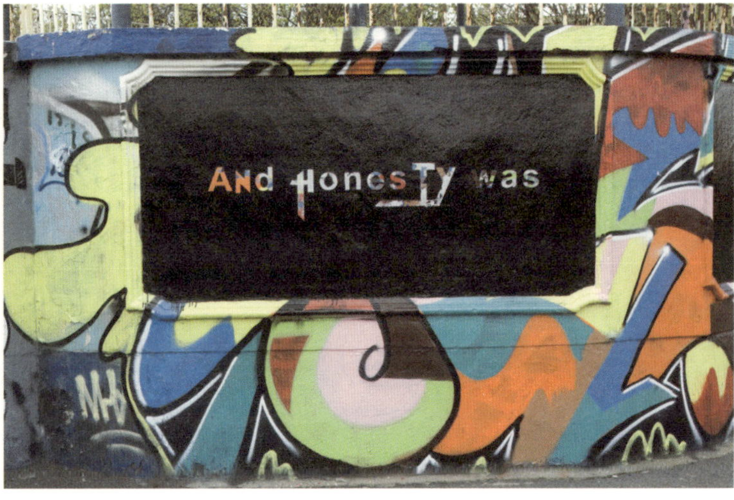
AND HonesTY was

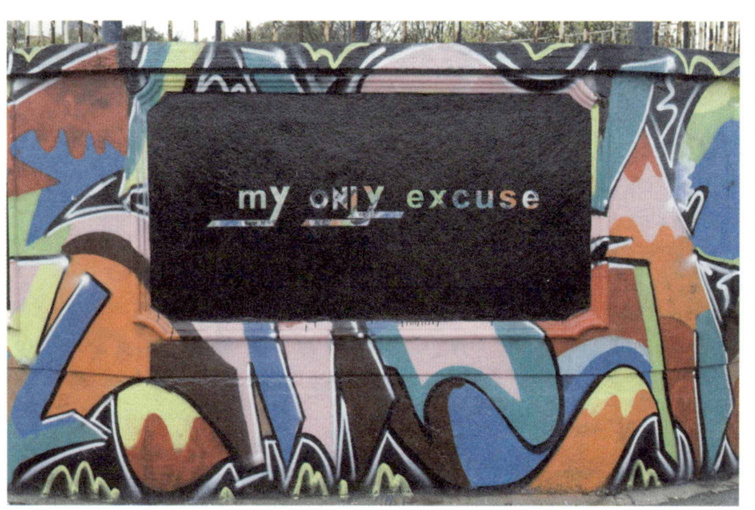
my ONLY excuse

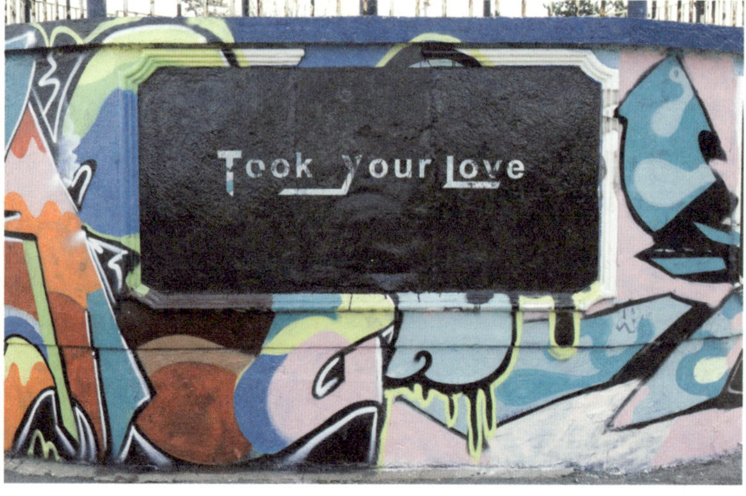
Took your Love

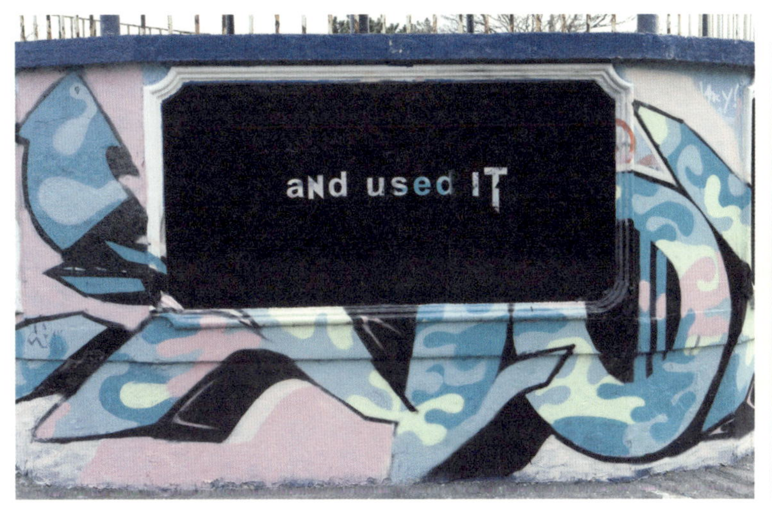
aNd used IT

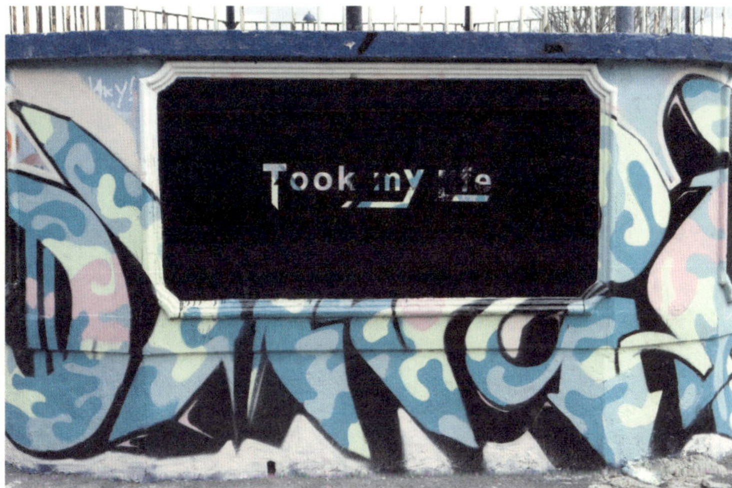
Took my

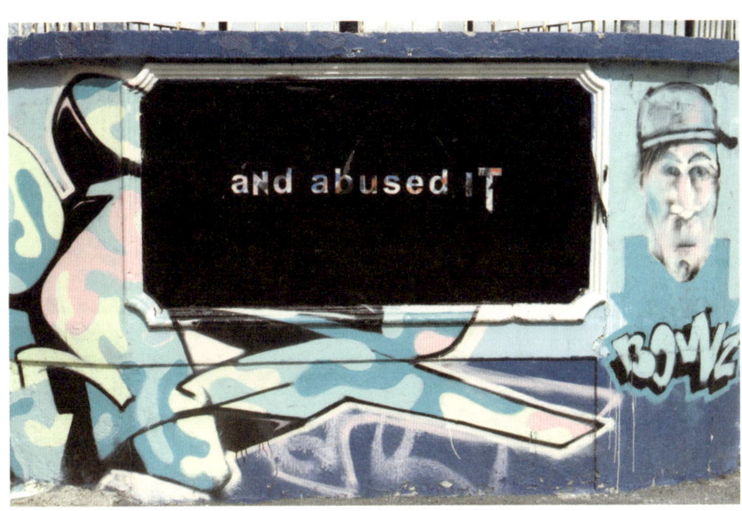
aNd abused IT

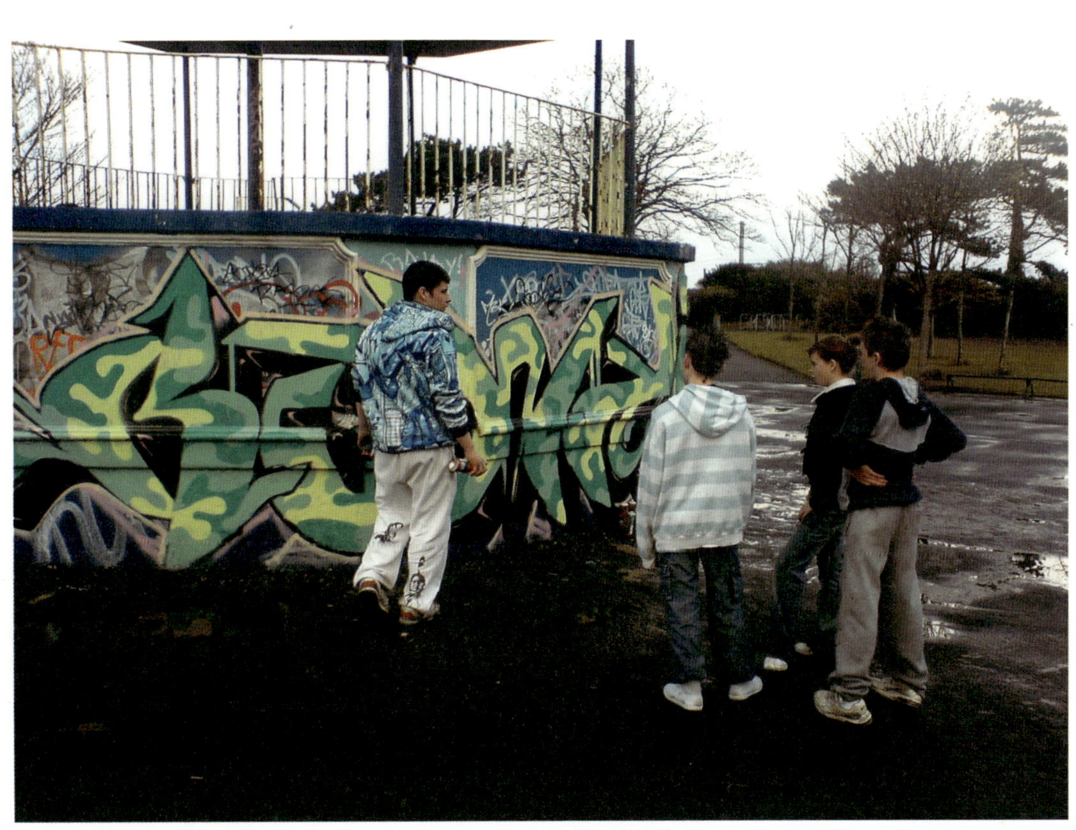

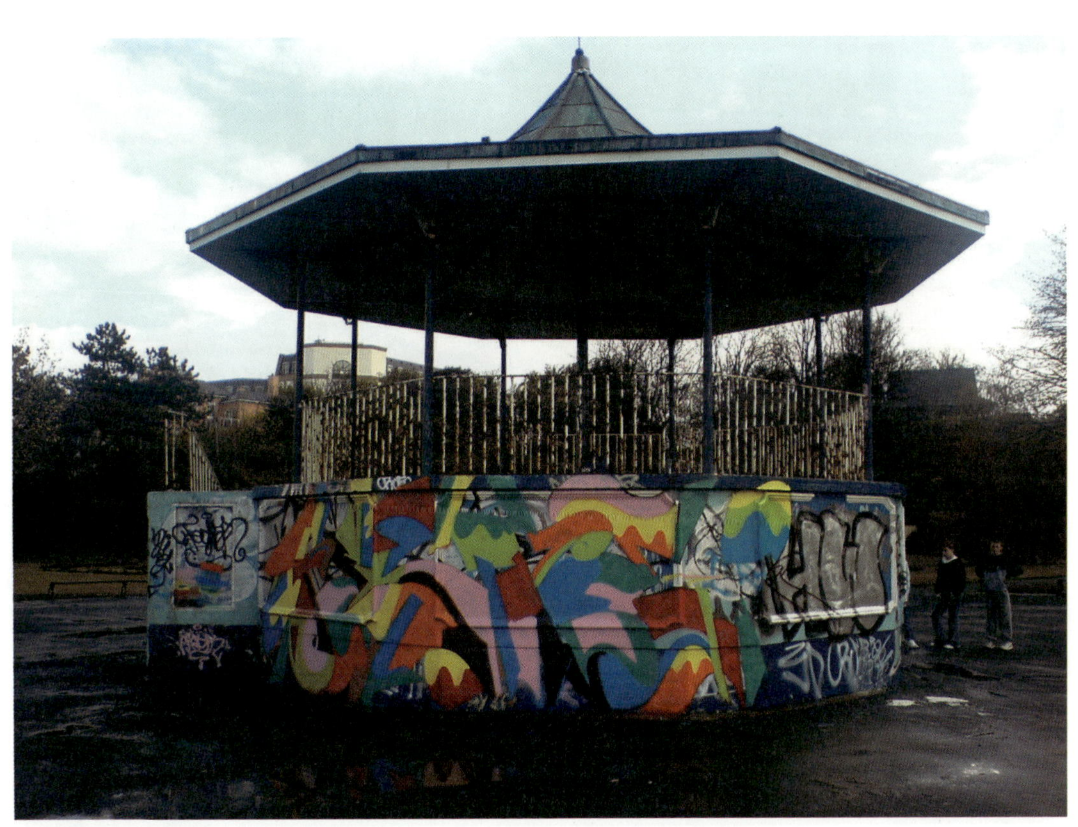

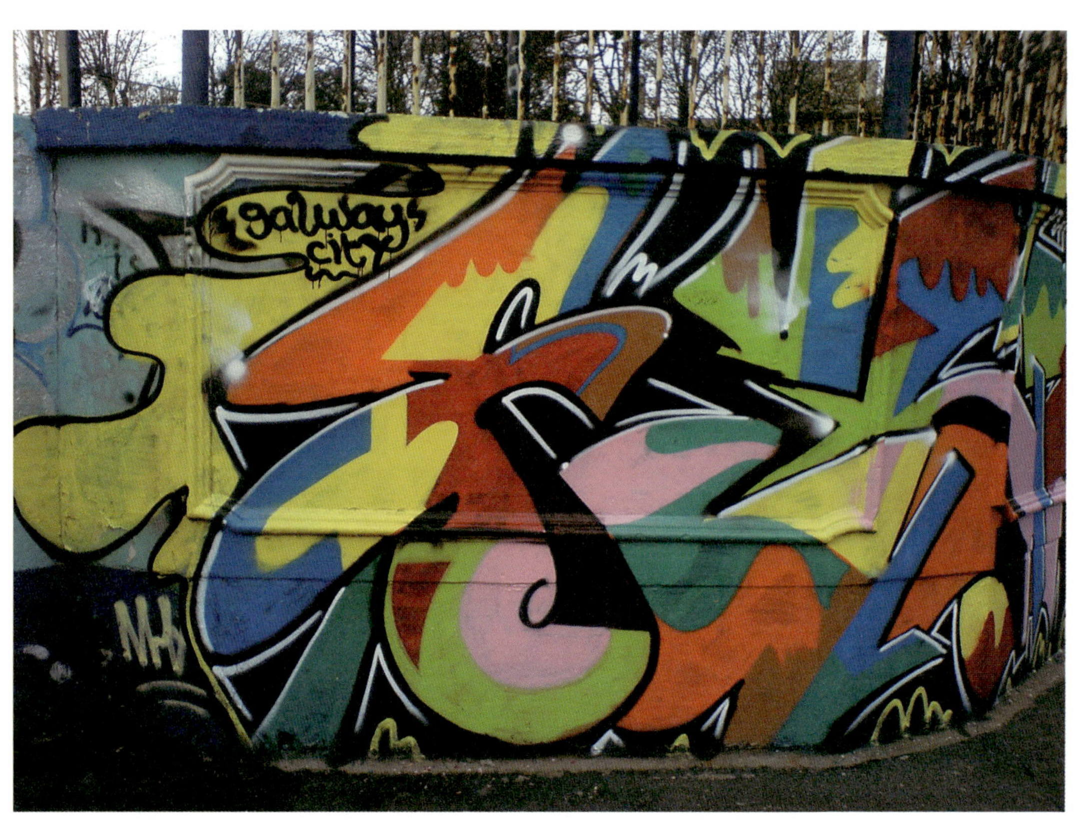
galways
city

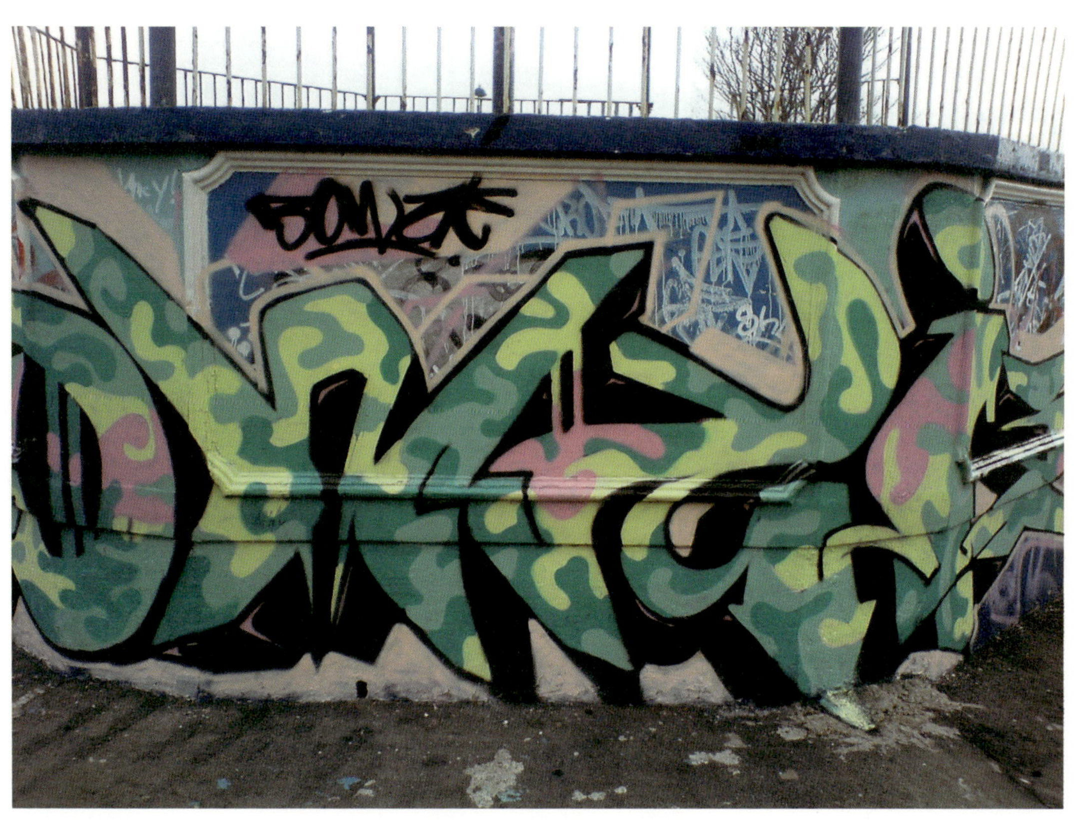

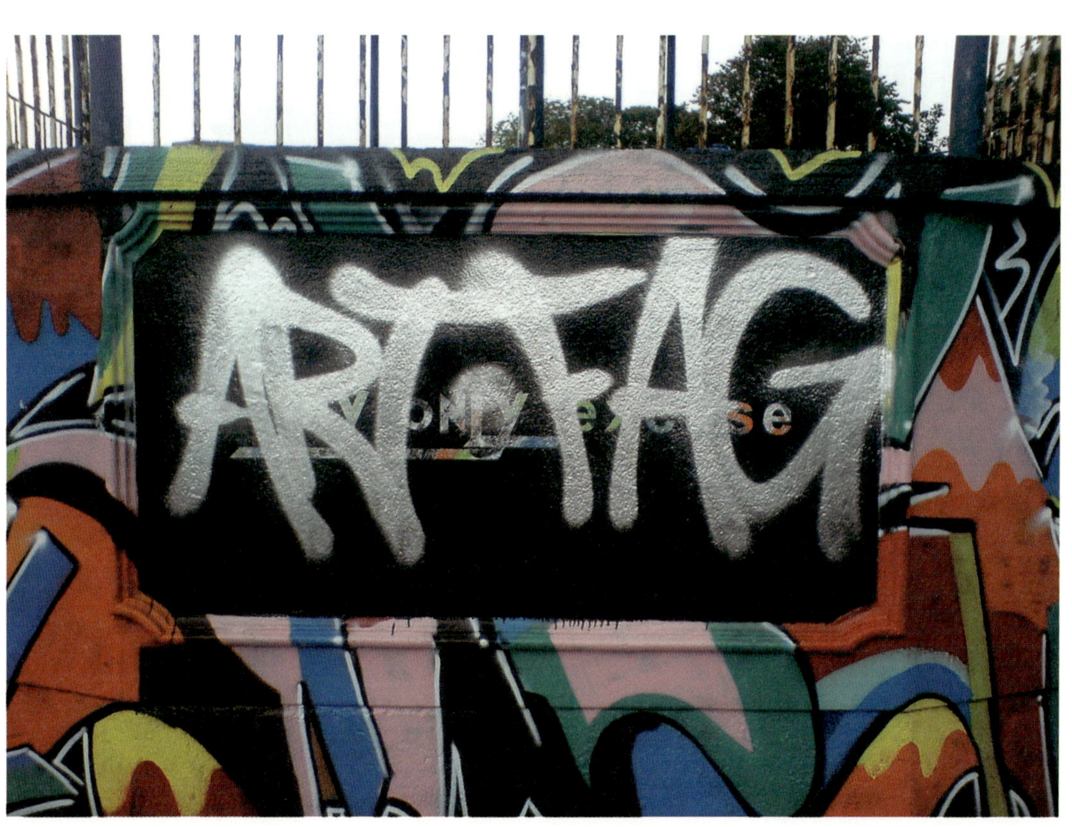
ARTFAG

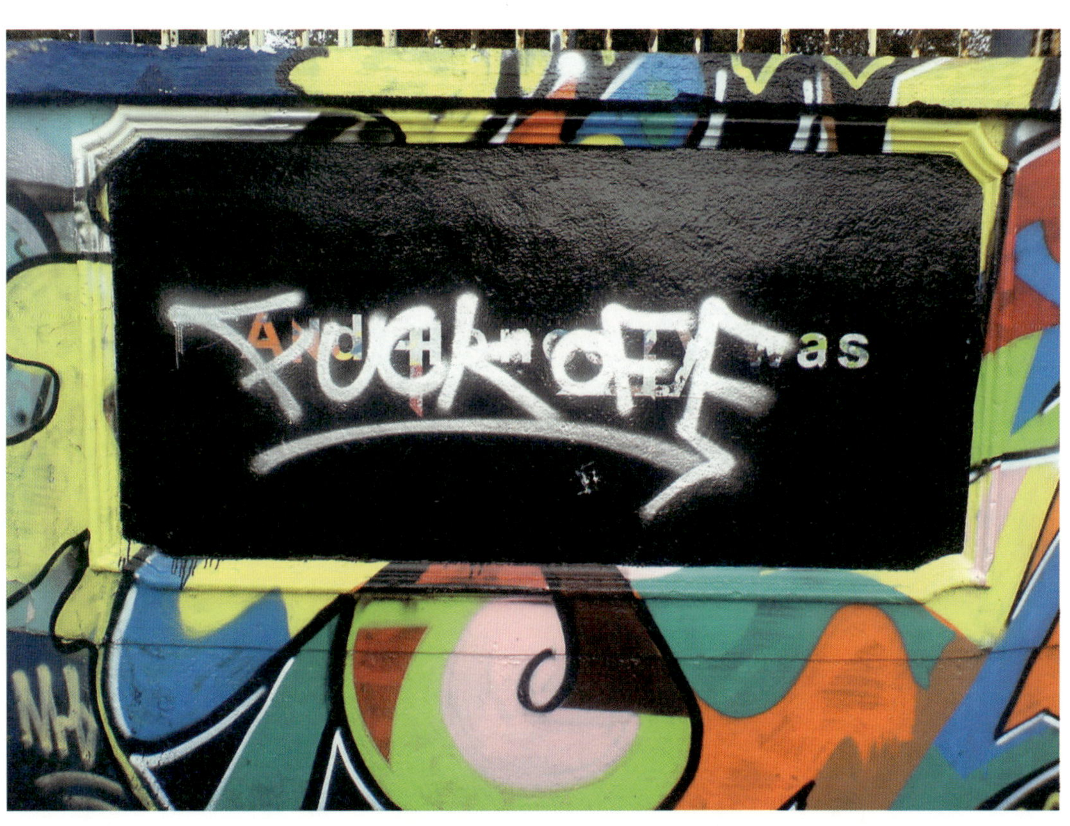
FUCK OFF
was

p.241

15

jouissance Seminar XX: Encore objet petit a
jouissance jouissance
Breaking the Waves? jouissance jouissance
reports jouissance
jouissance feminine without exception not
yet break out Ethics of Psychoanalysis
other completed all
incomplete feminine I am also
nothing higher than completion
not Encore violate/transgress its
prohibitions: simply to do what is allowed
obeying it thoroughly fulfil the subject
is actually 'in' (caught in the web of) power only and precisely in so far as
he does not fully identify with it but maintains a kind of distance towards it
his own partner Ransom
The Usual Suspects striking at himself
Moses and Monotheism? École freudienne de Paris
subject je ne sais quoi
object [agalma] agalma
une vraie femme Medea Beloved
Beloved Beloved kill
Sophie's Choice Sophie's Choice
not ethical modern
abstaining [Versagung] not
par excellence? suspends this exception of the
Thing sacrificing (also) the Thing itself out
of her very fidelity to them suspension
intersection masculine political
Antigone ate sine qua non
renounce the
for whom perverse happy
The Marriage of Figaro The Shawshank Redemption
hear I the light? hear the light
see the voice the Absolute appears
Figaro qua look as if we have seen a ghost

p.244

Bent, 2008
archival paper, toner, EVA glue, metal exhaust, balsa wood, cocktail sticks
65 x 95 x 140 cms

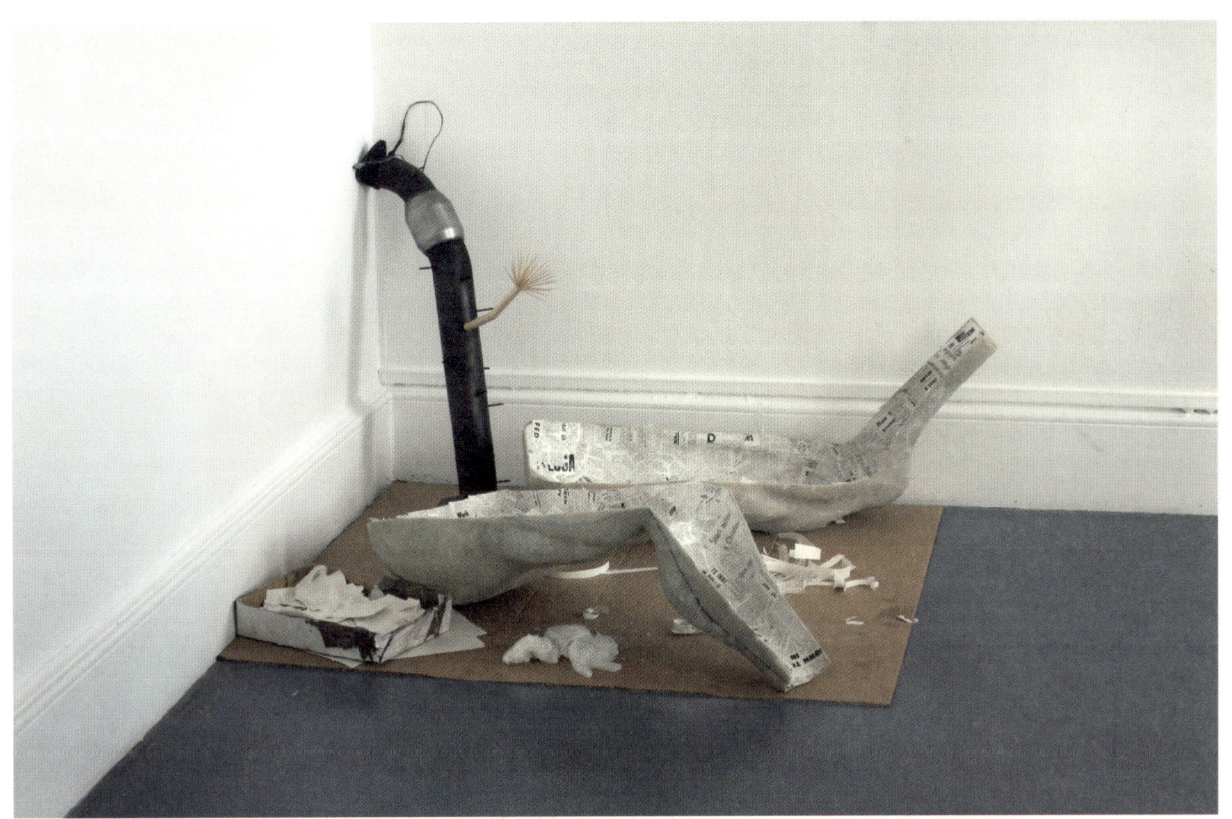

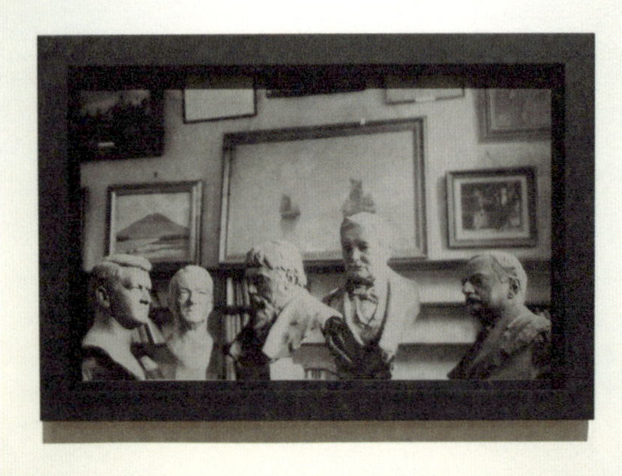

Information deficit blended-in as a tree, 2006
metal, wood, newspaper, PVA glue, balsa wood, cocktail sticks, polystyrene, clay, paint, varnish, polish, photograph
300 x 200 x 350 cms

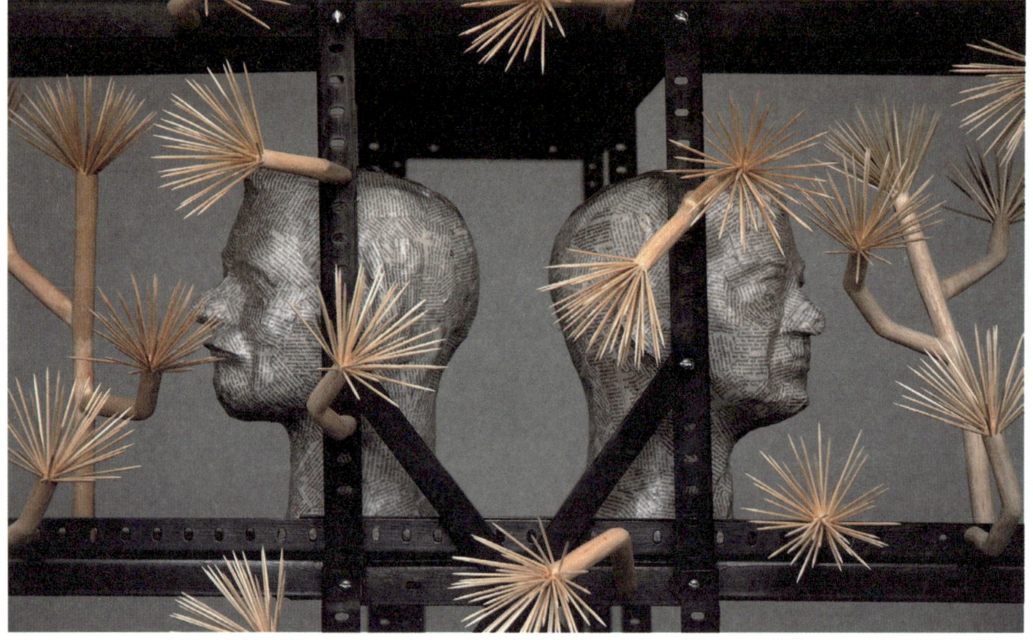

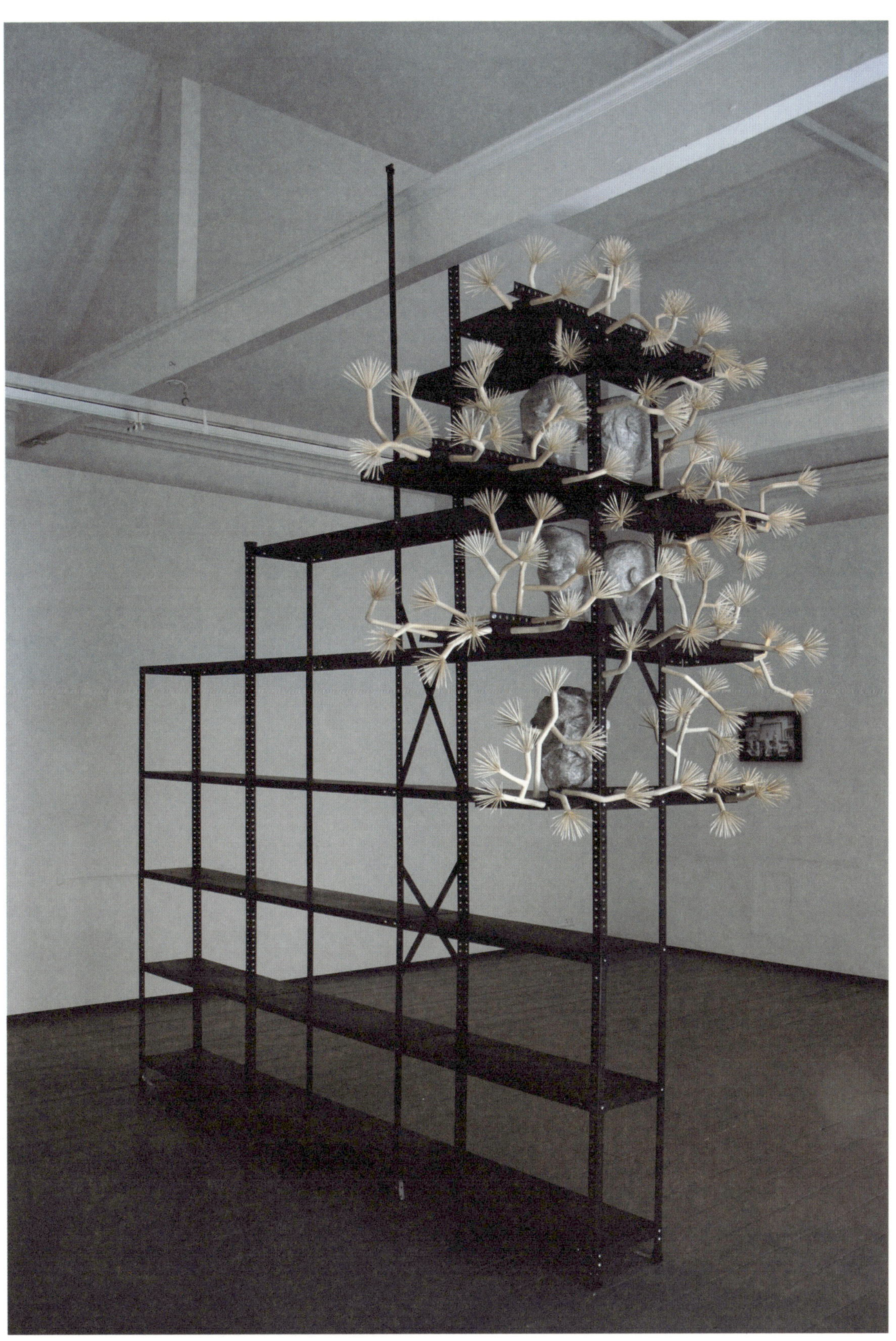

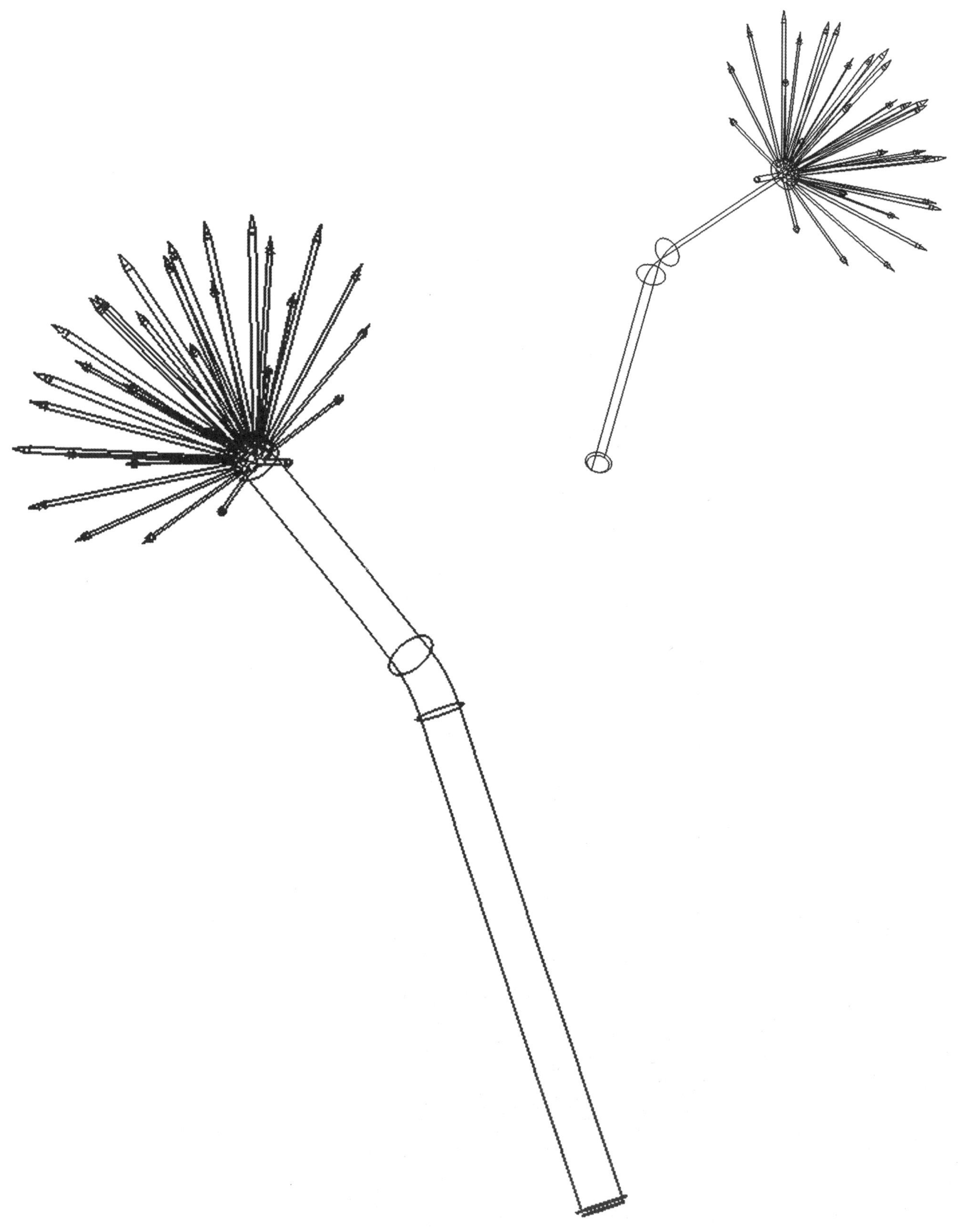

CAD design of twigs by Goran Krstić, 2006

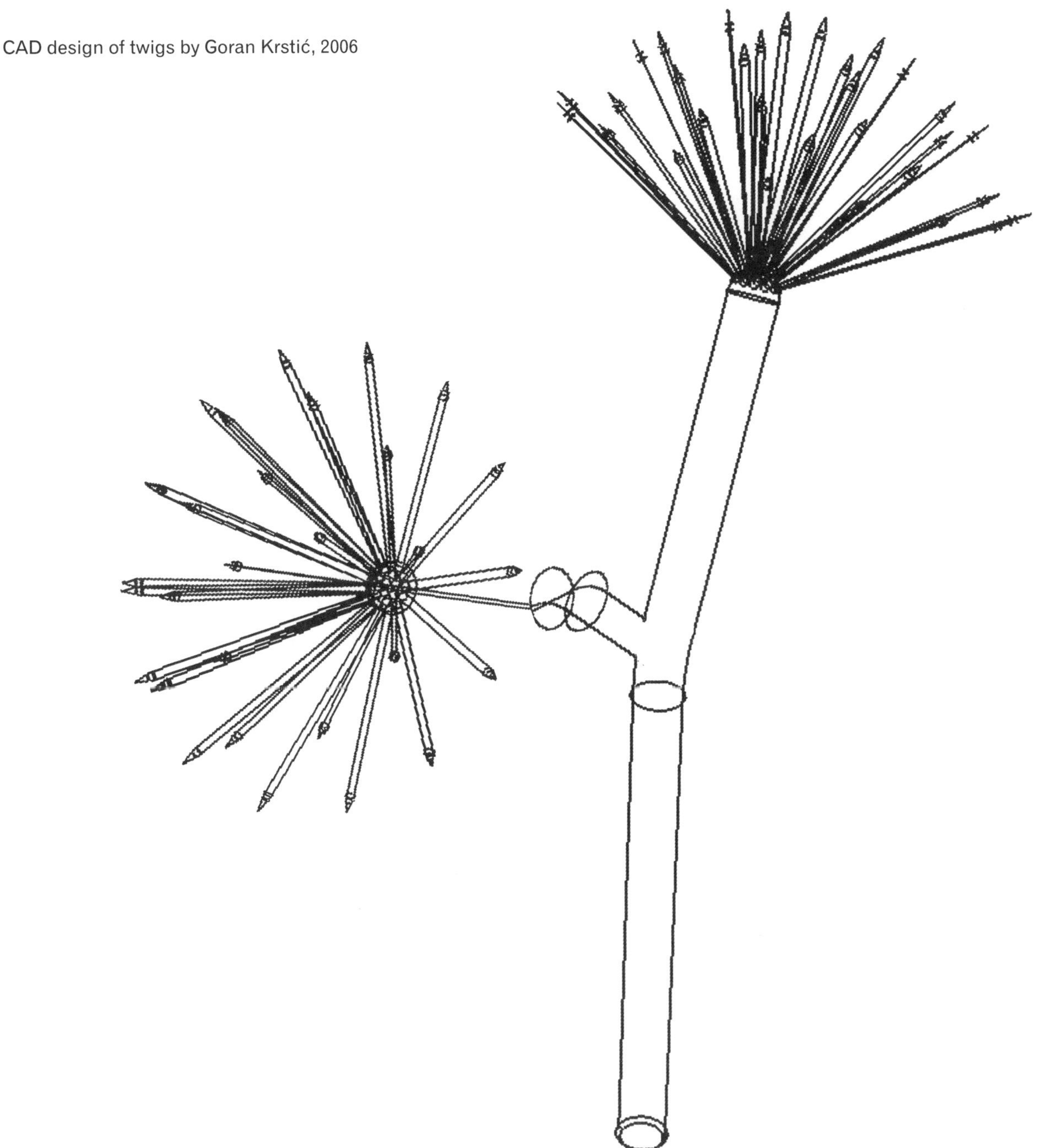

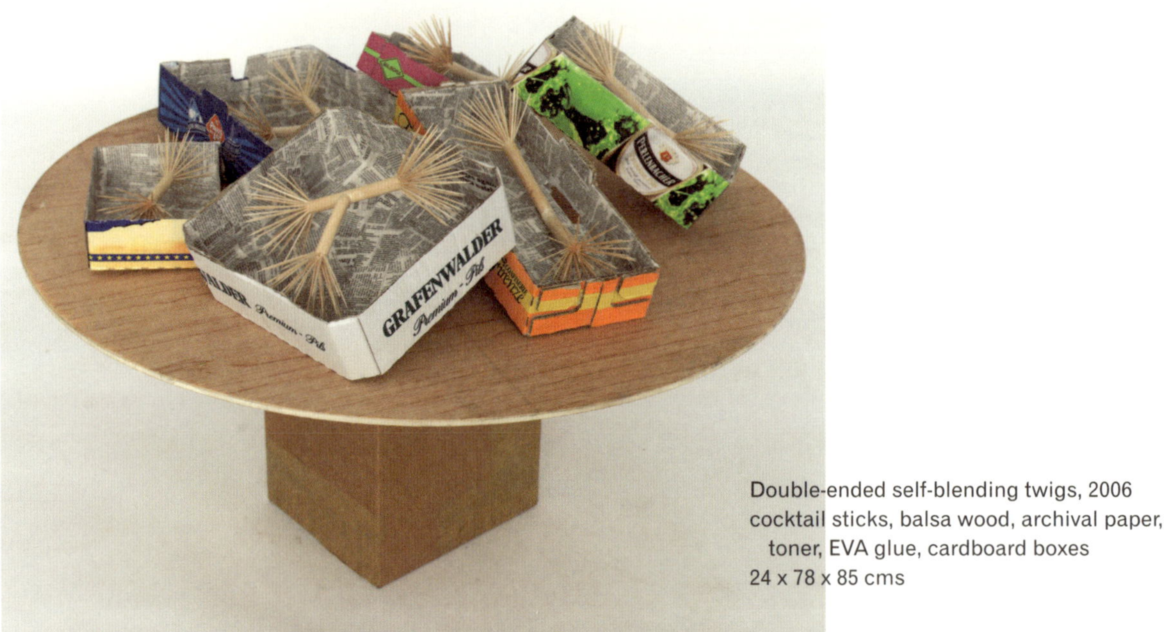


Double-ended self-blending twigs, 2006
cocktail sticks, balsa wood, archival paper, toner, EVA glue, cardboard boxes
24 x 78 x 85 cms

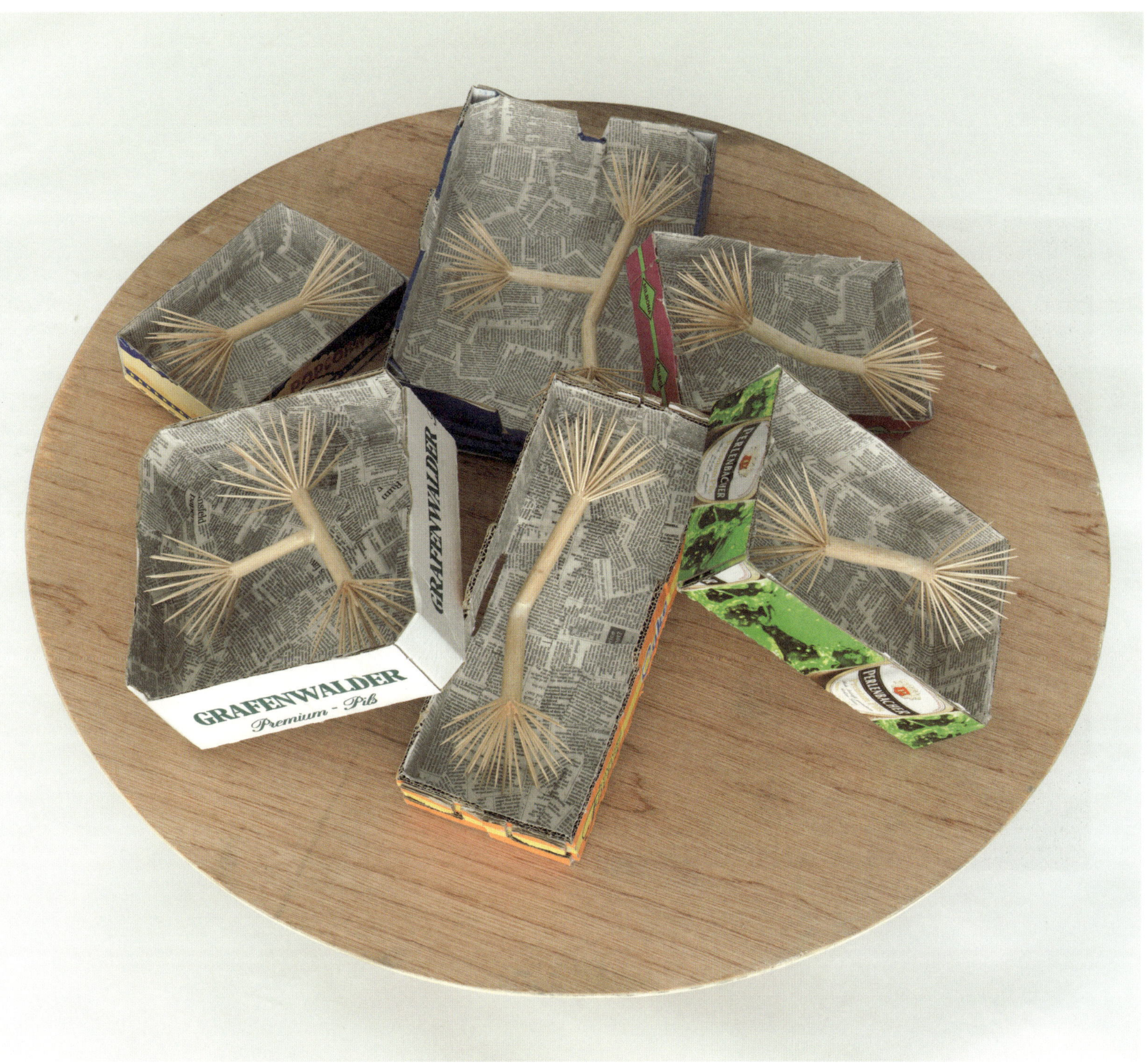
GRAFENWALDER
Premium - Pils
GRAFENWALDER

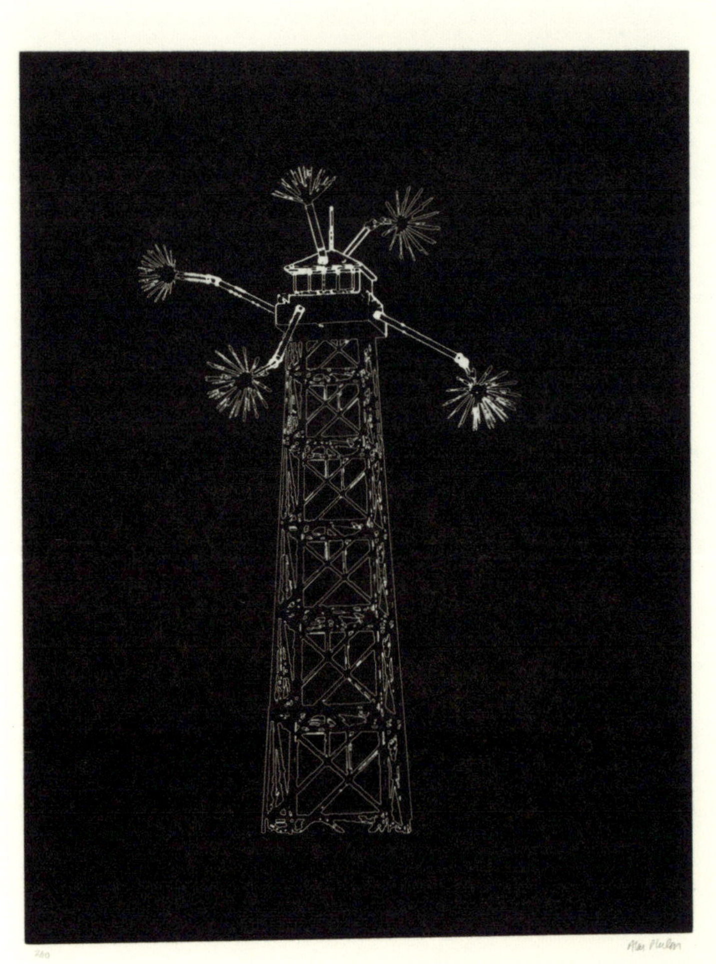

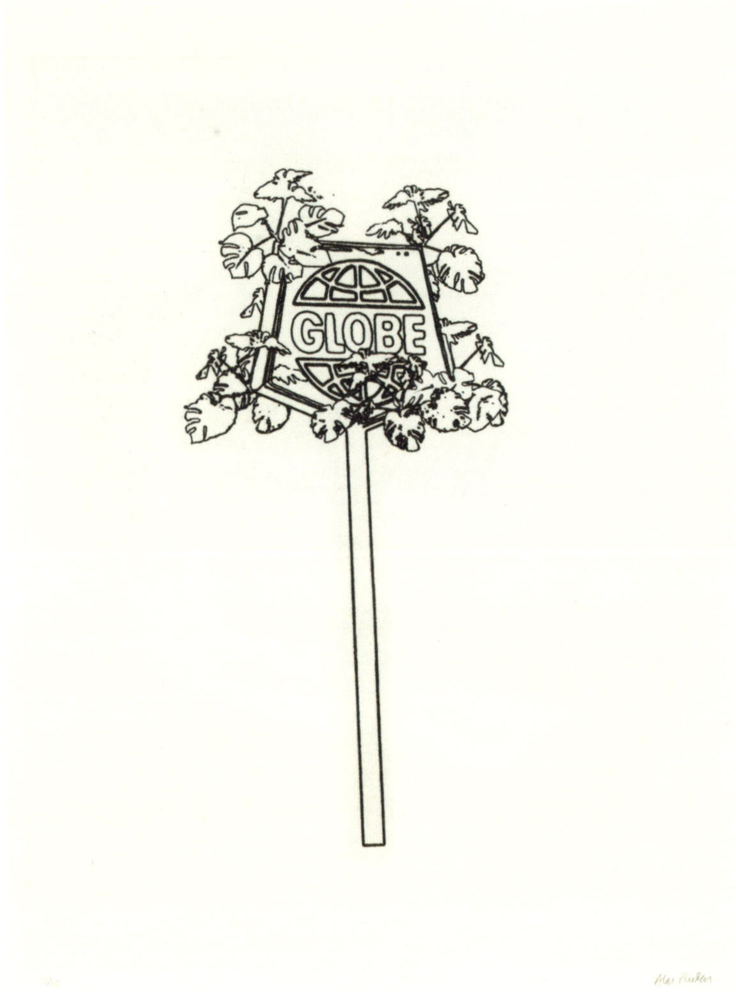


Blend-blend tower, 2006
intaglio print
63 x 50 cms

Blend-blend globe, 2006
intaglio print
63 x 50 cms

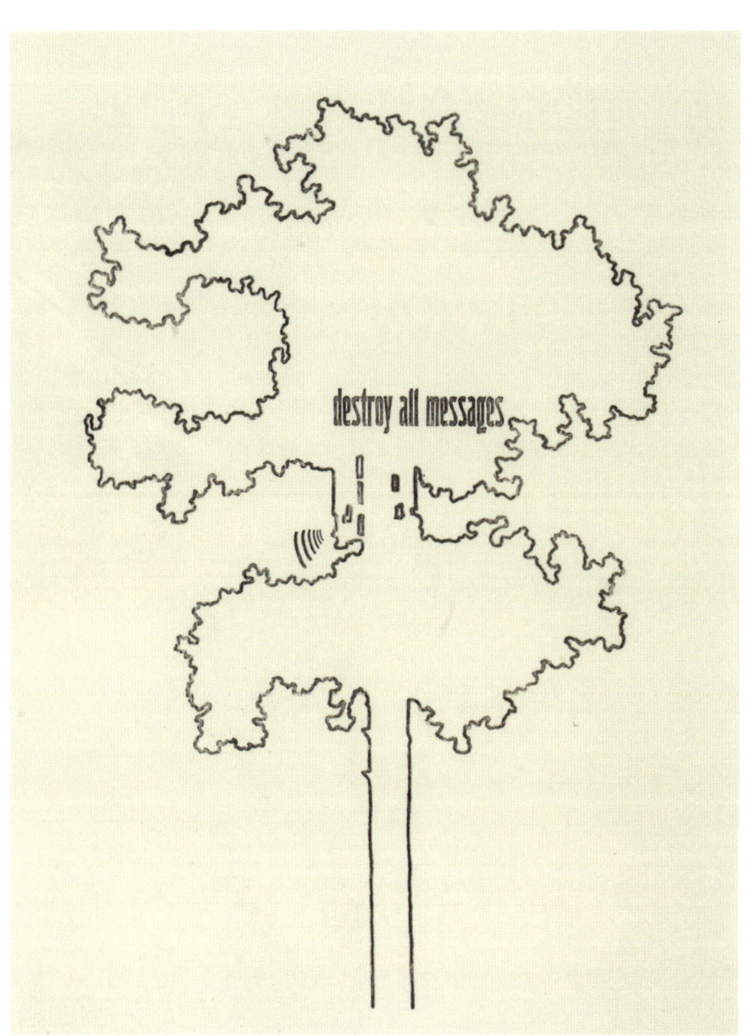


destroy all messages, 2006
toner on paper
70 x 50 cms

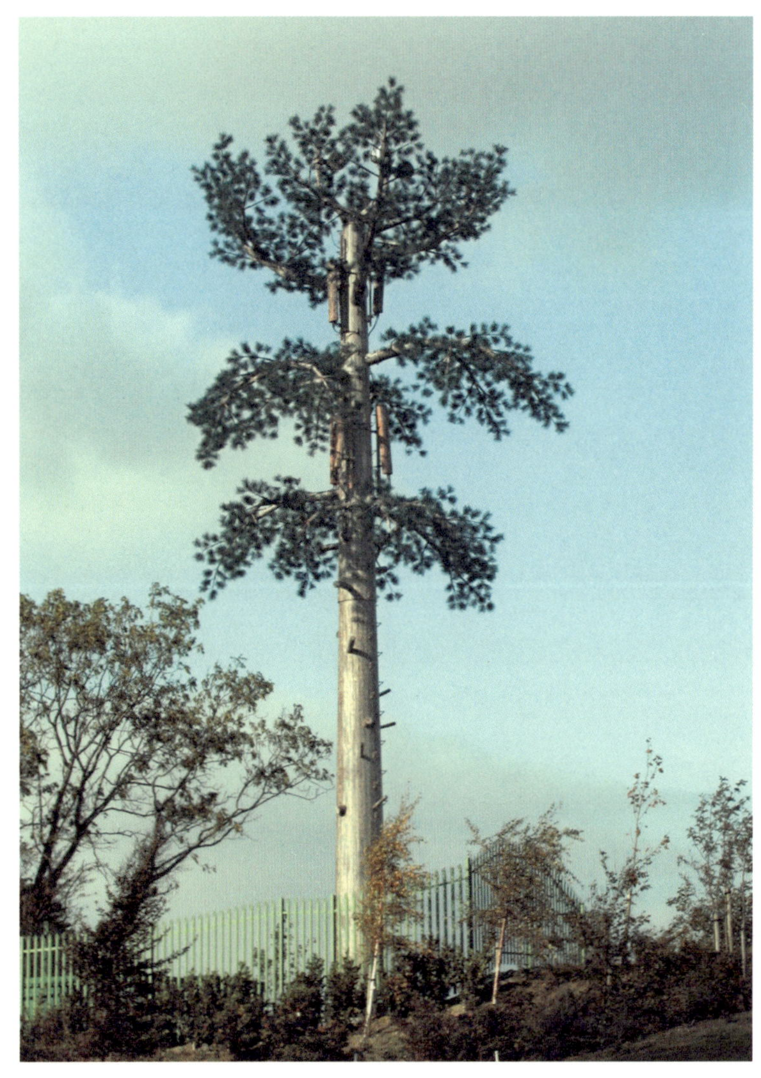

source image for Headline Drawing 1918, 2005

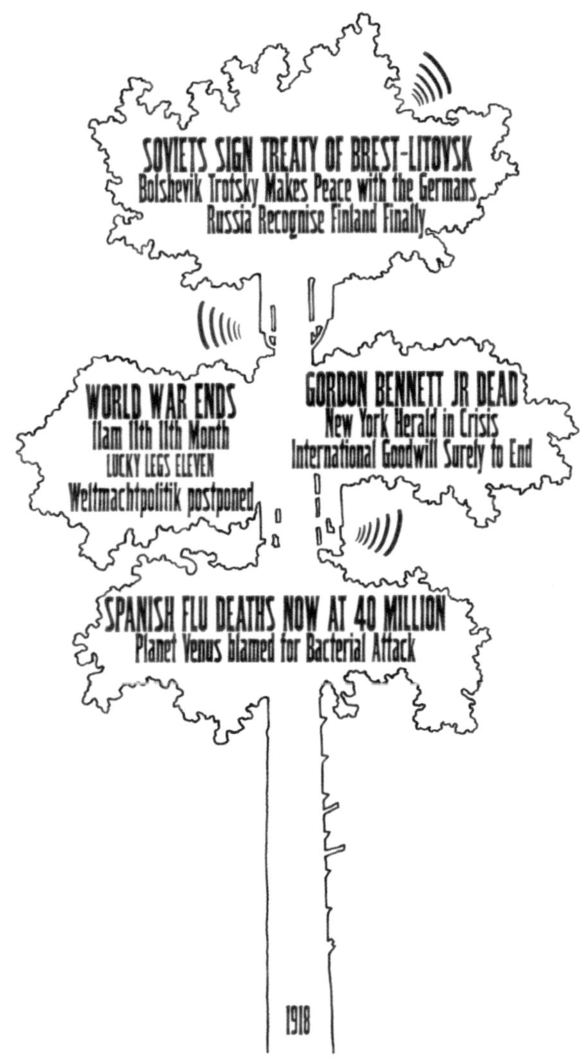


Headline Drawing 1918, 2005
archival inkjet on paper
29 x 21 cms

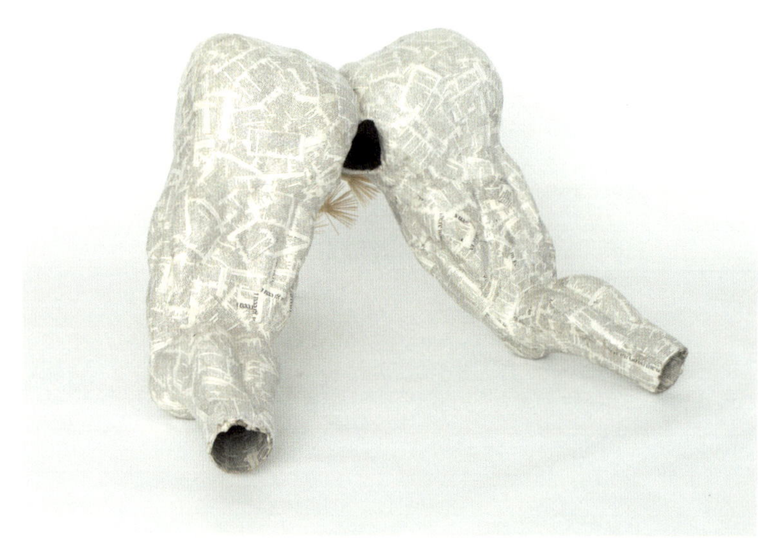

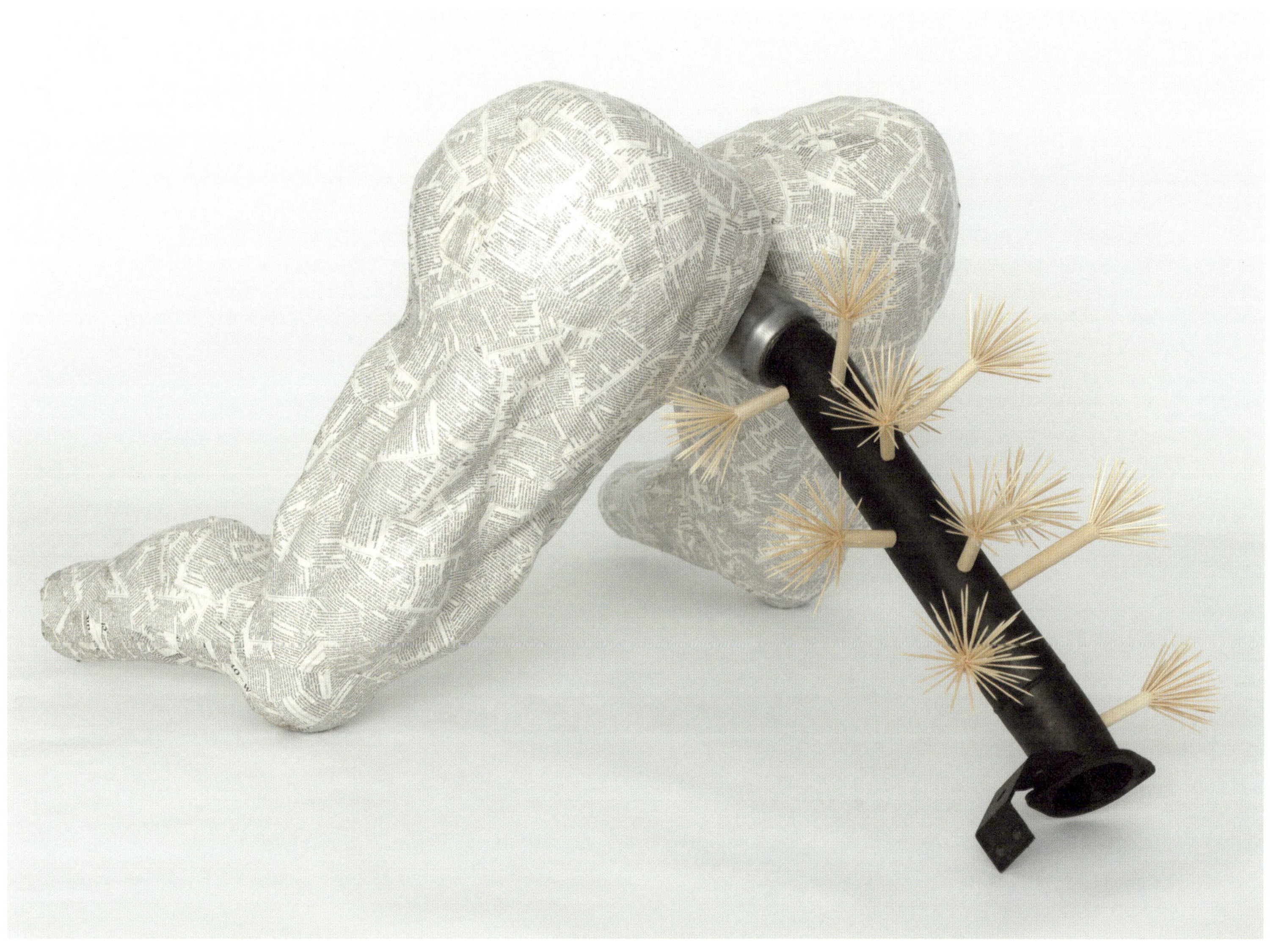

Bent (striking at himself), 2009
archival paper, toner, EVA glue,
metal exhaust, balsa wood,
cocktail sticks
65 x 95 x 140 cms
(papier-mâché made from articles
from the Ross O'Carroll-Kelly
column in the weekend Irish
Times)

/

# Alan Phelan

/

## Biography

/

**Born 1968, Dublin, Ireland**

1994 Rochester Institute of Technology, Rochester, New York, USA. Master of Fine Arts (Imaging Arts, Photography).

1989 Dublin City University, Glasnevin, Dublin. Bachelor of Arts (Communication Studies).

1996 George Eastman House, Rochester, New York. Certificate in Photographic Preservation and Archival Studies.

### Solo Exhibitions and Projects

2009 “Fragile Absolutes”, Irish Museum of Modern Art, Dublin; Limerick City Gallery of Art, Limerick; Chapter, Cardiff.
2007 “Ralph Eamon Odo Barbara”, mother's tankstation, Dublin.
2006 “Bio Bits”, The Lab, Dublin.
—— “Fading Fast” and “The Second Gordon Bennett Memorial Show & Shine - Modified Car Event”, Millennium Court Arts Centre, Portadown, Northern Ireland.
2005 “GB and the Western World”, Galway Arts Centre, Galway and Letterkenny Arts Centre, Donegal.
2004 “newtownwhowhatwhere?”, DCMNR broadband commission www.broadbandart.ie.
—— “Gordon-Bennett”, Grennan Mill, Kilkenny Arts Festival, Thomastown, Kilkenny.
2003-4 “newtownwhowhatwhere? archive”, Tulca Festival of Visual Arts”, Galway Arts Centre, Galway.
2001 “Three Stories”, South Dublin County Council and Artworking, “in context” public art project.
2000 “Enthalpic Everything”, Limerick City Gallery, Limerick.
—— “Enthalpic Pleasures”, Triskel, Cork.
1998 “Self-Rescue Mechanism”, Arthouse, Dublin, with Jim Dingilian.
1994 “Behind and Ahead”, SPAS Photo Gallery, RIT, Rochester, New York.
1993 “Egon and Ireland”, Gallery of Photography, Essex Street, Dublin.

### Selected Group Exhibitions and Projects

2009 “Reading the City”, EV+A curated by Angelika Nollert and Yilmaz Dziewior, Hunt Museum, Limerick, March.
2008 “Shuffle”, “I-Podism: Cultural Promiscuity in the Age of Consumption”, curated by George Bolster, Tulca, Galway.
—— “The Space In Between”, curated by Fiona Mulholland, Basement Gallery, Dundalk.
—— “Fifteen Fragile Absolutes”, The Process Room, part of the Artist's Residency Programme, IMMA, Dublin.
—— “Concourse Offsite”, curated by Claire Power and Carolyn Browne, DLR, Blackrock Park, Dublin
—— “Points of View – In Transition”, curated by Ciaran Bennett, Solstice Arts Centre, Navan.
2007 “The Art World”, Feinkost, Berlin.
—— “Platform II: Dis-[re]-place”, curated by Niamh Smyth, Knockbride House, Bailieborough, Co. Cavan.
—— “Oh show me your beauty when the witnesses have gone”, curated by Noel Kelly, ŠKUC, Ljubljana, Slovenia.
—— “Artist Exchange: process, practice and the audience, ResCen and Create”, Soho Theatre, London.
2006 “X-mas the spot”, curated by Nevan Lahart, Draiocht, Blanchardstown Shopping Centre, Dublin.
—— “Seconds: the imperfect artwork”, invited by Aileen Lambert, Wexford Arts Centre, Wexford.
—— “The Square Root of Drawing”, Temple Bar Gallery & Studios, Dublin.
—— “Fresh: reimagining the collection”, curated by Pippa Little, LCGA, Limerick and West Cork AC, Skibbereen.

—— "Mother's Ruin", curated by Finola Jones, mother's tankstation, Dublin.
—— "Test Pieces and Blend-in Moments", curated by Sandra Grozdanic, SKC Gallery, Belgrade, Serbia.
2005 "Fused", 'Gordon Bennett Sound Off', South Dublin County Hall, Dublin.
—— "Strata", curated by Ann Mulrooney and Tim Davis, Kells, Ireland and Pontrhydfendigaid, Wales.
2004 "Thinking of Ideas", Golden Thread Gallery, Belfast.
—— "Small: The Object in Film, Video and Slide Installation", Whitney Museum of American Art, New York.
—— "Country", curated by Noel Kelly, Equrna Gallery, Ljubjana, Slovenia.
—— "Imagine Limerick", EV+A, curated by Zdenka Badovinac, Limerick City Gallery, Limerick.
2003 "Appendiks 1", Thiemers magasin, Copenhagen, Denmark.
—— "Painting without Numbers", Cluain Mhuire, Galway Arts Festival, Galway.
—— "The National Gallery", The Return, Goethe Institut Inter Nationes, Dublin.
—— "Affinity Archive", The Metropolitan Complex, Broadstone Studios, Dublin.
—— "Permaculture", curated by Grant Watson and Vaari Claffey, Project, Dublin.
2002 "Crawford Open 3", Crawford Municipal Art Gallery, Cork.
—— "Perspective 2002", Ormeau Baths Gallery, Belfast.
—— "Love 2 Love", Catalyst Arts, Belfast.
—— "Fabulations of Form", curated by Sarah Pierce, Arthouse, Dublin.
2001 "Intermedia", Triskel, Anglesey Street Garda Station, Cork.
2000 "Absolutonic", Sculptors' Society of Ireland, Dublin.
1999 "Freeze II", curated by Anya von Gösseln, Arthouse, Dublin.
—— "Sculpture in Context", Irish Management Institute, Dublin.
—— "Office for Contemporary Art", Paul Kane Gallery, Dublin.
1998 "EV+A", juror Paul O'Reilly, Gaeltacht Cleaners, O'Connell St., Limerick.
—— "Art/Exchange Fair", New York, USA.
—— "Excellent Dynamite", Pallas Studios, Foley Street, Dublin.
1997 "Quadrant '97", curated by Caomhín Mac Giolla Léith, Belltable Arts Centre, Limerick.
—— "SSI/Ireland and Europe: International Visual Art Event", Iveagh Gardens, Dublin.
1996 "Artist Garden Project", Highland Park, Rochester, New York, USA.
1995 "Alternatives '95: Zenophobia", jurors Doug Ischar and Kaucylia Brooke, Ohio University, USA.
—— "Alien Artists II", Attleboro Museum, Attleboro, Massachusetts, USA.
—— "Fragile Landscapes", Centre for Photography at Woodstock, New York, USA.
—— "Signal", Bug Jar, Rochester, New York, USA.
1994 "Small World-Small Works", Galerie + Edition CAOC, Berlin, Germany.
—— "EV+A", curated by Jan Hoet, Limerick City Gallery, Limerick.

Curated Projects

2007 "inter-changes", Farmleigh Gallery, Phoenix Park, Dublin and Highlanes Gallery, Drogheda.
—— "Pilot:3 - live archive for artists and curators", Venice Biennale, collateral event.
2005 "Another Monumental Metaphor", Printed Project, issue 5, editor/curator (launched at the 51st Venice Biennale).
—— "Felons", Royal Hibernian Academy, Dublin (artist-curated project).
2004 "No Respect", Dublin, public art exhibition co-curated with Jane Speller, various locations Dublin city.
2001 "Stand Fast Dick and Jane", Project, Dublin. Co-curated with Tom Keogh.
1995 "Project X: Boundaries", Pyramid Arts Centre, Village Gate Square and the Mall at Greece Ridge Center, Rochester, New York, USA. Co-curated with Alex Miokovic.

## Awards

2008–09 The Arts Council, Visual Arts Bursary (multi-annual).
2007 The Arts Council, Visual Arts Bursary.
Short-listed for the AIB Art Prize.
2006 The Arts Council, Visual Arts Bursary.
2004–05 The Arts Council, Travel Award.
The Arts Council, Commissions Scheme (2005).
2003 The Arts Council, Projects Scheme (2004).
The Arts Council, Exhibitions Assistance Scheme, No Respect .
2001 The Arts Council, Publications Grant.
1998 The Arts Council, Visual Arts Bursary.
1995 Arts for Greater Rochester, Special Opportunity Stipend.
1991–94 Fulbright Scholarship.
RIT Graduate Scholarships and Assistantships, awarded quarterly.
1993 RIT Graduate Scholarship for "Best Show" of Winter Quarter Review.
1992 The Arts Council, Post-Graduate Scholarship.
1991–01 The Arts Council/Aer Lingus Art Flights.
1991 John F. Kennedy Fund Graduate Scholarship.

## Residencies

2007–08 Artist Residency Programme, Irish Museum of Modern Art, Dublin.
2006 Belgrade Residency, organised by Sandra Grozdanic, funded by Culture Ireland.
2002–05 The Fire Station Artists' Studios, Residential Studio.
1997–98 Artist in Residence, Arthouse, Dublin.

## Catalogues

2008 "Points of View – In Transition", essay by Ciaran Bennett. Solstice Arts Centre
2007 "Mother's Annual", essay by Chris Fite-Wassilak. mother's tankstation
2006 "Fresh: reimagining the collection". LCGA
2006 "Mother's Annual", essays by Sarah Pierce and Alan Phelan. mother's tankstation
2005 "Bio", with texts by David Godbold, Jeanette Doyle, Cherry Smyth, Gemma Tipton, Mick Wilson, Sarah Pierce, Henriette Huldisch, Nataša Petrešin, Enda Leaney, Maria Fusco and Ciarán Bennett. Tulca/GAC/MCAC/APN
2005 "Felons", catalogue with texts by Alan Phelan, Michel Peillon and Pelin Tan. RHA
2004 "No Respect", essay by Cherry Smyth, catalogue brochure. No Respect
2004 "EV+A 2004 - Imagine Limerick", 'Imagine Curating', LCGA
2003 "Crawford Open 1-4", CMGA
2002 "Enthalpic Whatever", essays by Ciarán Bennett and Lucie Foley. R4 Publishing
2002 "In Context", SDCC and Artworking. Essay by Mick Wilson. SDCC
2001 "Stand Fast Dick & Jane", introduction essay, text by Nayland Blake. OutArt

Reviews/Articles

| | |
|---|---|
| June, 2008 | "Park Life", Sarah Searson. VAI News Sheet |
| May 10, 2008 | "Art in the Park", Gemma Tipton. Irish Times |
| Spring, 2008 | "Ralph Eamon Barbara Odo", Charlotte Bonham-Carter. Circa Art Magazine |
| March, 2007 | "Driving Yugo to Dublin", Dejan Novacic. Evropa (Serbia) |
| Sept 23, 2006 | "Boy racer art theme", Jenny Lee. The Irish News |
| Sept 22, 2006 | "Fading Fast...", The Ticket, Aidan Dunne. The Irish Times |
| Spring, 2006 | "GB and the Western World, Galway", Gavin Murphy. Circa Art Magazine |
| July 27, 2005 | Motor News, "A gleam in a modified eye", Kieran Fagan. The Irish Times |
| Spring, 2005 | "Belfast: Thinking of Ideas at Golden Thread Gallery", om lekha. Circa Art Magazine |
| Winter, 2004 | "Dublin: Marking the Underpass at the Vaults", Aaron Lister. Circa Art Magazine |
| Aug 12, 2004 | "The art of the possible", Aidan Dunne. The Irish Times |
| Summer, 2004 | "Limerick: EV+A", Ciara Finnegan. Circa Art Magazine |
| June, 2004 | "EV+A 2004", Niamh Ann Kelly. Art Monthly |
| Feb 23, 2003 | "Pressed for Space", Medb Ruane. The Sunday Times |
| July 15, 2001 | "Outer Limits", Medb Ruane. The Sunday Times |
| Winter, 2001 | "Cork", review. Circa Art Magazine |
| May 30, 2001 | "Alan Phelan, Three Stories", Mark Ewart. The Irish Times |
| Sept/Oct, 2000 | "Enthalpic Everything", Jason Oakley. SSI Newsletter |
| Winter, 1998 | "EV+A" review, Annie Fletcher. Circa Art Magazine |
| March 20, 98 | "Jim Dingilian and Alan Phelan, Arthouse", Luke Clancy. The Irish Times |
| April 6, 1995 | "Scenes from a Mall", review of "Project X - Boundaries", Elizabeth Forbes. D & C, Rochester, NY |
| Nov 13, 1993 | "A Pleasure to Behold", Joseph Masheck. The Irish Times |

Writing and Publications

| | |
|---|---|
| 2008 | "Knowing that audience is not enough", essay. Ground Up |
| 2008 | "PILOT: third edition of critical questions. PILOT |
| Spring, 2008 | "The Case of the Midwife Toad... Conor McFeely", review. Circa Art Magazine |
| 2007 | "No Borders Just News", catalogue essays on Nina Canell and Brendan Earley. AICA |
| Winter, 2007 | "Artist-writers, writer-artists: An anonymous vox pop". Circa Art Magazine |
| 2007-08 | "Info-Pool", I'm Thinking of Getting a Studio", and additional text for "Art Handling". VAI website |
| 2007 | "Vuumph Orality", catalogue essay on Vanessa O'Reilly. Pallas Heights PCP |
| 2007 | "Vanessa O'Reilly", "PILOT:3", short text and selection. PILOT |
| April, 2007 | "A Network is Born", feature. VAI News Sheet |
| 2006 | "Mother's Annual", texts on Petri Ala-Maunus, 'Mother's Ruin' and Ciarán Murphy. mother's tankstation |
| Spring, 2006 | "Confident but Self-Questioning - Scotland", feature. Circa Art Magazine |
| Autumn, 2005 | "Exhibiting in Dublin - Closed Shop, Open Door or Back Alley?", feature. Circa Art Magazine |

p.263

| | |
|---|---|
| 2005 | "Passive Subversion", catalogue essay on Tom Molloy. Rubicon Gallery |
| 2005 | "Jingoism in the Decoy of Collecting", catalogue essay on Abigail O'Brien. George Moore Society |
| Summer, 2005 | "Models of Resistance Report", review. Contexts |
| 2005 | "Noel Bowler", review. Source |
| 2005 | "Printed Project", issue 5, guest editor/curator Venice Biennale issue. Printed Project |
| 2005 | "Top Biennale Themes", Eriteema: biennaalid. Kunst.ee |
| Spring, 2005 | "Silent Commitment", article. Contexts |
| 2004 | "Place and Non-Place", edited by Michel Peillon and Mary Corcoran, ill. p.183. IPA |
| Spring, 2004 | "Fabien Verschaere", review. Circa |
| 2003-2006 | "Column", issues 1-11, 13-21. VAI News Sheet |
| Sept, 2003 | "Blind Lip Sync", Venice Biennale review. Printed Project |
| Autumn, 2003 | "Dan Shipsides", review. Circa |
| May/June, 2003 | "Architecture Schmarchitecture", review. SSI Newsletter |
| Feb, 2003 | "The Metropolitan Complex, Roundtable Discussion", conversation. The Metropolitan Complex |
| March, 2003 | "Process", article. SSI Newsletter |
| Autumn, 2002 | "Caroline McCarthy, AIB Prize Exhibition", review. Circa Art Magazine |
| Winter, 2000 | "NSF 'Public Art - Making it Work' Conference", review. Circa Art Magazine |
| Winter, 2000 | "Dublin 1", review. Circa Art Magazine |
| June, 2000 | "Things We Do", catalogue editor. OutArt |
| Spring, 2000 | "Cologne", Germany, review. Circa Art Magazine |
| Autumn, 1999 | "SMAK, The Opening", Ghent, Belgium, review. Circa Art Magazine |
| 1998 | "A Long Player of Many Parts", catalogue essay on Mike Fitzpatrick. Galway Arts Centre |
| Autumn, 1997 | "Skulptur Projekte in Munster", Germany, review. Circa Art Magazine |
| Sept/Oct, 1997 | "Tomorrow is only a day away", interview with Liam Gillick. SSI Newsletter |
| July-Dec, 1995 | Art editor for several reviews and articles. Signal Magazine |

Represented by
mother's tankstation,
Watling Street, Dublin.

/

# Colophon

/

Published on the occasion of

**ALAN PHELAN**
**FRAGILE ABSOLUTES**

Irish Museum of Modern Art
21 July to 1 November 2009

Exhibition curated by
Seán Kissane

**IMMA Exhibition Team**
Enrique Juncosa, Director
Rachael Thomas, Senior Curator: *Head of Exhibitions*
Seán Kissane, Curator: *Exhibitions*
Marianne Kelly, Curatorial Assistant: *Exhibitions*
Cillian Hayes, Technical Supervisor
Joe Stanley, Technician

**Catalogue**
Editor: Seán Kissane
Assistant Editor: Marianne Kelly
Copy Editor: Michael Freeman

Designed by Ajdin Bašić

Printed by Formatisk d.o.o. Ljubljana

ISBN 978-8881586428



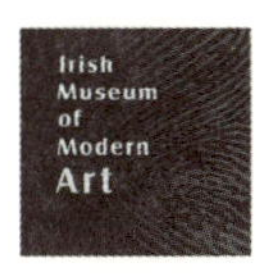


Irish Museum of Modern Art
Áras Nua-Ealaíne na h-Éireann
Royal Hospital, Military Road
Kilmainham, Dublin 8
Ireland

tel + 353 1 612 9900
fax + 353 1 612 9999
email info@imma.ie
website www.imma.ie

Photography credits

p. 13, 19, 54, 65, 84-91, 115, 118-119, 124, 131, 138-140, 146, 148, 150-151, 176, 182-183, 189-191, 203, 214-215, 233, 250-253, 256-257
David Monahan

p. 15, 38, 61, 109, 137, 184, 245
Liam O'Callaghan

p. 16, 18, 41-48, 50, "0" insert, 55, 56, 58-59, 64, 66-67, 68-78, 82, 106-107, 111-113, 116-117, 126-128, "Hill of Shouts" insert, 195, 200-202, 206-208, 220, 229-230, 235, "Bandstand" insert, 254-255
Alan Phelan

p. 17, 129, 218
mother's tankstation

p. 25, 122, 130, 210-211,
Courtesy Oregon State University Archives

p. 57, 155, 204-205, 236-240
Michael Durand

p. 60
Photo William Hederman

p. 80-82, 248-249
Goran Krstić

p. 83
Dragana Jurišić

p. 120
Courtesy Wexford Arts Centre

p.126
Archy Wang

p.141
AP Photo/Sang Tan

p. 174, 177-181
Courtesy NASA/JPL-Caltech

p. 184, 213, 217, 219
Courtesy Solstice Arts Centre, Navan

p.187
Photo by Mary Silver

p. 192-193
Eammon O'Mahony, Studioworks
Courtesy e v+ a - the exhibition of visual+ art, 2009

p. 205
Courtesy of Mercury Music

p. 230
Patrick Browne

p. 246-247
Matt Gidney

Book distributed by

Edizioni Charta srl
Milano (Italy)
Via della Moscova, 27 - 20121
Tel. +39-026598098 / +39-026598200
Fax +39-026598577
Email charta@chartaartbooks.it

Charta Books Ltd.
New York City (USA)
Tribeca Office
Tel. +1-313-406-8468
Email international@chartaartbooks.it

www.chartaartbooks.it

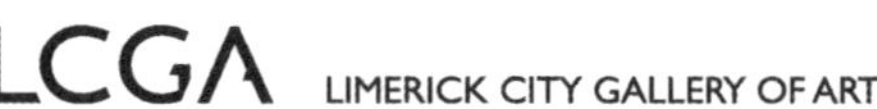


Director/Curator
Mike Fitzpatrick

Audience and Access Curator
Pippa Little

Care of Collections and Exhibitions
Siobhan O'Reilly

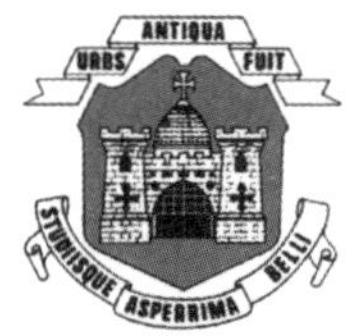


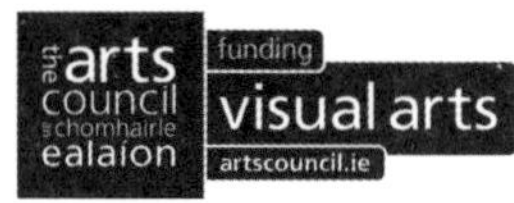


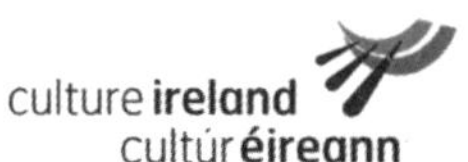

# p.267

/

# Artist's Acknowledgments

/

I would like to acknowledge all the people who have in many ways contributed to this project which will continue beyond this publication. Enormous thanks must go to Seán Kissane for believing in my work and making this project much more than it could have been. A huge thanks to Enrique Juncosa and the many staff at IMMA who has worked on the exhibition, from technical through to curatorial departments, with a special mention for Marianne Kelly for all her hard work over the past few years. I am most grateful for all from Zastava and Kragujevac who worked on the car project with enormous gratitude to Goran Krstić and Marija Aleksandrović and their family and friends who made both myself, Seán and my mother most welcome to their homes and places of work.

I am grateful to Mike Fitzpatrick of Limerick City Gallery of Art and Hannah Firth of Chapter Arts Centre for collaborating in this exhibition project.

Finola Jones and David Godbold at mother's tankstation for their support.

The following have contributed to the project in various ways: Patricia Kelly, Tony White, Pippa Little, Tricia Perrott, James Phelan, Tiah Edmunson-Morton, Miha Štrukelj, Alenka Gregorič, Dawn Williams, Paula Sutton, Medb Ruane, Mark Crames, Jim Dingilian, Kathryn Koran, Sarah Pierce, Manic-Motorz, Megan Johnston, Michael Dempsey, Harriet Phelan, Helena Drnovšek-Zorko, Dejan Novačić, Dragana Jurisić, Dušan Bjelić, Sandra Grozdanić, Nataša Bokić; Janice Hough, Claire Power, Carolyn Brown, Špela and Filiep Drnovšek-Zorko, Archy Wang, Gemma Tipton, Anthony Boylan; Tamas Szabados, Sheena Barrett, Alice Maher, Patrick Phelan, Maria Fusco, Philip Stone, Maria Bauermeister, David Skinner, Joe Stanley, Ed Kiely, Noel Kelly, Grant Watson, Sheila Gallagher, Bernard Nally, Nevan Lahart, Jacinta Lynch, Ciarán Bennett, John Davis, Rachael Thomas, Belinda Quirke, Mary Cloake, Claire Doyle, Eugene Downes, Hugo Jellett, Vanessa O'Reilly, Fiona Mulholland.

The Artist would also like to acknowledge the support of the Arts Council/An Chomhairle Ealaíon

For
Noel
Harry
Pat
Patricia
for all their love and
vital support always

# Supporting IMMA

/

**Honarary Patrons**

Maurice and Maire Foley
George McClelland
Eoin & Patricia McGonigal
Gerard O'Toole
Lochlann & Brenda Quinn
Brian & Elsa Ranalow

**Patrons**

William & Laura Burlington
Daniel Caffrey
Mairead & Finbar Cahill
Joe Christle
Moya Doherty & John McColgan
Ivor Fitzpatrick & Co
Maureen O'Driscoll-Levy
Noel Smyth
Mark Adams Fine Art
Bank of Ireland
de Blacam and Meagher
Kerlin Gallery

**Benefactors**

Campbell Bruce
Frank X Buckley
Dr Abdul Bulbulia
Brian Coyle
Therese Coyle
Donall Curtin
Steven Doody
Grainne Dooley
Niamh Donlon
Bernard Dunleavy
Olga Filippova
Phil Gibbons
Margaret Glynn
Tom E. Honan
Sophia Ledingham
Brian McMahon
Cormac O'Malley
Lorcan O'Neill
Louis O'Sullivan
Sandra Phillips
Anna Walsh
Jane Williams
James Adams & Son
Solomon Gallery
Smurfit Kappa Group